MW01277453

This book is dedicated to Sarah
whose patience, understanding and wisdom
helped me regain my sanity at a time
when I was close to losing it.
Thank you my friend.

ACKNOWLEDGEMENTS

Though my memoirs have been written strictly from my own recollection of events that occurred throughout my life and without the aid of notes or reference books, I am indebted to all who have provided me with the inspiration to put these events on paper.

Many thanks to Keith Woodcock, Artist, for permission to use the painting of a Wellington Mk. II on the front cover, and to Frances Litman, Photography, for permission to use the beautiful wedding photographs, also my very good friend David Price, who played a big part in my life and assisted with proof reading and setting the record straight.

Thanks also to Reverend Glenn Sim, Pastor of St. Mary's Anglican Church, Saanichton for his support and encouragement; and to Alex Peel, my Author Services Representative at Trafford Publishing Company, for her assistance.

And very many thanks to Roy Diment of Vivencia Resources Group who provided the cover design and book layout, and very useful advice.

Photos, other than the Woodcock painting and the wedding photos, are from the author's collection.

Veronica Bennett-Butcher
Saanichton, BC
2005

Contents

List of Photographs

PROLOGUE

An Introduction to my Parents

My father, Ronald Reginald Bennett, was born August 3rd, 1905 to Jack and Olive Bennett in Kitsilano, a beautiful seaside suburb of Vancouver, British Columbia, Canada. Jack and Olive had both left England as teenagers to start new lives in Canada. Olive was an accomplished seamstress who held various jobs in that capacity, while Jack sold pianos, among other things, and moonlighted as the pianist in the lounge of the Georgia Hotel, on Georgia Street, in Vancouver.

They moved to Victoria, the capital of British Columbia, on Vancouver Island when Ronald was about two years old, and lived in a little house on Toronto Street in James Bay, one of the original residential areas of Victoria.

The world famous Empress Hotel opened in the Inner Harbour of Victoria in 1908, and Olive was housekeeper there for several years, while Ronald attended South Park School. Jack and a friend opened a fish and chip shop adjacent to the house on Toronto Street, but Olive couldn't stand the smell and that enterprise was short-lived.

When Ronald was about 8 years old, the family moved back to Vancouver. Olive opened a dress shop featuring her own line of dresses and was very successful; however, the marriage was falling apart, and the couple divorced the following year. Ronald and his mother returned to Victoria where he continued his schooling. Having inherited his father's musical talent, he had chosen to learn all the wind instruments and became an excellent saxophonist, playing in the school band as well as other dance groups.

By the time Ronald was 18 he and his mother, who had remarried, returned to Vancouver and were living in a beautiful home on Hollyburn Mountain. Ronald was attending the University of British Columbia when he and a friend decided to spend the upcoming sabbatical on a ship going anywhere, just for the experience. They were to meet at dockside on a certain day, but while Ronald showed up early, complete

Ronald Bennett

with his saxophone, his friend was a no-show, so the ship and Ronald left without him. Evidently Ronald's mother was unaware of their plans, and thought her son had run away from home.

She contacted her sister, who had married a rather wealthy gentleman in England, asking her to meet the ship when it arrived in Southampton. Of course, Ronald didn't have the necessary papers for him to land in England. But money talked, and his aunt and uncle actually bought him off the ship and took him to their magnificent estate in Surrey.

He was a good looking but very shy young man, quite tall and slim with blond hair and hazel eyes. He was unsure of what was going to happen next, he really wanted to go back to Canada. His Uncle had other ideas and wanted to put him to work in his business, which was the first Ford dealership in England at that time, but Ronald refused and took off again by himself, heading for London with very little money and no idea where he was going. First he needed a meal but was too shy to order, then he needed a place to stay and didn't know where to start looking. He saw several signs reading 'To Let', but had no idea what that meant, so knocked on a door to enquire.

There were two young ladies watching from an upstairs window. They both decided they wanted to meet this good looking young man and raced each other to the front door. It turned out that this was a boarding house for ladies only, but the poor young fellow looked like he was about to drop, so they invited him in, gave him tea and cake and decided there was a little room in the attic which he could use, at least for a couple of nights. It actually turned into several weeks.

Amy Doody

One of the young ladies took him under her wing and found him a job as an office boy in the office where she worked. The young lady's name was Amy Jane Doody, born in Prittlewell, England, September 24th, 1895. She was a feisty little lady, just 4 feet 10 inches tall, with beautiful auburn curls and twinkling blue eyes. Her Irish father was a politician in the British House of Commons, and her mother a wonderful home maker. She was raised, along with her brother and sister, in Southend, Essex and she excelled as a sports woman as well as a scholar, and was an excellent pianist.

She was single and, since it was not fashionable to be single at age 29 and be termed an 'old maid', she was definitely looking for a husband. Although there was a ten-year difference in their ages, they very soon fell in love.

Six weeks after they first met, Ronald and Amy were married in the church of St. Martins in the Field in London, and just seven months later I was born in Charing Cross Hospital on May 31st, 1925, exactly nine months after my Dad celebrated his 19th birthday. It took me a few years to figure that one out, but I do believe it accounts for a lot of the things that have happened in my life.

Anyway, whatever the reason, they spent 64 years together, travelling the world and sharing a wonderfully fulfilling life. They became proficient archers, winning many trophies both in England and Europe. Dad received the Scorton Arrow from King George VI. It was a twelve inch silver arrow awarded for the highest scoring shoot. They travelled all over the European Continent either by car or motor bike, climbing mountains, exploring caves and visiting Ronald's ancestors in Norway.

In the early years their love of music found them forming a little orchestra, with Dad on his saxophone or another of his wind instruments, Mum on piano, my Aunt Nellie (Mum's sister) on violin, her friend Clint on bass and Uncle Harry on drums. They played tea time music, as was fashionable in restaurants in the 1920's, and were very popular at this and other venues.

Dad stayed in the job Mum found for him in the office where she was Secretary, and he rose from office boy to office manager, until he voluntarily joined the Royal Air Force in 1938, several months before the Second World War began. He started out as a Balloon Technician, and soon became a Sergeant in charge of balloon sites in and around London. Later on he joined a Pathfinder Squadron, then became an Air Traffic Control Officer with 617 Squadron, which became known as the Dam Buster squadron.

Three months after the war ended in 1945, he finally returned to Canada introducing Mum and me to his native land and his mother, whom he had not seen for nearly 21 years.

He died in his 82nd year and Mum followed him five years later when she was 97. Their love for each other endured many hardships. I was very proud of them, they were my parents and I loved them.

1

CONVENT LIFE

Nanna Doody and Veronica, age 3

Can you imagine being three years old and being enrolled in a boarding school, a convent no less? Well my Mother could, and there I stood screaming my head off, not because I was scared, but because my new high button boots were pinching my tiny feet, and staring into a massive door, somewhere behind which a bell clanged as my mother pulled on an iron ring. Soon, high above my head, a small door opened and a voice asked, 'May I help you?', to which Mum replied that she had brought her daughter for her first day of school. The massive door opened on creaky hinges, and I was promptly grabbed by the hand and almost dragged into what was to be my home for the next three years.

This was no kindergarten, our play-times were strictly controlled by women, dressed all in black whom I was told to call 'Sister', and another woman who was to be called 'Reverend Mother'. In those three years, I found out that, as a boarder, once the Sisters learned your name you were the scapegoat for any misdemeanours, and I found myself being punished for events I knew nothing about. They were not the happiest of times but I survived, and do believe that those first lessons learned have helped me get through many adversities as life progressed.

One night, as I was trying to sleep, I heard a noise which really startled me. A group of nuns were chattering very excitably, and running through the dormitory waking everyone up. They grouped us in front of the big windows, and soon we saw what it was that they were so excited about. A huge silver balloon glided past our windows, very slowly. It was really quite an eerie sight. I later learned that this was in fact, the 777 foot British dirigible # R101 making its maiden flight to India. Soon after we saw it, it crashed in the woods near the French town of Beauvais and nearly all on board were killed instantly. I remember the special service that was held in the

1

chapel. I was only five years old, and did not understand the historic importance of this event until much later when I watched a re-enactment documentary film.

While at the convent, I was experiencing some very bad earaches, but the nuns would just put warm drops in my ears, and a wad of cotton wool, and tell me to go to sleep. But the earaches would persist, and started interfering with my school work. Eventually, the pain was so bad they sent for my Mother who took me to the hospital where I was admitted immediately. She was told that I had the beginnings of mastoids, and would need an operation. Evidently my Dad had also had mastoids, and a small scar behind his right ear from his operation. Mum was adamant though, and refused to let them cut into my head; however, they did something which necessitated bandaging around my head, and cut my hair around the top of the bandage, like a skull cap.

Veronica studying, age 5

The following day when Mum came to see me, she couldn't find me anywhere. It was bath time, and the nurse who was assigned to bathe the boys, soon discovered that I was not one of them. Seems my new haircut caused a case of mistaken identity, and I had been moved into the boys' ward. Fortunately, the diagnosis was not mastoids, but myringotomy (which I always thought sounded like a girl's name), and was a collection of fluid, which they drained. This was not a cure though, and about every four years, until I was sixteen, I'd get a swelling behind my ears and have to go through the draining process. Some of my teachers thought I had mumps, which of course is very catching, and would send me home. I didn't mind that a bit. Thank goodness I eventually grew out of that problem, although it did leave me with a slight hearing loss in both ears.

I mentioned that once the nuns knew your name, they never forgot it….. Well, one day during the afternoon lesson, one of Reverend Mother's assistants came storming into the classroom disrupting everyone, especially Sister Mary our teacher, whom I thought was very pretty and much too nice to be shut away in a convent, and having to wear that awful black and white outfit. This nun whispered something in Sister Mary's ear, and they both looked in my direction. Immediately I felt guilty, but of what I had no idea, until Sister Mary announced that the whole class was being kept in until someone owned up to writing the rude word on the toilet wall.

Needless to say, nobody did and it was getting near time for the day scholars to go home. I knew their mothers would be worrying about them if they were not on their regular busses and we boarders would probably not get our dinner, so I kept hoping somebody would 'fess up. When 5 o'clock came, I couldn't stand it any longer, so I said I had written the rude word on the wall, even though I didn't even know what the word was. I was kept behind while everyone else was allowed to leave. I was not only scolded severely, my punishment was to clean everyone's shoes and not having any dinner. None of the girls in class would speak to me and I was thoroughly miserable.

A few days later, Sister Mary asked me to stay behind after class was dismissed, and I felt sure I was in trouble again. It seems she had played detective and checked the toilet to see for herself what was on the wall, only to discover that I could not possibly have written that, even if I had stood on the toilet seat. It was much too high up for me to reach. First she hugged me and said she knew why I had confessed, then gave me a long lecture about taking the blame for others being the wrong thing to do. It was a

Nanna Doody, in 1931

lesson I should have learned, but didn't, especially when I knew my middle name was 'Trouble', and I'd probably be blamed anyway. I managed to get myself thrown out of that convent I'm pleased to say, though I probably shouldn't be.

It was Easter, and I was almost 6 years old, all dressed up in white for my confirmation, which had just taken place. As I passed by the chapel, I could hear organ music and smell the fragrance of lilies, and was overpowered by the feeling of peace and beauty. So I entered the chapel, and floated down the aisle, pirouetting towards the altar, where I knelt and said a prayer of thanks. However, that ethereal feeling was very short lived. Little did I know that there were nuns in the choir loft, and the next moment I was being whisked away to the Reverend Mother's office, where I was strongly reprimanded for 'dancing in the chapel' – obviously a no-no. And I thought I was a little angel! Within the hour, my Mother and Father arrived, and I was hurried off the premises, never to return.

Alas, it was 'out of the frying pan and into the fire', as I spent the next couple of years, 1931 to 1933, at a 'council' (public) school, being teased constantly by a couple of school bullies of the female variety. My long blonde ringlets were a great source of delight, as they were dipped into the inkpot of the bully who sat behind me in class.

Veronica, age 5, learning to follow in Dad's footsteps

To my dismay, Mum decided it was easier to cut off my blonde locks, rather than keep washing my hair and the clothes that were dripped on.

My school satchel, which was a rather nice, real leather one that I carried on my back, also received the attention of the bullies, who lay in wait for me and snatched it off my shoulder on my way home from school, emptying the contents into the road, hoping a bus or two would run over the books and pencils. Fortunately, two very nice young men (boys actually), came to my rescue one day, and from then on, escorted me to and from school.

I did fairly well at this school, despite the teasing, and was beginning to enjoy the freedom a council school afforded. Being home every evening, and sleeping in my own bedroom, making friends, and visiting other children's homes as well as inviting them to mine, were all new to me and, the best part of all, I didn't have to wear a uniform.

Mum was a reasonably good seamstress and made most of my clothes. One outfit that was my favourite was a skating dress she had knitted on circular needles. It was pale blue with white bunny fur trim and the skirt flared out when I spun around in circles. Dad and I had joined the ice skating club at Wembley Stadium and spent Saturday afternoons together. It was a lot of fun and he was an excellent skater. He had learned to skate on the lakes during the winters in British Columbia when he was a child and I loved to watch him. Of course, if I tried to do what he did I always ended up flat on my back.

Dad had joined a well known dance band and was playing his saxophone at dances and weddings on a regular basis, while still keeping his day job. Twice a week the band would be at our house for rehearsals. I loved these times, learning all the tunes of the day and dancing along as they played. We had an extensive library of 78 rpm records with all the well known singers and orchestras, and I knew all the words to just about anything the band played. Too bad they don't write music like that any more.

The following year, 1934, a few months before my ninth birthday, Mum presented me with a little brother, but she was very sick and had to stay in the hospital for almost the entire year, keeping the baby with her, so I only got to see him once in a while. Dad took care of me, with the help of our upstairs neighbours for the first couple of months, but I soon found myself moving in with a married couple whom I really did not like. Their name was Pickett, and I used to say (under my breath of course), 'You'll never get well if you pick it!' The Picketts worked at the local women's prison and were pretty tough themselves, so once again I found myself being restricted, and they were very strict disciplinarians. I wasn't allowed to see my friends other than at school. At the time I didn't understand why I had been sent to live with them, and thought my parents didn't want me any more now they had a little boy.

Fortunately the year passed quickly, Mum finally left the hospital and I was able to return home. My little brother was absolutely adorable, with curly blonde hair, bright blue eyes and a deep dimple in each cheek, and I loved him very much. Mum had to stay in a wheelchair for a few months after she returned home and I was so happy to be able to take care of Adrian. I learned how to hold a tiny baby and bathe him, as well as dress him and change diapers which, of course, were the big square terry cloth ones that had to be folded diagonally and secured with an enormous safety pin.

I would take him out in his pram and show him off whenever I could, as if he were my own little baby. Christmas was the best time, when my Dad bought Adrian a train set (or was it for himself?), and we put sparklers in the smoke stack and set it off on it's journey around the dining table, with Adrian's infectious little giggle setting us all off laughing.

Soon after Christmas 1934, we moved from our basement flat in London to a new house in Rayners Lane, a pretty little village about 40 miles from London, which we fondly nicknamed Rainy Lane. This was a brand new housing development with only three houses completed. Ours was the middle one of the three which were joined together, rather like a triplex. The landscaping had not been finished when we moved in, and it was not unusual to receive a visit from some hungry sheep at the kitchen door.

The house had been the 'show house' and was completely decorated throughout and very attractive, although Mum decided right away that the awful wallpaper in the hall would have to go. It was rather hideous with huge bunches of cherries on a dark greeny brown background, and soon got changed to something much more cheerful.

Here we each had our own bedroom, lots of rooms to play in, and eventually, a lovely garden. I helped my Dad plant flowers and veggies, and watered and watched every day to see how our garden grew. We discovered that the soil was excellent. All we planted grew very quickly, especially the grass. Every other weekend Dad had me mowing the lawn with an old fashioned push type mower. It was hard work but I kept going and got quite a thrill out of seeing the nice straight lines of grass appear as I went backwards and forwards from one end of the garden to the other.

Our garage was at the end of the garden with double doors out to the alley that ran between the houses on our street and those on the adjacent street. We did have a car which was usually parked out on the road because Dad used the garage for growing mushrooms. My job was to follow the horses and pick up their droppings in a shovel and deposit them in a wheelbarrow, which then got emptied into trays in the garage for the mushrooms to grow in. Did you know that mushrooms were grown in horse manure?

A lot of interesting things happened while I was living in Rayners Lane. Every Saturday a gentleman would come to the door with a suitcase full of sweets of all kinds. I'd keep him standing there while I tried to make up my mind what to spend my three pence allowance on. Usually I'd end up with a bar of Cadbury's white chocolate which tasted just like condensed milk, and I loved it. We could hear the milkman coming with his horse drawn wagon, as well as the Eldorado Ice Cream man on his tricycle ringing his bell and yelling 'Ice Cream' at the top of his voice.

The coal was also delivered by a horse drawn wagon. We had to put newspapers on the floor when the coal man brought the sacks of coal through the house from the front door and through the kitchen to the back door, then outside to the coal bin where he dumped about five sacks of coal. The house smelled of coal dust for quite a while after his deliveries. There was also a tinker and knife sharpener, who had all his wares on a huge wheelbarrow. He made quite a noise with all the metal pots banging together as he pushed his way along the street.

Although the year was 1936, surprisingly enough, very few deliveries were made in motorised vehicles, and even fewer after the war started in 1939 as, not only was petrol (gasoline) scarce, but cars were confiscated so the metal could be used for the war effort. They even took away the decorative chains and railings that surrounded the front gardens along the street.

When Mum was well enough, she went back to work as a secretary, and I attended another council school. Adrian spent the day at a babysitters until I picked him up on my way home. I'd feed him, and then start getting dinner ready for my parents, who were both working in London, and travelled back and forth by train. Adrian was becoming a very alert young man, and would sit beside me asking questions as I did my homework, our blonde heads bent over the books together, engrossed in whatever subject was at hand. Although I was eight years older than my brother, he managed to keep up with me in everything we did, and we enjoyed each other's company.

One sunny afternoon, I decided to stop by the park on the way home to enjoy the swing set. Adrian was giggling his head off as I pushed him higher and higher, when something attracted my attention and I looked away. The next thing I knew, I was flat on my back, seeing stars. The swing had hit me square in the mouth and cut my lip very badly. Fortunately, a lady had been passing by (it was she whom I had turned to look at) and saw what happened, and came to my rescue. Poor Adrian was frantic, seeing the blood pouring from his big sister's mouth, and the giggles had turned to tears.

With a pretty little handkerchief, the only thing the lady had to quell the flow, held firmly against my mouth, Adrian and I walked the three miles home, and the pain was excruciating. By the time my parents came home I had managed to look more normal, and had dinner ready for them, but was unable to eat mine. It was then that my Mum realized I was hurt, and rushed me to the doctor, but it was too late to stitch the wound. It had to heal by itself, and I still have the little lump on my lip to remind me, certainly a lesson learned the hard way.

My mode of transportation to the council school was by roller skates. The school was about two and a half miles from home through a fairly busy residential district. Double decker busses were frequent, as well as motor cycles, and the only place to skate was in the road because the sidewalk was made up of 18 inch concrete squares with about one inch space between them, so that it was impossible to skate on the sidewalks. Not being a very good roller skater (I was much better on ice), I needed someone with me, and in this case it happened to be two young boys who lived on my street and were in my class in school. They loved to tease me and would be on either side of me holding my hand and pulling me along at what I thought was breakneck speed, then they'd let go of me and I'd go sailing off, unable to stop.

Usually I would deliberately sit down to stop, but that became quite painful, so I started strapping a cushion to my behind to soften the blow. On one such occasion when they let go of me I went flying across an intersection just as the bus was crossing from the side street and I made it through by the skin of my teeth. I think that scared them so much, they were a bit more cautious after that. They'd learned a lesson, but the teasing kept up. One would ask the other, 'What's for lunch today?' and the other would answer, 'Ham sandwich' which was the cue for them to smash me in the middle, me being the ham in the sandwich. I never did manage to duck in time and usually suffered a bruise or two, all in good fun of course.

Dad had sold the car, and had a motorcycle and sidecar at that time, in which we travelled to and from Southend in Essex, to visit my Grandmother (my mother's Mum). Mum and I used to vie for the pillion seat behind my Dad, but I only won if it was raining, for reasons which became painfully obvious. By the time we reached our destination, I would look like I had chicken-pox from the beating of the rain in my face.

One occasion, when I was in the sidecar with my little brother wedged between my knees, became my most embarrassing moment. When we arrived at my Grandmother's house, I realized I was sitting in a pool of water, and since Adrian was still in diapers, I was sure he was the culprit. Alas though, t'was I – my lower extremities had become numb during the trip, and I was completely unaware that I had wet my pants. Dad thought it was very funny, which just added to my embarrassment.

Grandad Doody at the gate of Loretto

My Grandmother's house was called Loretto, and it was the only house my Grandparents had lived in since they married. In fact my Grandfather had the house built as a wedding present for Nanna. There was a front parlour, a sitting room, large dining room, huge scullery (kitchen and larder), five fairly big bedrooms, but no bathroom and no outhouse either - what were they going to do? He decided there was room for a bathroom on the landing at the top of the stairs. And that's where it went, big enough to hold a six foot bathtub and a toilet. The only problem was, you had to walk in backwards and sit down immediately as there was no room to turn around, and to get into the bathtub meant standing on the toilet seat and stepping in and out the same way, as there was no room to stand between the tub and the wall. Definitely an afterthought!!

Grandfather Doody was a wonderful man, with a lilting Irish brogue, and twinkling blue eyes. When I was very small, my most favourite thing to do was stand on the seat behind him in his wing backed chair and brush his beautiful bushy, white hair. Sometimes he would say, 'Ouch', and I would get hold of his nose, turn his head round and ask, 'Did I hurt you Gaga?'. I loved spending time at Loretto, playing in their huge garden which smelled of lavender and lilac. There were apple trees, cherry trees, and plum trees, as well as gooseberry and blackberry bushes. My Grandfather had hung a swing from one of the apple trees, which was quite secluded from the house. I spent many quiet times there during my growing up years, swinging back and forth, and day dreaming.

Much earlier, until I was almost three and started school, I had lived with my grandparents, while my parents lived and worked in London, visiting Loretto on weekends. During this time I became sick with milk poisoning, and was not expected to live. My bed was the bottom drawer of a chest of drawers in the sitting room, which had been converted into a bedroom for me. While my grandmother was out shopping one day, she saw a man selling colourful balloons and brought several home, tying them to something that would be in my line of vision when I woke up. She says those balloons saved my life as I got quite excited when I saw them, and my health improved rapidly from then on. I missed my Grandparents terribly when I started school at the convent, and I always looked forward to spending a school vacation with them.

We were settled and happy in Rainy Lane in our new home, and expected it to continue for some time. I had made friends with several of the new neighbours as the houses were built and occupied. It wasn't long before there was quite a little 'gang' of us racing up and down the street on our bikes or roller skates. However, my folks had other ideas. I found myself once again enrolled as a boarder in a convent, and Adrian was sent off to a Grammar School, which was actually a military academy. He was just three years old, and I could remember what I went through at that age.... my heart hurt for him, and it would be quite a long time before I saw him again.

My new school was not much better than the first one in that, once they knew my name I became the 'mischief maker' or so I was called. I came to the conclusion, that no matter what I did, it would be wrong, and I guess I gave up trying to be 'good'.

In the six years I spent at this convent, I found that I was either the oldest of the juniors, and so was expected to be a leader, or I was the youngest of the seniors, and didn't know anything. I felt more comfortable with the former, and enjoyed teaching the little ones to dance, or play games, and even wrote a few little skits for them to enact on Parent's Day.

There came a time though, when I had to act as the senior I really was, but I was not popular with the rest of the seniors, who were rather a 'snooty' bunch. Most of them came from wealthy families. Their parents were either employed in government jobs overseas, or lived in mansions somewhere in the English countryside, while my parents were very hardworking, middle class people.

The rest of the boarders wore brand new gym slips with crisp white blouses and a burgundy tie, while I was the recipient of hand-me-downs from students who had either grown out of them, or left the school. My only brand new item was the straw Panama hat which I positively hated. If I didn't have ears, I'm sure it would have been down over my eyes.

We were supposed to wear felt 'overshoes' over our walking shoes, to protect the highly polished wood floors, but for some strange reason mine would always be missing, and I'd find myself praying to Saint Anthony, the finder of lost items, to help me find those darned overshoes. Needless to say, they (the overshoes) would turn up as whatever class I had just missed was breaking for recess, and I would have to stay behind to catch up. I always suspected that one of the seniors had hidden them but could never catch her in the act, or prove it, and the teasing went on.

We also had a 'tuck shop'. That was a large cupboard which was kept padlocked and only opened once a week. It was stocked with all sorts of sweets and other items on which we could spend our weekly allowance. My favourite was Turkish Delight, a hard jelly square full of nuts and covered with icing sugar. My three pennies would buy me two of these squares. I'd nibble one very slowly and tried to save the other, but since I had nothing in which to wrap it, I'd end up eating that one also and have to wait all week to repeat the process.

There were two priests who alternated early morning Mass and afternoon Benediction, which was also time for 'Confession'. As we knelt in the chapel with our arms resting on the rail we noticed when it was the turn of Father Damien, who was young and quite good looking, to take the confession, it was mostly the younger nuns who had plenty to confess, and we would be looking at our watches, whispering, 'Sister so and so has been 20 minutes'. We had not yet learned about the birds and bees but our little minds worked overtime wondering whatever could be taking her so long, whereas when it was Father Cuthbert, who was much older, confession was over quickly and very few nuns had anything to confess.

There was no school on Wednesday afternoon so the boarders were taken on an outing, usually to a very nice area where there was a pond, and we could feed the ducks. We had to walk to this place with a nun leading our procession, which we called a crocodile, and another nun at the rear. We were paired up with a partner and had to hold hands as we kept in strict line until we got to our destination. The area also had a big grassy knoll where we were allowed to run free and play 'tag' or 'hide and seek', while the nuns in charge kept an eagle eye on us to make sure we didn't get out of hand, or (heaven forbid) try to run away.

This place grew lots of watercress, which we collected and took back to the convent kitchen where the nuns would give it a cursory wash, and we would have gritty watercress sandwiches with our tea. Watercress grows in very marshy, muddy areas around the edge of the pond. The mud collected on our shoes and sometimes, if we lost our footing, on the rest of us as well. So after depositing the green stuff in the kitchen, it would be a quick but much needed bath (by the way, we wore a chemise when we bathed, no nude bodies allowed!). Other times, for our outings we would be taken to the local swimming pool for the afternoon, but of course, the nuns did not go in the pool with us. On these occasions, one of the seniors would be 'in charge'.

To make up for our Wednesday afternoon outings, we would have classes on Saturday mornings, and Dad would come to pick me up at noon. One Saturday afternoon, a party was going to be held for one of the seniors who was graduating and going to become a nun, so Dad would not be picking me up until about 6:00pm.

After lunch I joined the other girls in the gym, where we could enjoy some playtime. My choice of play was a skipping rope which, apparently, one of the other girls wanted. I hung on as she pulled, until finally, she kicked me in the stomach and I doubled over in pain, letting go of the rope, and off she went, happily skipping around the gym. The Sister in charge wanted to know what was wrong, and through my sobbing I told her what happened. However, she didn't believe me, and with a resounding smack to the side of my face, told me not to lie. When I protested that I wasn't lying, she landed another smack to the other side of my face.

By this time I was really sobbing, and was banished to the music room. I was already learning to play the piano, but still not very well, and the music sister was waiting for me. First came the scales and the mistakes. Each time I hit a wrong note, I'd get a whack on the knuckles with her baton, and soon my hands were getting sore and the whacks were getting more frequent.

This lasted for about an hour, then the first sister returned to the music room and announced that I would have to write certain chapters from our history book. Well, our history books were written rather like the bible, in two columns of very small print, with all the pertinent dates down the margins. I tried to write, but by this time my hands were quite swollen, and I couldn't hold the pen, plus tears were dripping onto my paper, and smudging what I did write. This being the age before ball point pens, I had to keep dipping my pen-nib in the ink pot, but it was a hopeless cause, and doomed to failure.

As I was mulling over my sad situation, I looked out of the second storey window, and suddenly realized that if I got out of the window onto the sloping roof below, I could give a mighty leap and clear the fence, landing on the pavement *outside* the convent walls and into *freedom*, anticipating of course, that I would land safely on two feet. I opened the window, had one leg over the sill, and was just about to pull the other leg out, when the door opened and in came the Reverend Mother carrying a yardstick. The next hour (which was probably only ten minutes), I received several hits with the yardstick, mostly on my shinbone which, as you know, can hurt like anything, and I collapsed in a screaming heap. All this episode took place from about 1 pm to almost 5 pm, and it was time for the party to begin.

I was escorted limping and still sobbing, to the refectory where everyone was gathered, but I was not allowed to join them and had to sit outside and listen to them having fun. I was given a piece of the celebration cake, though I was sure it would choke me if I dared take a bite!! Finally, and thank God, Dad came to take me home for the rest of the weekend, but not once on the way home, did he ask me why I looked such a wreck.

One of my favourite things to do when I spent Saturday night at home was to undress in front of the fire in the living room before climbing the stairs to a cold bedroom, and my PJ's would be laid out across the hearth to get warm as I disrobed beneath a dressing gown. For the first two Saturday nights I took my PJ's and got ready for bed in my bedroom because I didn't want anyone to see my wounds. I know Mum was thinking I was growing out of my little girl habit, but one Saturday I forgot and she saw the bruises on my shins, which were turning all shades of purple and yellow by this time. Of course she asked how I got them, and I started to tell her, when Dad interrupted and said , 'You must have done something wrong or they wouldn't have caned you'. Of course the other girl, who was the cause of all my grief, got off scot free.

Despite the fact that I was always in trouble, I was a good student academically and usually managed to finish among the top three in my class, although my favourite subject was Phys. Ed. The whole school was involved in this. About 100 students, from grade two up, were lined up in rows on the tennis court, and we did some very rigorous calisthenics. Did I mention it was an all girl's school? For an hour, twice a week we worked hard until we were ready for Parents' Day, which came at the end of a term (semester).

Judges were seated at a head table and they watched for the best performance by a student, rewarding her with an ivory cross on a red ribbon, which was proudly worn around her neck for the rest of the term, and she got to keep it. I was so sure I was going to win on this particular occasion and had worked my heart out to be the best, but it was not to be, and I was devastated. The cross went to a girl who had missed most of the school year through sickness, and had only returned to school a few weeks earlier. The rule was, that you had to have attended a certain number of classes to be eligible, and I knew she hadn't. Oh well, that was the way it went sometimes, I guess you had to know the right people!

During the summer when we had our six week vacation from school, I spent time at another convent, sometimes at Littlehampton, where we were close to the ocean, and although we had lessons on most days, we also went to the beach and had fun. Another convent I spent vacations at was in Canterbury right next door to the Archbishop of Canterbury's residence. I'd join some of the other boarders peeking over the fence to see if we could see the Archbishop when he strolled around his gardens.

If he spotted us, he usually stopped to chat and would give us an apple or other fruit from his orchard. The nuns at these convents were not nearly as strict as those back home and I always looked forward to spending time with them.

When my brother was still an infant we had an Austin 7 automobile, which was rather like a square box on wheels, and very small. My parents were great ones for camping out, and Dad would drive all over the countryside, stopping at a farmhouse and enquiring if we could pitch a tent in their field. On one such occasion when I was lucky enough to be spending a vacation with them, we had driven to a place called Bratton St. Muir (pronounced Seymour), near Wincanton in Somerset. We were in farm country and the smell of new mown hay was in the air, along with the aroma of pig sties and horses of course.

Discovering the seashore and its seaweed (also on back cover)

We soon stopped at a very pretty farmhouse with the usual enquiry.

The farmer and his wife were only too happy to let us camp in their field, and I helped my Dad set everything up. As the tent was only big enough for two people to stretch out in their sleeping bags, my brother and I had to sleep in the car. He being so small, was fine, but I was folded up like a concertina on the back seat and not at all comfortable.

Some time during the night the rains came, and were teaming down along with thunder and lightning. When I rubbed a hole to see through the steamed up window, I could see the water pouring down the steep hillside we were parked on, and into the tent. The farmer and his wife came running out with flashlights and ordered us all into the farmhouse, which fortunately had several unoccupied bedrooms where we not only spent the rest of the night, but the rest of the week, and were much more comfortable.

This was the beginning of a great friendship between our two families and I was invited back to spend some of my school vacations, with or without my parents, from then on. They also had a young son, just two years older than me, who taught me how to ride a horse, build a haystack and drink apple cider, which we hid in earthenware jugs under the bushes, to be retrieved later. He taught me how to milk a cow and collect the eggs from the bantam hens. There were also turkeys and geese, and a pig sty which I helped muck out. I really loved the farm and looked forward to my times there with great anticipation.

On one of my vacations there I was invited to play the piano for a children's dance to be held in the church hall. By this time I was a somewhat better student and had learned a few tunes that the young people could follow. As we were leaving the farmhouse, I was coming down the wide wooden staircase carrying a lighted oil lamp with a very tall chimney, when I tripped and the lamp went flying. The glass chimney shattered into a thousand pieces and the oil spilled over the hall floor, still alight. I was terrified the house would go up in flames but fortunately, Mrs. Hill (the farmer's wife) rushed out of the kitchen with a sack of flour (hav-

Three cousins at play, left to right, Veronica, Monica and April

ing heard me yell FIRE) and threw it over everything, dousing the flames. She was more concerned with the small cut I'd received to a finger than the fire, and after applying a bandage, we left for the church hall, and continued to enjoy the evening like nothing had happened.

Down on the farm, left to right, Monica, Veronica, Adrian and April

That same vacation, John (the farmer's son) caught shingles and was in a lot of pain, confined to bed. I would do his chores for him and then visit his room and read or do a jigsaw puzzle with him as there was no television then, and no radio in his room. When he was well enough to get out of bed, he wanted to take my picture sitting in the windowsill with the view of the garden behind me. The door to his bedroom was at his back and just as he was about to take the picture, his Mother came into the room and immediately got the wrong impression, since he was standing there in his PJ's, holding the camera in front of him with both hands and his head bent looking through the viewfinder - well, I'm sure you can use your imagination to jump to the same conclusion. And we were all innocence!!

A few days later, when I was visiting John, I happened to lean out of the window and rested my hand on the bottom of a broken milk bottle, almost cutting my left index finger off. I could see the white bone, but it didn't bleed, at least not right away. I should really have had stitches to put it back together, but we were miles from anywhere so had to make do with a tight bandage and eventually it held with no more than a lasting scar; I wasn't able to play the piano again on that vacation, which had turned into one calamity after another. I wasn't sure I'd be welcomed back again, but there were no hard feelings and I did spend several more wonderful vacations on the farm.

2

THE WAR YEARS

In 1938 there was a lot of talk about someone named Adolph Hitler, the Chancellor of Germany, who had a hidden agenda to take over the countries surrounding Germany, as well as England, and had already invaded the smaller countries. It seemed that England was definitely going to be at war with Germany. We were issued gas masks and ration books, and there were posters everywhere declaring, 'Your Country Needs You'. People started volunteering for the army, navy, or air force, rather than waiting to be 'called up'.

Dad announced early in 1938, that he had joined the Royal Air Force and was going to be trained as a Balloon Barrage Technician. One day he arrived home in his new RAF uniform, looking very handsome indeed, and very young too. With his blonde Norwegian good looks, he cut quite the figure. He had left his job at the London Brick Company where he had worked in the office for several years and was now serving full time in the air force, and training other balloon barrage operators at a place called Bridgenorth. He was able to spend just one weekend a month at home with us, where we were still living in Rayners Lane.

Our school was being evacuated to the country for the 'duration of hostilities', which meant the students were going to be separated from their parents indefinitely. There were a lot of emotional outbursts when they realized this and a lot of the students refused to go. I managed to graduate the following Easter, at the tender age of 14 and with honours no less, so avoided being evacuated, thank goodness.

Now it was into the 'real' world, and I actually got my first job on my 14th birthday. Mum had made me a rather nice two piece outfit of dress and jacket in a soft pink, and I wore it to my one and only job interview, which was with a company called, Twentieth Century Fox Furnishing Fabrics. This was in a very big building situated in the heart of London. I sat before the President of the company with my ankles crossed and hands in my lap, as we convent girls had been taught, while answering a lot of questions in a rather shy manner. Evidently, I must have made a good impression, because he said, 'Wonderful Veronica, can you start on Monday?' and I promptly forgot my manners and jumped up with a WHOOP, 'It's my Birthday', which made him laugh, and we became friends.

It was a fairly easy job, packing up large swatches of material for distribution to the Twentieth Century Fox film studios, who then chose the fabric they wanted to use for their stage sets, draperies or upholstery, and even carpeting. I worked alongside two older ladies who taught me how to wrap a bundle of swatches properly. Of course, as the junior, I also had to make the tea (it was England after all), and take it around in cups and saucers to the various department heads, then collect them again ten minutes later, wash up, and put things away, before returning to my swatch packing. Sounds a bit boring, but I was really feeling very independent and grown up.

I had to travel to and from London by tube train, getting up really early to be at the job by 8:30 am and leave there at 5 pm, sometimes not arriving home until nearly 7 pm or later. It made for a long day and, on arrival at home, I would have supper and a bath and go straight to bed to sleep like a baby. I was happy and it seemed I had finally grown out of my middle name of 'Trouble'.

A few months later, war was declared at 11:15 am on September 3rd, 1939. As we listened to Neville Chamberlain, the Prime Minister at that time, giving his "We are at war with Germany" speech on the radio, my mother was talking over the fence with our neighbour, and I was standing on top of the coal bunker. Suddenly, we heard a plane overhead, and thought it was probably from Northolt Airport, which was just a couple of miles away. I looked up to wave to the pilot as I had done so many times before, I could see him quite clearly in the cockpit. But it wasn't one of ours, it was a German fighter. I saw the cross on the fuselage and the swastika on the tail of the aircraft. Even before I could register the fact, there was a loud explosion. The fighter had deliberately crashed into a hangar at Northolt airport. We later learned that several aircraft had been destroyed, as well as some people killed. The war had begun, and these were the first casualties.

From then on we spent our nights sleeping on a mattress under the dining table which was solid oak with good sturdy legs, praying that the bombs we could hear dropping, would not drop on us, and we were scared. We were already prepared with our blackout curtains, which had to be tightly closed at night, so not a chink of light showed outside that could possibly be seen from enemy aircraft overhead, and the only illumination was from the wireless (radio) dial which we kept on all the time in case of emergency instructions. Anderson Air Raid Shelters of corrugated steel and concrete had been built at the end of several gardens. Although we did not have one of these, my cousin, who lived in the house behind ours, did. So if necessary, and if we had time, we could all pile into theirs.

At night the sky was lit up with searchlights weaving in search of enemy planes, and the Bofors Guns which were placed on flat cars on the nearby freight line tracks went off with a resounding WOOMPHA – WOOMPHA, which shook the whole house. Air Raid Wardens wearing tin hats, blowing whistles to warn us to take cover, were racing around the neighbourhood on bicycles. They too suffered casualties as they were always the ones in harm's way. When a bomb dropped close by, the percussion caused a wave of suction that, in one case, sucked the clothes right off one poor air raid warden who, fortunately, was otherwise unharmed, except for his dignity.

Rationing was something that became a way of life very early on and there were shortages of almost everything. Ration books were issued and a coupon represented one week's portion of meat, fish, or butter and cheese. Real eggs were unheard of, and were substituted by a powdered variety which tasted terrible. Toilet paper was nonexistent so newspaper became a necessity, though it's a wonder we didn't all get lead poisoning from the print! Bananas, oranges and other fruits were only available if you were under 16 years of age. Sweets of any kind, as well as sugar and flour were also unavailable, and my Candy Man was out of business. The only good thing about rationing was the fact that most people were healthier than they had ever been.

We were also issued with gas masks in little cardboard boxes, and tin hats, which we had to carry with us at all times. Babies too, had a type of gas mask, but as you can imagine, trying to get one to stay on a baby was an impossibility. Fortunately, we never had to wear the gas masks, but there were times when the tin hat came in handy.

With the war already started, the young man who was our postal clerk at Twentieth Century and took care of the mailing, was enlisted into the army at very short notice - here one day and gone the next. I applied for his job, and moved upstairs to his desk right away, learning a lot of new things all at once. First came the old Smith Corona typewriter, which wasn't too bad, since I had actually started taking a business course.

Although I didn't get very far in the course, I did know the keyboard, and soon learned the hunt and peck method of typing. Then there was a mimeograph on which I had to print hundreds of forms, but managed to get more ink on myself. Then came a Gestetner print machine, again a very messy project, an Addressograph, which was a big clunky thing that you fed metal plates into on one side, and envelopes on the other, pull down a handle, and the plate and envelope met, imprinting the address thereon (I didn't like that one).

Of course there was the inevitable filing, and lots of it, and relieving on the switchboard. That really scared me. It was the old style of plugging in here, flip a switch, answer the incoming caller, plug another plug into their extension number on the board, flip another switch to ring it through, and keep your fingers crossed that it connected. Sometimes, all the lights would go on at once, and all the wires would get crossed, so that it was impossible to see which call had terminated, and who was still plugged in. Thank goodness it was only for lunch time or tea break, and not all day long - I think I'd have thrown in the towel very quickly. As it was, all the different things I learned there stood me in good stead for future jobs, and I chalked it up to good experience

One night, after the air raid warning had sounded, Mum and I were looking out of her upstairs bedroom window, and were shocked to see the entire skyline aglow. It was the London Docks and the Battersea Power Plant being totally destroyed by incendiary bombs, and everything was on fire as we watched in horror. The bombs dropped, and fire raged all night, and well into the next day. It had been impossible for fire engines, or any rescue vehicles to get through the inferno and debris.

The most amazing sight was the aftermath of this raid. The underground tube stations throughout London became home to thousands of families who survived this and other raids, but had lost their homes and entire possessions. Most of the men had been called up, or joined the military, so it was the women and children, the young and the old who spent their days and nights, huddled on the platforms, eating and sleeping where they could find a spot. They were always cheerful and uncomplaining, despite the fact that all they had managed to salvage filled a paper bag. The Underground became their home for the duration of the war, babies were born and people died during this ordeal.

I mentioned about combing my Grandfather's hair when I was very small, which somehow translated into an ongoing desire to be a hairdresser and beautician. My mother attended a beauty salon close to where she worked in London, not because she was vain, but because it was not always convenient to wash hair at home - no soap, it was rationed, and no hot water, it cost a shilling in the meter and sometimes a raid would have caused the gas to be shut off. After one of her visits to the salon, she announced that they would take me on as an apprentice, and I would get on-the-job training. I left Twentieth Century Fox to start what I hoped would be my future career. I found myself mixing the bleaches, holding the papers for perms, and passing out clips, serving refreshments and, of course, cleaning up after everyone, but I never touched anyone's hair.

One day, while assisting a hairdresser who was preparing to give a permanent wave to a customer with very long hair, and using the thinning shears to thin the hair out, the phone rang, and the hairdresser left to answer the call. When she returned, she picked up the scissors, grabbed a handful of hair, and chopped the whole thing off - she had picked up the wrong scissors!! Somehow or other, she managed to keep working without letting the customer know, and when the final comb-out was done, the mistake was well hidden in the curls. I often wondered if that customer ever discovered her short patch.

There were some very interesting customers too, such as Ginger Rogers, the movie star who was always partnered with Fred Astaire and was such a wonderful dancer. She had been entertaining the troops in France and was stopping over in London before her return to the United States. She was so beautiful. Others were movie stars, Olivia DeHavilland and Vivien Leigh, who played Scarlett O'Hara in *Gone With the Wind*. I was still a teenager and was fascinated with these glamorous women.

Unfortunately, I didn't stay at the beauty salon very long and didn't learn very much. We had sold the house in Rayners Lane and were supposed to move into some rooms in a house close to Mum's office near Regents Park in London. But before we could move in, the building received a direct bomb hit and was demolished, along with all our possessions, which we had left there in suitcases. For the next few weeks we were gypsies, staying with friends and dodging the bombs. Like the people in the tube stations, all we had was in a paper bag.

This all took place in 1940 when London was being heavily bombarded. I had to change jobs several times when the building I had been working in the day before disappeared overnight in a pile of rubble. Many times we'd be on our way to find somewhere to eat, when the siren sounded and the air raid warden or police would rush us into a shelter, only to find the restaurant gone when we resurfaced. The Battle of Britain had begun and it was an amazing sight to see the fighters of both the British and German air forces chasing each other around the sky, but although there were many losses on both sides, we were winning this part of the battle. Sir Winston Churchill (whom I believe saved our hides) made the now famous speech, "*Never in the field of human conflict, was so much owed by so many, to so few.*"

Even though there was a war going on, the circus was still performing at Earls Court in London. Dad took my brother to see it, and they were unable to get home because the train tracks had been bombed, so they had to spend the night in one of the crowded tube stations. There was a lady sitting beside them on the platform, sound asleep, wrapped in a knitted shawl. My darling brother noticed a thread of wool hanging from it, and started pulling, more and more until he had almost completely unravelled the entire shawl, so carefully that the lady did not wake up before my Dad noticed what he was doing. When the lady did wake up, and saw what had happened, she was naturally quite upset. Dad apologized most profusely, as well as paying the lady some money, and Adrian got a good scolding, but all he said was, 'Well, she still has the wool, she can knit it up again'. That was the logic of a five year old!

Earlier in the day Dad and Adrian had been shopping at the famous Selfridges Department Store on Oxford Street. At one point they were in a lift which was being operated by a young lady in a very smart uniform, when she suddenly turned to my Dad with a disgusted look and proceeded to take the lift to the top floor. When she opened the door she indicated for Dad and Adrian to follow her, and marched them into the manager's office.

There she told a disjointed story of an incident that had just happened in the lift. Dad had no idea what she was talking about and was finally allowed to leave. When they arrived home and Dad related the story to Mum, Adrian cut in with, 'I know what happened, the lady trod on my toe so I pinched her bottom, HARD!!'. I guess that explains that situation.

After a couple of years, during which Dad had been training others to be Barrage Balloon Technicians, he was promoted to Sergeant and was posted to a place called Byfleet, in Surrey. There were two major aircraft factories on either side of Brooklands Race Track, and he was the Sergeant in charge of several balloon crews protecting these factories from daily bombing raids. The 'balloons' were large dirigibles which had to be sent aloft on cables attached to a winch and flown high enough to deter low level and dive bombing attacks by enemy planes on vulnerable targets.

About 231 V-1's, or flying bombs were brought down by these balloons. On some occasions the balloons would get shot down and crash in flames, doing as much damage as a bomb. Dad received commendation on two occasions when such disaster struck his site, and received the 'Oak Leaves and cluster' from King George VI at a Buckingham Palace investiture.

Since there were no permanent living quarters attached to this posting, Dad was staying in a boarding house in the village of Byfleet, but wanted to find a place for us to be a family, although my brother was still away attending Taplow Grammar School. Dad had been looking around in the village and found the perfect place. Finally, we were able to leave London and the constant noise of bombs, sirens and danger, although nowhere in England was really safe.

Our cottage in Byfleet was actually the carriage house to a mansion, and was quite large for a cottage, having five bedrooms, two bathrooms, a library, lounge and huge kitchen which became the gathering place for quite a number of the Canadian Signals Corps, the first Canadian regiment to arrive in England. The soldiers were billeted in the huge houses on the golf course across the main street from us, which had been commandeered for use by the military. I did tell you my Dad was born in Vancouver, British Columbia didn't I, so of course he welcomed his fellow countrymen into our home, and it became their home away from home. There were always a few dropping in to share their letters, whether it be good news, a 'dear John', or a parcel of goodies, these young men were always welcome.

We had a very large garden with many apple and pear trees, as well as a pond for ducks and a few chickens which supplied us with much needed eggs. It backed onto Brooklands Race track, where Sir Malcolm Campbell won many races in his mini sports cars, prior to hostilities. The track had been covered with wire mesh and camouflage, so that it could not be a landmark for enemy aircraft.

Just about 100 yards from our cottage was the Vickers Aircraft factory where Wellington bombers were built, and I got a job there as secretary in the Free Issue Stores. Actually, I wasn't in the 'store' which supplied things like nuts and bolts, clamps and hoses for the people building the planes. I was in the office learning to use a clunky old teletype machine, answering the phone and typing orders, using an ancient Smith Corona upright typewriter similar to the one I had used at Twentieth Century Fox. I was still using the hunt and peck method of typing. My boss would stand behind me and watch as I typed, shaking his head in disbelief since by this time I could type quite fast without too many mistakes. He said it looked like I was playing the piano, but he couldn't figure out the tune!

Vickers had received a direct bomb hit just two weeks before I started work there, and the dust was still flying. Much damage had been done to a walkway between the hangar and the cafeteria, and several people on their way to lunch had been killed. The air raid siren was going off frequently. When it did, we all had to evacuate across the street to an underground shelter until the All Clear sounded and we could return to work, hoping we still had jobs to go back to.

This was a huge shelter, built into the side of a hill, and could hold about 200 people comfortably, with plenty of food and water. Invariably, someone would start singing, and before long everyone would join in and make the best of a bad situation, not knowing what we would see when we left the shelter. Fortunately, the factory did not receive any more direct hits, but there were 40 incendiary bombs dropped in the garden of our cottage one night. How they missed the house, we'll never know, but thank God they did.

During lunchtime in the (makeshift) cafeteria on my first day at work, I met two Canadian airmen, whom I learned were there to take a two-week course on aircraft engines, and I also learned that they did not yet have a place to stay. Knowing that we had several bedrooms and only two in use, I naturally invited them home – oh! I forgot to mention, this was the day my Mother was moving into the cottage. She was actually pleased to see them, and set them to work unpacking and making things work. They stayed for the two weeks, and enjoyed Mum's cooking and hospitality. She always managed with the aid of their ration books, to come up with plenty to eat and invariably enough for second helpings.

Dad also helped out a lot. When he was doing his rounds of the balloon sites at Brooklands first thing each morning, there were always plenty of rabbits scurrying around and he would manage to bag a couple to bring home for dinner. Mum's rabbit pie and rabbit stew were delicious and always evoked words of praise from whoever was lucky enough to be there for dinner.

Word soon spread that our house was the place to stay, and from those first two airmen, it became four, then six, then eight, for the next four years, and believe me, there was never a dull moment. We still entertained the Signals Corps, and then the Navy joined in when they started attending courses at the Hawker Aircraft factory, on the other side of Brooklands Race Track. Since our house was always full of young men, the local young women were not far behind, and impromptu parties were happening on a regular basis. It was hard to remember there was a war going on, but it seemed appropriate to enjoy oneself today, we didn't know what tomorrow would bring.

I joined the local Air Cadet Squadron and found myself learning Morse Code and being taught precision drilling. My uniform consisted of a grey skirt, pale blue shirt, black tie and shoes, and a forage cap of grey with the Air Cadet Badge. We met one evening a week unless there was an air-raid and we couldn't get to headquarters, which happened all too often. Although I never used the Morse Code at any time, my training became the ground work and stayed with me for the future.

I worked at Vickers for a couple of years, during which time I met Sir Barnes Neville Wallis, the inventor of the bomb used to destroy the German dams in the famous Dam Buster raid led by Squadron Leader Guy Gibson of 617 Squadron. The initial prototype plane for the raids on the Dams was a white Wellington with no markings which I watched being built at Vickers, but had no idea for what purpose at the time.

Just before I left Vickers to go to work at Hawker Aircraft, the 'other' factory, where the Hurricane fighters were built, I took a day off, and together with my Dad, we took a train from Weybridge to Taplow where my brother had been boarding at Taplow Grammar School. We had been advised that Taplow was on the 'front line', and being so heavily bombarded that the students were spending all day in the air raid shelters, not learning very much, so they were closing the school for the duration of hostilities.

On the way to the railway station, my boss at Vickers passed us on his way to work. We said a cheery, 'Good morning', to each other, and continued on to the station. When I went in to work the following morning, I was greeted with, 'When you want a day off to spend with your boyfriend, at least be honest about it'. I realized he had assumed my Dad was my boyfriend (I mentioned Dad looked so young in his uniform). Well, I called headquarters and relayed a message for Dad to stop by my office when he did the rounds of his balloons on the aerodrome, and we soon cleared up the confusion when I introduced him to my boss, although I'm still not sure my boss was totally convinced, and he continued to tease me. Incidents like this happened quite frequently and became quite embarrassing at times, especially if I happened to be out somewhere with Dad and ran into one of my boyfriends. It took a bit of explaining and I wasn't always believed, but then had to invite the boyfriend home so he could meet Mum too. That usually set the record straight.

It had been almost three years since I had last seen Adrian and it was so good to see him again, he had certainly grown into a good looking young man, now eight years old, and almost as tall as me. He was glad to be home again too, and quickly adjusted to his new school in the village, and was way ahead of other children his age. I'm sure he was a genius, he was so smart. His two best friends were twin boys who lived close by, and the three of them spent a lot of time together creating new games. One of Adrian's special accomplishments was writing poetry, he could compose a rhyme about almost anything.

On the other hand, I preferred to take long bicycle rides, and my girlfriend and I would head off on Sunday mornings, armed with a big tin of home made cookies we intended to deliver to one of the many military bases scattered within a 25 mile radius of home. We usually just kept cycling until we got tired (probably the full 25 miles), and then found the nearest camp to deliver the cookies (or biscuits, as we called them).

On one of these Sunday mornings, when Adrian had been home about six months, he came into my bedroom demanding that I get up and take him to his favourite swimming hole. This was part of the River Wey which ran through the village of Weybridge, the next village to ours. There was a lovely area there called The Blue Lagoon, which was a very popular swimming and picnicking spot for off-duty military personnel stationed in the area, and it was always crowded, despite it being wartime. However, I already had plans to go a little further afield to a new camp of Canadian soldiers that had just arrived and deliver our special cookies, so he left in a huff, and I went back to sleep. I'm sorry to say, that was the last time I saw my little brother alive.

When I arrived home much later than I should have been, because my bike had a flat tire, Dad was waiting at the gate. I thought I was going to be in trouble for being

Byfleet 1941, just one week before Adrian drowned.
Rear, Nanna Doody; centre, left to right Mum,
Adrian age 8½, Veronica, age 16; front, Bonzo the dog

late, but instead, his first words were, 'We've lost Adrian'. I thought he meant they couldn't find him at the Blue Lagoon, so I was ready to jump back on my bike and go to look for him. I said, 'I know where he is, I'll go find him', but Dad stopped me and said, 'No, Adrian has drowned, you won't find him'. Needless to say, I was shocked and couldn't believe what I had just heard. I was still ready to go and look for my little brother, but Dad restrained me and took me into the house.

The beautiful spot where so many people had enjoyed swimming and picnicking was actually the point where two rivers met past a mill, above which were sluice gates. Someone had opened those gates, allowing water to rush through, causing a whirlpool in which my brother was caught. Only being eight years old, he didn't have the strength to fight his way out, and his body was carried down stream. It would not be recovered for five days, despite the efforts of many of our Canadian soldier friends and others. No-one ever owned up to opening the sluice gates, but I always felt guilty for not being with him although, according to eye-witnesses, nothing could have been done to save him.

It seemed that wherever I went after that, whether at work, at home, or shopping in the village, people seemed to be whispering and pointing at me, and I wanted to hide where no-one would find me. About a month after Adrian drowned, my girl friend and her family moved away. I really missed her so one day I raided my piggy bank, packed a small suitcase, and hopped a train to where she was, but I was also very sick at the time. When I arrived at her house, her Mother made me go straight to bed, where I stayed for the next three days. I was sure Mrs. Wilson would have called my parents or the police, but she hadn't. However, the police did arrive on her doorstep asking questions. I later learned that the station master at Weybridge had informed the police of my destination. Mrs. Wilson didn't let on that I was there, but she did make me get up and dress. She fed me lunch and then insisted that I get the next train home, which I did. I know she then called my Mother at her office, because

Mum was at the station to meet me.

Definitely not a 'welcome home' greeting though. She handed me the house key and a penny – to buy a bun, in case I was hungry! I had to walk the three miles home. Another surprise awaited me – all my photos had been turned face down, and my clothes removed from my bedroom, as well as my bed being stripped. That was just about the last straw, but rather than let it totally destroy me, I set about straightening my photos right way up, and making my bed, as well as having dinner ready when Mum came home. For the next six months I said very little, and did nothing that would cause any kind of trouble.

I had to find another job because I had walked out of the one at Hawkers and, not unexpectedly, they had fired me. The Canadian government had opened a library adjacent to where the Signals Corps was billeted and I applied for a job there, but I wasn't happy either at work or at home. The atmosphere was strained to say the least, and I couldn't wait to turn 17. That would happen in just a few more months and I was already plotting my next move.

3

WOMEN'S AUXILIARY AIR FORCE

The months couldn't pass quickly enough and in May of 1942 when I turned 17, I tried to join the Women's Land Army. These women, as the name implies, worked on the land, taking the place of male farm workers who had been called up into the military. I had wanted to work with horses at Epsom Downs Race Track, but when they wanted me to report at 5 am I chickened out, that was just a wee bit too early for me. Then we were notified that one of the airmen who had been billeted with us had been shot down over the North Sea on his way back from a bombing raid, and despite the efforts of Air Sea Rescue, they were unable to find and rescue him. This prompted me to want to join the Women's Royal Navy in the Air Sea Rescue Division, but I had to wait another six months until I was seventeen and a half, which was the minimum age for volunteering.

The six months dragged on and the very day I was 17½ years old, (I'd counted out the days), I went to the nearest recruiting office, which was on the Kilburn High Road, but to my dismay, the Navy office was closed; however, right next door was the Women's Auxiliary Air Force recruiting office with its doors wide open. So, not to waste my trip, I went in there and signed up. Actually, I almost wasn't allowed to as they thought I was only 13 years old, and gave me a form to take home for Dad to sign, giving his permission for me to join the air force.

I had passed the math test and the questionnaire, and signed up as a Flight Mechanic, Aircraft Engines. Dad did not like the idea of me in uniform, but he signed anyway, with the remark, 'I can't wait to see you as a mechanic, you don't like getting your hands dirty helping your Mother'. Wow! Such enthusiasm made me even more determined, and I could hardly wait to be called up.

I didn't have to wait long. Just a couple of weeks later on the day I was summoned to report to Innsworth WAAF Station, Gloucestershire, it was pouring with rain, a miserably cold January morning in 1943. By the time I arrived, having changed trains twice and waited on uncovered platforms, I was soaked, and wearing my best hat and coat which were ruined. They still were not dry the next morning when I had to find the canteen for breakfast, and then join all the other recruits to be fitted with

First picture in the WAAF
(also on back cover)

uniforms. I say 'fitted' because there were only two sizes, big and bigger. I only weighed 98 pounds, and was five feet tall, so you can guess where it fitted.

It was pitch dark and, of course, with the war still on, all buildings were Blacked Out, so I got hopelessly lost trying to find the canteen, and was even beginning to wish I was back home. Fortunately, a guardian angel came to my rescue and steered me back to my billet. Although I didn't get any breakfast, I was in time to join the others and be marched to the issue stores for our uniforms.

Everything was stuffed into a kit bag, grey wool stockings, garter belt, sanitary belt and a bra which I would never be able to fill, and bloomers. Oh my, those bloomers were the source of many jokes. We used to call them Passion Killers. They were certainly enough to cool anyone's ardour, with elastic around the legs and waist which you could pull up to under your armpits, and down to below the knees, one of the many 'one size fits all' items we received that day.

Once back at our billet, the next job was to mark everything with our name and service number, in indelible ink. I still had labels from my convent days and sewed them onto everything, and printed my number in indelible ink on white tape, sewing that on beside my name. I was feeling very proud that I was actually about to wear a uniform that had nothing to do with convents. Hopefully, that part of my life was far behind me.

From then on, we were either at attention or at ease. We were being yelled at constantly, to fall in or fall out, go here or go there, stand up or sit down, go to sleep or wake up, and actually waking up was the worst part, being blasted out of bed by the tannoy loud speaker trumpeting reveille.

Then there were the lectures on what to expect, how to behave, whom to salute, whom to call Sir or Ma'am, a lecture called Ranks and Badges, and a whole lot of other stuff which I was sure would be totally useless. This went on for the next three days, during which time we were getting used to wearing our uniforms, cleaning brass buttons, and polishing shoes till you could see your face in them, while the rain kept pouring down. But there was worse to come.

At the end of that first week of orientation, we were being dispatched to various parts of the country for the next phase of our training. Our kitbags were packed and, according to regulations, carried on our left shoulder (they weighed a ton). Our orders were to march to the railway station, where we would board our designated train. We had been handed our first pay package, which was only a few shillings, and our instructions for reaching our final destination.

In my case, along with a few other recruits from my entry, we were being housed in civilian quarters which was a private house not far from the ocean at Morecombe, on the north west coast of England, north of Blackpool, Lancashire. We never did get to enjoy the sights and sounds of that lively place, nor did we ever get to the beach, mainly because the entire beachfront was covered with barbed wire in case of an enemy landing. It was still winter, and bitterly cold, with the wind constantly blowing off the Irish Sea.

We were supposed to be 'square bashing'. That is, we were being taught how to form columns of three, and march with precision to the barked orders from our drill instructor, who was an enormous sergeant, built like a tank, with a voice like a boom box. Definitely not a pretty sight and a force to be reckoned with, along with the gale force winds which, at times, actually blew us off our feet. Many a new hat was lost during these drill sessions. Other times, we were attending lectures in the local cinema, until one day the roof blew off and we had to find a new place to listen to more of the same.

The house in which we were billeted was fairly comfortable, but the meals left a lot to be desired. The young couple who owned the house, and were supposed to be feeding us, had been issued with ration books for each of the new boarders. We soon discovered however, that most of the food was going into their own kitchen for their consumption and we were getting powdered eggs on soggy toast almost every day. One day, I actually saw half a side of beef being taken into the house. I thought maybe we were finally going to receive a good meal, but that didn't happen. Knowing how my mother provided such great meals for the airman billeted with her, I had to say something. Naturally, that didn't go over too well with the housekeepers, and I was promptly moved to another billet which wasn't much better. But I survived, and kept my thoughts to myself, realizing the situation would not be lasting that much longer.

By the time we were ready to leave Morecombe, our band of raw recruits was beginning to shape up, and we were looking forward to marching in the 'passing out' parade. That was where everyone (nearly 300 of us), marched past the saluting stand in formation, to a military band playing a rousing Air Force march. Our spirits were high, chests were out, arms swinging high to the waist of the girl in front, just as we'd been taught, but it was also a sad moment, because we knew we would all be going in different directions again, depending on the trade we had enlisted in. But first came a much needed week's leave.

As a WAAF Flight Mechanic, Engines at age 18 (also on front cover)

Mum had moved again, so instead of going to our new home, I decided to spend my first leave with my cousin April, in Romford. Actually, that was not a very safe area, being so close to Biggin Hill, a major fighter base and the target of many very heavy air raids.

While in Romford, we spent a lot of time in the air raid shelter. Old Gerry (our name for the Germans) always managed to arrive at meal time, just as we were about to sit down to eat. The siren would sound, alerting us to an impending air raid. April, her mother and I would head for the shelter at the bottom of the garden with our meal on a tray, but there were lots of spiders in the shelter. Spiders and snakes are two creatures I can't stand, so April and I would sit on top of the shelter, and watch in silent horror as one plane after another was shot out of the sky, our food totally forgotten.

Romford was a nice little town where April and I would spend a lot of time browsing the street markets. Both she and her mother were great seamstresses. We'd buy a piece of material in the market, take it home, and in no time a new dress would be made and worn that evening to the local dance hall. I always enjoyed the time I spent at this house, until a land-mine exploded in the next street, and the front of the house was heavily damaged by the blast. As a result they moved from Romford to a safer area, although nowhere was really safe. Most of England was under constant bombing raids. London alone had lost more than a million homes by this time.

When my leave was over, I boarded a train to Rugely, in Staffordshire. It turned out to be a troop train, packed to the rafters with young men in uniform, and all their gear, headed for God knows where. All they knew was that they would be on the 'front line' before very long, and facing other young men, who would be called 'the enemy'. Most of the men on the train were about the same age as me and I felt their anxiety, but I too was heading into the unknown, so we tried to cheer each other up in the usual British way, by singing. Gracie Fields and Vera Lynn were the Forces sweethearts at that time, and their songs were on everyone's lips, so we sang, 'We'll meet again don't know where, don't know when, but I know we'll meet again some sunny day', knowing of course, that we probably wouldn't.

I left the train at Rugely, and discovered there were about 30 other airwomen also headed for their Flight Mechanic Training Course. We soon realized that we were on our own as far as finding our way to the camp, which happened to be some distance from the railway station, up a very long steep hill, which we christened Kit Bag Hill, although I doubt that we were the first ones to call it that. By the time we checked in at the guard house we were ready to drop, and still had to go through a lengthy signing-in process.

Eventually, everything was taken care of and we were assigned to our billet, a long wooden hut with 7 or 8 two-tier bunks along either side to accommodate 30 airwomen. A small coal burning stove in the centre, and two long tables with benches were before and after the stove. To one side of the entry door was the Corporal or Sergeants Room, which was off limits to all we 'erks'.

Our so called mattresses, were actually three squares, 24 inches by 30 inches, called 'biscuits', filled with straw, as was the only pillow, two rough sheets (definitely not percale), and two heavy khaki blankets. These items had to be folded exactly a certain way, squared off each morning and placed on top of the three biscuits at the top end of the bed. Beds could not be made up again until after 6 pm. We were also issued eating utensils, a mug, shoe polish, button cleaning items, and a whole mess of other necessities which, when 'kit inspection' was called, had to be placed 'exactly so' on the made up bed, which also had to be 'exactly so'.

The Inspecting Officer would make a careful study of everything on the bed, and if there was something he or she didn't particularly like, it could result in all manner of disciplinary action. More serious misdemeanours could result in 'Jankers', which meant peeling potatoes or carrots in the Sergeants mess for a week, or scrubbing the ablutions (toilets).

Other than the above daily routine, we were learning to become Flight Mechanics. I must say I thoroughly enjoyed the hours spent in the hangars, climbing over aircraft engines and discovering what made them work, or not, and learning how to fix them. I am proud that I was among the first one

An aircraft being refuelled by unidentified airwomen

33

hundred women Flight Mechanics of the second world war, and I was determined to show my Dad that I really didn't mind getting my hands dirty.

Once we had taken an engine apart and put it back together again, we had to install it on the aircraft. We worked as a team of five, each with our own particular job to do, and after it was finally installed and the check list signed by each of us, came the ultimate test – would it start.

Unidentified Flight Mechs at work on an aircraft

There was an old aircraft, a Fairey Battle, outside the hangar. We had been working on the engine of this aircraft, which looked quite menacing from where I stood underneath the nose. Having just finished putting on the cowling, and then the nose cone, the test was to begin, but first came the cockpit 'drill', which we called BUGS, meaning, 'Brakes, Undercarriage, Guns, Gills and Switches'. All of these had to be checked before we could yell to someone on the ground, 'Magneto ON'. Now came the hard part: 'Swinging the Prop'. When you are only five feet tall it's easier said than done, but I had to do it. By jumping up and grabbing one of the three propeller blades nearest to me, and pulling down, not to forget to step back immediately, the engine should now start. Oh, Happy Days when it did, and Oh Hell when it didn't, which I am glad to say, was not very often. Fortunately, this aircraft was not intended to fly, but we did have to check everything to make sure we had done the job properly.

There was also an old Anson, with a different type of engine which we had to learn about and test in the same way, as well as lectures, and written tests almost every day. We were trying to cram into 3 months, what most engineers say should take two or three years to learn, so studying and paying attention were our a major priorities.

We did have some fun too though. Rugely was also a Fleet Air Arm Station, where sailors were learning to be Flight Mechanics, so it was not unusual in our off hours to run into some of these Navy types. Up to now, I had not been into a public house (the minimum drinking age was 18), so on my 18th birthday, my group decided I should be initiated. We met up with a young sailor, also celebrating his 18th birthday at the same time and in the same manner. The two of us got rip-roaring drunk, and had to be carried back to camp. I don't think I ever knew his name. I wonder if he remembers that evening?

The time came to graduate as a fully-fledged Flight Mechanic/Engines, and I eagerly awaited news of my marks, and where I was going to be posted. My goodness, the nuns would be having a fit because I'd graduated third in my class, and without having to use one word of their stupid Latin. I always knew that would be a waste of time. Needless to say, we REALLY celebrated that night, and the next day were handed our posting orders. Once again, we had to be separated from the friends we had so recently found, but there was a war on, and so it goes.

WAAF Flight Mechs at work on a radial engine

My next posting was to No.15 Operational Training Unit, Harwell, near Didcot in Berkshire, but almost immediately, I found myself being trucked to the satellite station at Hampstead Norris. Glad I didn't have to carry my kitbag all that way, although there was no Kit Bag Hill thank goodness. Things were very different here. I found myself living in a tent with three other airwomen, where mice could be heard skittering around in our pillows which were filled with straw. Everything was very primitive and uncomfortable for the first several months, until billets were erected for us, similar to those at Rugely.

While we were still in the tents, we had a terrific rainstorm that lasted for a couple of days, and everything we owned got soaked. Since there was nowhere warm for us to hang anything to dry, they stayed wet for some time, then began to smell mouldy and started to rot, but we had a very hard time getting replacements. Our boots particularly, which we had to wear every day with our battle dress, were beginning to fall apart. I stuffed mine with brown paper until the new issue of shoes arrived. I don't think our mother base at Harwell realized what drowned rats we were. Of course, we nearly all came down with bronchitis, or worse, and no time to get sick, we still had to get to work and keep the planes flying.

Speaking of which, I was now working on Wellingtons, the same planes I had been involved with at Vickers Armstrong in Byfleet. I held a special affinity for each one. Here was where every nut, bolt and tightened screw really mattered, as these aircraft were being flown by aircrew training for future combat with the enemy in bombing raids over enemy territory. The Wellington, or Wimpy, as it was fondly nicknamed, was one of the few bombers available at the beginning of the war in 1939, when it became the backbone of the Royal Air Force's Bomber Command. The light but strong geodetic framework of crisscrossing tubes under doped fabric skin enabled it to keep

A liquid cooled Merlin engine, a type on which I worked

flying through very heavy attack. However, by 1943 the 4-engine bombers such as the Lancaster and Halifax had taken over the more concentrated bombing raids on Germany and the Wimpy was used mainly for training.

It was powered by either two Pegasus radial or two Merlin in-line engines. I much preferred the in-line engines, where the cylinders were placed so they were easy to work on, with valves, pistons and tappets in two straight rows, as opposed to the radial engines which, as implied, were in a double circle of cylinders, hard to get at, and caused many skinned knuckles from the sharp fins that encircled each cylinder.

A crew of five airmen, consisting of a pilot, navigator, bomb-aimer, wireless operator/air gunner, and rear gunner flew in the aircraft on training flights. They depended on the ground crew which consisted of the engine mechanics, the airframe fitters who took care of the 'skin' of the aircraft, instrument technicians, electricians and others, to keep their aircraft in perfect condition, and of course, the very necessary parachute packers. We all worked together as a team to ensure their safe return as far as the aircraft was concerned, but there was always the possibility of running into an enemy attack or accident, and we did suffer losses.

A memorial to lost aircrew somewhere in Scotland, including a radial engine, another type on which I worked

Our work attire consisted of a battledress top and trousers over the regulation air force blue shirt, with starched collar and black tie, black socks and heavy leather boots. As if that wasn't enough, we had to wear a boiler suit over all that, and instead of our 'dress' hats, the women wore berets, while the men wore their usual forage caps. During the summer months, we could discard the

36

battledress top but were still covered with the boiler suit, and in the winter, when it was particularly cold working in an open hangar or outdoors, it was not unusual to see a couple of inches of pyjama legs showing beneath our trousers. It was our way of trying to keep warm.

Wellingtons at rest in the snow, from the painting by Keith Woodcock © (also on front cover)

The Flight Mechanic who worked on an engine was required to fly on the test flight after the maintenance job was completed, sitting beside the pilot in the co-pilot's seat, keeping an eye on the instrument panel and an ear out for any changes in the sound of the engine. One of the pilots I flew with quite often was from New Zealand, a real daredevil. On one occasion, he flew over a field where a farmer was busy building a haystack, and flew so low that the slipstream blew the haystack to pieces. I can still see the farmer's look of rage, as he waved his fists at the aircraft.

This pilot had a girlfriend who lived in one of the mansions not far away. She always knew when he would be flying, and would be standing on the balcony ready to wave her hanky as he flew over, but to her horror this time he seemed to be flying right for the balcony, and only pulled up at the last minute. I'm quite sure she needed to change her underwear after that – I know I did!!

There was another episode that got us both into trouble. This same pilot went a little further afield than usual, and we found ourselves over the City of Reading. After buzzing the city at low altitude, giving the local population a real scare, he then flew *under* the bridge crossing the River Thames. When we arrived back at the airfield, both his Commanding Officer and mine, along with my sergeant, a very forbidding character, were waiting for us.

The pilot was whisked off to parts unknown, while I was severely reprimanded for being in the aircraft *without a parachute*. Actually, I never did fly with one, because the 'chute' store was way around the other side of our field and I was just too lazy to walk all that distance, though regulations said I mustn't fly without one. There had been a few times with this particular pilot when I really thought I might need a chute, but he said, 'Not to worry - you can sit on my lap when we bail out'. I can just see me flying off into space when his chute opened, so was very glad we always managed to land safely.

I almost forgot to tell you that when it came time to land after our Reading episode, the landing gear would not come down, and we had circled the aerodrome several times, before finally managing to use the hand pump to lower it. So that accounted for the fact that we had been chased along the runway by the fire truck and ambulance. I often wonder what happened to that pilot. I never flew with him again, and I think he was probably posted elsewhere. I just hope he survived the war.

Life at Hampstead Norris was not all work and no play. Although our days started at 6 am and sometimes didn't end until nearly eight pm, while we waited for a plane to return from a test flight, we found time for dating, dancing, roller skating, and generally getting up to a little harmless mischief. We had the usual NAAFI hut, a canteen for socializing, selling the necessities of life, along with weak tea, terrible coffee, stale cakes and cookies. We also had a weekly dance in this building. Ballroom dancing was something I always enjoyed, and I was fortunate to find a really good partner, who twirled me around the floor on a regular basis. Since we were in full uniform, that meant I was wearing heavy flat heeled shoes, not the most comfortable shoes for doing a quickstep or jitterbug, but a good way of breaking in a new pair.

There was also another building that had been empty for some time, and a group of us who also enjoyed roller skating (the old fashioned way), decided this would be a good place for us to use as a rink. The only problem was that it had a cement floor, and it wasn't long before the surface of the floor became churned into dust. By the end of an evening of skating, we all ended up with white hair, but we didn't let that deter us, there was a war on, and this was our way of letting off steam for an hour or two.

We became one big happy family, everyone knew everyone else, nobody got left out. Some of the WAAF had boyfriends in the Army, on the front line, or Navy, or aircrew actively engaged in bombing raids. Several times news would arrive, advising them that something had happened to their loved one. It affected all of us, and we supported each other in times of need. Easter 1943, I was the recipient of such news when my mother wrote and told me that my favourite cousin, an officer in the Royal Ulster Rifles, had been killed during a raid on Rommel's headquarters in Tunisia.

I remember the last time I had seen him was the leave I spent in Romford when he was also on embarkation leave. His regiment wore kilts, and of course we girls were curious to know what they wore under them, since we had heard they didn't wear anything. His sister April and I went through his kit bag, but we couldn't find any underwear, so what we heard must be true and we teased him unmercifully, but all in good fun. He was a great sport and I was very sad that he was gone.

Just before June, 1944 we sensed that something was different around the camp. Leaves were cancelled, and there seemed to be an air of suspense. It wasn't long before the news came that our beloved Hampstead Foo (our pet name for Hampstead Norris), was being closed down, and we were all being sent to our mother base at Harwell.

This was an interesting occurrence too. On the day we were to depart for Harwell, we were given orders to 'fall in' with our bicycles at 8 am at the guardhouse. Having loaded our packed kit bags onto trucks, we were then ordered to, 'Mount bicycles and start pedalling'. For the next few hours (which seemed like days) we, that is about 100 of us, all ranks and trades on various types of bicycles, tried to keep up with the NCOs. Being such a small person, I had a small bike and ended up as Tail End Charlie.

It was probably about 22 miles from Hampstead Norris to Harwell, but not that day, I swear it was more like 50. I arrived at Harwell in the dark, not knowing my way around (shades of Innsworth) but, at least it wasn't raining! Fortunately a couple of friends had hung back with me and, together, we finally found the canteen, and were lucky enough to get something to eat. Then we had to sign in, retrieve our kitbags and find a place to sleep.

This turned out to be the old married quarters, not exactly home away from home, and we hoped we were not going to be here very long. There was the barest minimum of furniture left by the previous occupants, so we had to scrounge around for bedding and a few other things such as coal or wood for the fireplace. Unfortunately there was none available, and it was freezing and damp. We couldn't even get any hot water for a bath to warm up. Complaining did no good either - we were reminded that, 'There's a war on, you know!' Of course, there were a lot of people much worse off than we were, at least we had a roof over our heads.

A skeleton crew had been left behind at Hampstead Foo to tie up loose ends. Among them was my dance partner, who arranged to continue having dances in the NAAFI on a weekly basis, for as long as he could. One of these occasions happened to fall on the same night as our Domestic Night. That was when we had to clean our living quarters from stem to stern, and wait for it to be inspected by the Orderly Officer of the day. Apparently we didn't meet this officer's standards, and had to stay and do it over again. Then again had to wait for her return to inspect and, hopefully, give us an AOK. This all took precious time, and we were anxiously eyeing the clock, hoping we wouldn't be too late to get to the dance. Finally all was done, and we passed OK, but now we had to find our way to Hampstead Foo.

By coincidence (?), there was a hole in the fence separating our billet from the main road. One by one, we 'three musketeers' crawled through undetected and flagged down a passing vehicle. We made it to Hampstead in time to enjoy a few dances. Now came the time to return to Harwell, and I got left behind (can't imagine why!), and it was after midnight before I was able to get a lift back to Harwell, and to the hole in the fence. Wouldn't you know it though, the guard just happened to be passing that very spot as I was crawling through, and shone his flashlight right in my face. Needless to say, I was on a charge, and spent the next few nights peeling potatoes in the officer's mess. And much to everyone's dismay, the hole in the fence was repaired.

There was new activity at Harwell, strange aircraft were being flown in by American pilots. Talk was, that they were taking over the base in preparation for an invasion. In fact this turned out to be the 8th Air Force of the United States Army Air Force. They were preparing to carry, and drop paratroopers over France for Operation Overlord, on what became known as D-Day, June 6th, 1944. Although we had still been going to work each day on the Wellingtons, we were suddenly ordered to attend a meeting in an empty hangar, where we received instructions to pack and proceed to transport, which would take us to our next posting. We didn't all get posted together, and once again we were separated from our friends.

A Wellington bomber

I was being posted to a place called Honeybourne, another Operational Training Unit, in Wiltshire, and would still be working on my beloved Wellingtons. The aircrew personnel here were mostly Canadian, with a few Australians and New Zealanders, but everything was geared to the Canadians, the entertainment, Red Cross canteen, etc.

Having a Canadian father, I too was Canadian, although I had not yet been there. I am sure, had the war not intervened, he would have taken my mother and me to Canada to live, but evidently that was not possible and we would have to wait a few more years. In the meantime I proudly wore the 'Canada' flash on my shoulder and felt I was part of their team. I didn't have to crawl through any holes in fences to attend the functions, I was always welcome.

My new home was the usual wooden hut, with 7 two-tier bunks on either side, the stove in the middle and two bench tables. We still had kit inspections, domestic nights, and spit and polish. One of the most unusual things we had to do, was actually dust and polish every lump of coal, and arrange it neatly in the bucket beside the stove in the billet. We also had to repaint the fire water buckets every week, red on the outside and white on the inside.

After one such exercise, there was quite a lot of both red and white paint left over, so we drizzled it, decoratively, over the rocks in the little rock garden we'd planted outside the billet door. On this occasion it was the Station Commander and the senior Medical Officer, as well as our WAAF Commanding Officer, and other visiting Officers who were being escorted on the inspection tour. When the Station Commanding Officer saw all this red and white paint, he remarked, 'Good heavens, looks like someone had a miscarriage out here!'. I thought our poor WAAF Commanding Officer was going to faint. Those of us within earshot of this remark could barely keep from giggling.

Later on that year, just in time for Christmas, I managed to have seven days leave, and spent it with my cousin Monica, who still lived in Rayners Lane. We decided to spend the day in London, browsing the shops. Despite the fact that London had been heavily bombed consistently, and there were gaping holes where stores had been, most places were gaily decorated for the festive season, and the tube train was crowded. We were exiting the station at our destination, looking ahead towards a large department store, when it suddenly exploded and the buildings on either side of us started to crumble. A V-2 rocket, a pilotless ballistic missile which travelled faster than the speed of sound and gave no warning, had made a direct hit on the store filled with holiday shoppers.

Monica and I dove under an archway of bricks which was still standing, to avoid being hit by flying debris. After a few moments she said that, since I was in uniform, perhaps I should get out there to see if I could help anyone. To say that I was scared was putting it mildly. I'd already seen the aftermath of a raid or plane crash, but this was different. I saw a lady running towards me, holding her arms as if she were cradling her baby, but there was no baby, it had been blown out of her arms. The little, lifeless body was on a pile of bricks on the other side of the street. There was nothing I could do for her. I also saw a man collapse and die in front of me, with a large shard of glass sticking out of the back of his head, which was almost severed. As I looked around I was helpless to do anything, and had to wait for the ambulances to get through the rubble.

My cousin and I, though unharmed, were in no state to continue with our plans for the day and eventually managed to get home. This was the beginning of the V-2 raids. They lasted for several months and did a terrible amount of damage to the major cities of Great Britain, causing the loss of many civilian lives. I was glad when my leave was over, and I could return to the RAF station where, strange to say, I felt a lot safer.

Honeybourne was about six miles from Stratford-on-Avon, the home of William Shakespeare and The New Shakespeare Memorial Theatre where his wonderful works are performed, also our favourite pub, The Dirty Duck, the sign of which actually had a White Swan on one side, and a Black Swan on the other (hence the Dirty Duck). Officers from our station, as well as those from nearby stations, frequented the White Swan, while we other ranks were relegated to the Dirty Duck, and never the twain shall meet, fraternizing being frowned upon.

My upper bunk mate and I were frequent visitors at the Dirty Duck, cycling to Stratford after our work day and chores were completed, parking our bikes across the street outside the Unicorn (another favourite pub). On one such foray, we came out of the Dirty Duck to discover our bicycles missing, stolen from almost under our noses, which happened often. Funny thing was, after the war was over and the local reservoir was drained, hundreds of issue bicycles were found rusting on the bottom. Each of them had to be paid for by the person it had been issued to because they couldn't turn them in, mine included.

Not knowing how we were going to get back to Honeybourne was a bit of a problem, until the driver of an American air force truck came to our rescue and offered to give us a ride. Unfortunately, he was not the saviour we thought, and deliberately took a wrong turn, heading in the opposite direction, and despite our demands to be let out had no intention of stopping. There were four of us squeezed into the front seat, the sergeant driver, me, Margaret, and beside her against the door, a corporal. Suddenly, she reached across in front of the corporal, and got the passenger side door open, pushed him out, grabbed me and pulled me out as she jumped, and when we picked ourselves up, started running like the wind, back the way we had come, knowing that it was unlikely they would turn the truck around and follow us - they didn't, thank goodness.

There was hardly any other traffic on the road and it was some time before a petrol truck came into view. The driver, a civilian Cockney, called out to ask if we needed a ride, which we gratefully accepted. Back to where we started from, we parted company with the petrol truck and our Cockney friend, and started walking again, along the road back to Honeybourne that we should have been on originally, but it was a very long way.

Eventually, a British Army truck came along with its load of revellers returning to their army base, stopped and offered us a ride. We were only too glad to stop walking at this point, but the revellers were a little too rambunctious and we were very relieved when they let us off, although we still had a long way to go and it was pitch dark.

At one point we found the railway tracks, and knowing they led us in a straight line to a point near our camp, decided to walk along them, but Margaret was scared a train might come along and hit us - though there wouldn't be one for a few hours yet, so we gave up that route and returned to the main road. We did a lot of walking after that without seeing any more vehicles. Dawn was fast approaching and the sky was beginning to lighten.

Suddenly, Margaret saw a vehicle approaching and pushed me into the ditch as she yelled, 'Bloody Yanks, get down', but we'd been seen, and the driver stopped. Thank goodness it turned out to be the newspaper delivery van. He took us to the bottom of the hill leading to our billet which I was never more glad to see. I never knew six miles could be so long.

We walked, or should I say crawled, into our billet as the tannoy was sounding reveille, and just had time to change into our working battle dress and get to the canteen in time for breakfast. Needless to say, there was a lot of yawning going on that day, and a hot shower and bed was all we could manage that night.

A few weeks after this event I found myself stranded once more in Stratford. I was still without a bicycle, so had travelled with a group of officers in their car from Honeybourne, and since I was not allowed on 'their' side of the pub, they forgot about me when it was time to return to camp. Margaret was on leave at this time and I had ventured out alone, which I was beginning to realize was not a very smart thing to do. A young Canadian airman offered to give me a ride back to Honeybourne on the crossbar of his bicycle and since it was the only offer in sight, I accepted with the knowledge that it was going to be a very slow and uncomfortable ride.

At first it was quite funny, we kept falling off after travelling only a short distance, but at one point we landed in a ditch after sliding quite a distance down a hill, and things turned ugly.

The next thing I knew, my hands were pinned behind my back and I could hardly breath as this person who was all of 200 pounds, pressed on top of me. I struggled to get free, but he weighed far more than I did and had the advantage, there was nothing I could do to stop him and I knew I was being raped. When I felt him relax I managed to kick him with all my might, catching him in the head with the heel of my shoe. I knew I had hurt him, and when he let go of me I could tell there was blood pouring from the wound I had inflicted.

I managed to crawl up the hill and flagged down a passing jeep which, fortunately was heading for Honeybourne, where they took me straight to the hospital. I too required some stitches and spent the next three days recuperating. I never told my parents or anyone else what happened, except the doctor and police, and from my description, he was identified when he reported to the medical section for treatment. He had betrayed the trust most service people had for each other in wartime, and I wanted to see him punished.

It was a long time before I went into Stratford again. That was definitely a life-altering experience, and a lesson learned the hard way. I was informed later that this airman was court-martialled and sent back to Canada where he received a dishonourable discharge.

There was a lady living in the village of Mickleton, close by Honeybourne, whose home was open to the WAAF to visit and have tea whenever we felt the need for Home Comforts. She also bred cocker spaniels, and a new litter of puppies had just been born. One of the girls in my billet had decided to purchase a puppy to take home with her, and asked me to go with her to choose one. We were invited to stay for tea and played with the puppies for a while. They were all so adorable that I decided to have one also. We each paid for our chosen pet and told the lady we'd be back to pick them up the day before our next leave, although we couldn't resist visiting every day in anticipation of taking them home, and of course, taking advantage of the tea and cake.

However, leave was cancelled at the last minute, and here we were with two puppies in the billet, not yet house-trained of course, peeing on everyone's bed. We were definitely not popular at that point. I decided to take my puppy to the Canadian Red Cross hut, where I knew the sergeant in charge, and he promised to take care of him for me, but it would be another three months before I could take the puppy home to my parents.

I couldn't believe my eyes when Wimpy, the name I had christened him, started to grow. He wasn't a spaniel after all but a shaggy dachshund, with his little short legs, and long plume of a tail, he was really beautiful. I loved him, and couldn't wait to show him off to Mum and Dad. However, when we arrived at my parents' home in Lincolnshire, Wimpy and I were met at the front door by two huge Whippet terriers. Their jaws were so large they could have eaten Wimpy for lunch. I was rather afraid for his safety but couldn't do anything about it as I was only home for the weekend, and dare not take him back to camp with me.

I was anticipating being home again in three months, but once more, leave was cancelled and it would be six months 'til I saw Wimpy again. I was amazed that he remembered me. He came racing up the garden path to greet me, tail wagging and tongue flopping. He was a beautiful sight. Seems that he and the Whippets held a healthy respect for each other, and were friends. It was so cute to see the way they all played together with Wimpy running in and out of their long legs, almost daring them to snap at him. Unfortunately though, the Whippets had to go. The local farmers were missing some livestock, blaming the two dogs for either chasing them off or killing them, so Wimpy lost his playmates but then, to compensate, was thoroughly spoiled by my parents.

Back at Honeybourne, despite the fact that we had been given a bad impression by those two Americans, we were treated royally by the U.S. Army Medical Corps personnel, who moved into a vacant hospital in Evesham a few miles away. Once set up, they erected a Nissen hut solely for entertaining, which they did on a grand scale. They held a monthly dance, with a full dance orchestra that played and sounded like the Glenn Miller Orchestra, definitely the favourite band of the era. Our WAAF wing was always invited, along with local Land Army girls and the Women's Army Corps. A large garry (truck) would be sent to pick us up.

One night, the garry was very late. The driver had managed to get hopelessly lost around the country lanes. We were beginning to think we were forgotten, so he was greeted with cheers when he finally showed up. As we arrived at the Nissen hut, we could hear clapping and the shout went up, 'Let the party begin, the WAAF are here'. They had actually held up proceedings until we arrived, what gents!

On the way back to Honeybourne after the dance, our driver swerved to avoid a couple of drunks wandering in the road, and the garry overturned and caught fire. One of the girls had been reading a love letter from her new American boyfriend by the light of an oil lamp hanging from the centre of the canopy. The letter got burned, as well as some goodies the Americans had given us, like sugar and butter, chocolates and cookies, all sorts of things that we were unable to get because of rationing. A stone lodged in my knee when I landed face down on the roadway, but thank goodness nobody was seriously hurt. The driver was terribly upset and after making sure everyone was alright, hiked all the way back to the hospital to get another vehicle, ordering us to stay put until he returned with another garry and replacement goodies. He became our special driver after that, and our hero.

I was really sorry to leave Honeybourne. The time I spent there had been most enjoyable, except for the one really bad experience which I was trying hard to forget, and the fact that there was still a war going on with bombs dropping on the major cities of Great Britain, and lives being lost. Occasionally a German plane would follow one of our planes back to the base and try to shoot it down, or unload it's bombs in a farmer's field. Being in the heart of the country and miles from the big cities, I somehow felt removed from it, while still being a part of it, and it was certainly very different from life in the convent.

My next, and last wartime posting was to RAF Wigsley, in Lincolnshire. This was known as a Heavy Conversion Unit, where aircrew were still training, but in heavier aircraft, such as the Halifax and Lancaster. From here they would go immediately to an operational station, starting their 'tour of operations'. The Wigsley station was sprawled across much of the countryside, in that the WAAF quarters were quite a long way from the canteen, as well as the hangar where I worked. I say 'I', because I found myself to be the only female mechanic in the hangar, much to my dismay and to the delight of the other mechanics, who thoroughly enjoyed making my life difficult.

To be able to work on an engine which was on the aircraft, it was necessary to use a trestle, rather like scaffolding, standing on the platform or on some occasions to actually sit on top of the engine. If I found myself in this position, invariably someone would move the trestle and I would have no way of getting down, jumping off the wing might have been an option, but it was much too high.

Another thing they did was open the hydraulic drain when I was working underneath and I'd get covered in glycol, which was rather like pink honey. Actually, I found out that it was good for the complexion, so I'd let that one go without complaining too much. However, opening the oil sump over my head was not a good idea.

There was always a certain amount of jealousy between the groundcrew and aircrew, who were rather unkindly called Brylcream Boys, because the ad for the hair product, 'Brylcream - a little dab'l do yah!' depicted a good looking man in air force uniform, wearing pilot's wings. But the aircrew trusted female mechanics to do a good job, and I have to admit, we did favour them over the male 'grease monkeys'.

I'd arrived at Wigsley early in the new year, 1945. At the time there had been several turning points in the progression of the war, and although we had lost a terrible amount of military personnel, both in the air and on the ground, as well as at sea, and civilian casualties had been in the thousands, it did look like the end was nearer and in our favour. We carried on doing whatever we did best, and kept our sense of humour. It is said the British don't have a sense of humour, but I can assure you, it's what kept us going at the worst of times, though there is absolutely nothing funny about war.

Returning from a date one night, we were amazed to see all the lights on in the buildings at the camp and music blaring from open windows. People were running around everywhere, shouting and laughing, as well as crying, but we didn't know what all the commotion was about until we checked in at the guard house, and it was yelled at us by Mr. Churchill announcing over the radio, that PEACE HAS BEEN DECLARED. The date was May 8th 1945, which became known as VE Day, or Victory in Europe.

The sergeants' mess, which was opened to all ranks, soon became crowded, drinks were free and the noise was deafening. I found a window seat in one corner of the room. Rather than drink myself silly, like everyone else seemed determined to do, I watched the scene, which was really quite emotional, but it was too soon to realize the enormity of the situation.

In a few weeks, those of us who had volunteered for the duration of hostilities, would be back in civvy street looking for work, a place to live and a resumption of family life as we had known it. For others, there would be nothing left to go home to and they would probably make the decision to stay in the air force and make it their career. But for now the celebration would continue, there was time for decision-making later.

Some people suggested finding their way to the city of London, where millions of people were already packing the streets leading to Buckingham Palace, though I doubt they would have been able to get there. We were nearly 130 miles away and it was midnight, so chances of hitch-hiking were remote. The whole country was celebrating peace at last. It had been six long years and we were ready, but it would be a few more years before we could give up our ration books and rebuild our cities. And the troops who were overseas didn't come home right away.

The following day, we had a much needed day off, no doubt the Commanding Officers also needed the time to recover from his and her hangovers, but it was back to work as usual the next day. Or was it? I arrived at the hangar ready to finish working on my aircraft, and was promptly told that I was obsolete, and no longer needed. So, rather bewildered, I walked back to the guardhouse to find out what was going on. My Commanding Officer was there, sitting at the old Smith Corona typewriter, trying with one finger to type something. As soon as she saw me, she asked, 'Can you type?'. Without hesitation, I said, 'Yes Ma'am', and found myself compiling lists of personnel who were to be repatriated back to their homelands.

It wasn't easy convincing them they had to leave though, several of them had fallen in love with English girls and wanted to stay in England. However, they were not allowed to marry (although quite a few did anyway). I had to do a lot of shuffling and delaying of the inevitable, but eventually, they would be on their way home.

On December 7th, 1941 the United States of America had been brought into the war with the bombing by the Japanese of Pearl Harbour on the island of Oahu, Hawaii, although Great Britain had been receiving aid from the United States for some time. The war in the Pacific lasted almost four years until the dropping of two atomic bombs by the United States Army Air Force, on August 6th and 9th which destroyed the cities of Hiroshima and Nagasaki, Japan. A few days later on August 14th, Japan surrendered and the Peace Treaty was signed on September 2nd, 1945. The war in the Pacific was over, and for the first time in six years there was peace throughout the world.

Not long after this event Dad was demobbed from the RAF, and decided it was time he too went back to his homeland of Canada, and to his mother whom he had not seen for almost 21 years. My 'demob' number had not yet come through, so he applied for me to be 'bought' out of the air force on compassionate grounds. That is to say, I was still a minor (under 21 years of age) and my parents' only surviving child.

This was being done without my knowledge, until I was called into the Commanding Officer's office one day, and handed a clipboard with several pieces of paper on it. I was told to go around the camp and get signatures from 'all the departments listed'. Having done this, I was then told to pack my kitbag, and handed a railway pass to Bridgenorth, where I was hastily demobbed and put aboard a train for Lincoln, my folks current home. It was all done so quickly, I really wasn't sure what was happening, but the next series of events led me to believe we were about to leave the country. This we did just one month later.

4

LEAVING DEAR OLD BLIGHTY

Wimpy, my beautiful little dachshund, was given to two spinster sisters who lived in the mansion in the village of Old Bolingbroke near East Kirkby, where Dad had been stationed. I was sure they would take good care of him. Dad's co-workers and friends gave us a big farewell party and the following day Mum, Dad and I headed by train to Cardiff, Wales where we spent a week in a hotel. During the week the two princesses, Elizabeth and Margaret, and their parents, the King and Queen, visited Cardiff. They went right past our windows, waving. I was sure they had come to see us off, what a wonderful gesture!

On November 17, 1945 we boarded the SS Trondanger, a Norwegian freighter, which carried only 12 passengers, the other nine passengers being the wives of senior crew members. We were on our way to Vancouver, British Columbia and our new home.

Our voyage took exactly four weeks, and it was an extremely exciting trip to this teenager. The Irish Sea and Atlantic Ocean crossing was very rough, as is normal in the winter season, and we rocked and rolled constantly for the first 14 days. As we crossed the Gulf Of Mexico we ran into a hurricane, and were tossed from one side of the cabin to the other. The waves were washing right over the ship, and the crew was not allowed outside unless tied to something to stop them from being washed overboard. We lost a lifeboat, a hatch cover, as well as radio contact, and water was pouring down the companionways. In the salon, our dining table and chairs were chained to the floor, and our table cloth was wetted so that dishes didn't slide.

The Captain warned us, 'When a big wave comes, hang on, and count seven more waves', then the shudder would come as the propeller came out of the water, and it settled down until the next big one came. The lady sitting alongside him was about to take a drink of water when a big wave started just as she raised the glass to her mouth. The Captain tried to grab the glass from her before she got soaked, but he lost his balance, his chair tipped over and he rolled into the corner. Being a huge man who resembled Winston Churchill, it was quite funny and I really wanted to giggle, but my father's foot touched my shin, and a look told me I'd better not. There were several seconds of silence before the Captain let out an almighty guffaw, and then we could all laugh with him. He wasn't hurt, but *very* wet and rather red in the face.

There were actually two dining tables in the salon, one headed by the Captain and the other headed by the First Mate, with one steward to serve both tables. The stewards' name was Armando Hernandez, a very handsome Latino, who was always impeccably dressed in white jacket and black pants. During the storm, he carried an enormous tray, loaded with the dishes from both tables. The salon was under about two feet of water, and as he sloshed through it, another big wave started. Undaunted, he did three perfect pirouettes, and landed the tray squarely through the hatch, only dropping one knife at the last minute. It was quite a performance, worthy of the round of applause we gave him.

Poor Armando. He requested an audience with my parents one evening, and asked them for my hand in marriage, saying he 'wanted to take me to Norse America and get me soused' (whatever that meant). Needless to say they declined his offer. Glad I didn't hear about that until much later, although it might have been an interesting experience!

Having survived the hurricane, it was on through the Panama Canal, but being an empty freighter, we had to disembark in Cristobal in order to avoid paying freight charges. We spent the first evening with the Captain and his wife touring the city of Cristobal by open barouche (a horse drawn wagon), and it was beautiful. All the stores were brightly lit, and were open all night. The little native children in their gaily coloured clothes were running around us and laughing, and their big brown eyes shone with happiness, it was the tonic we needed. Suddenly the skies opened up and there was a torrential rain storm. No-one ran for cover, it was so refreshing.

Armando, having been rejected by my parents, had gone ashore alone and as we turned a corner in the barouche, there he was in the middle of the road, waving his arms wildly for us to stop. He climbed aboard and passed around his bottle of Apricot Schnapps which was almost empty, and he was quite drunk. The Captain stopped the barouche and gently led him off to the side of the road, sat him down and told him to stay put, then got back in the wagon and we proceeded back to the ship, where he then sent someone to rescue Armando.

About 3 am we were awakened by quite a commotion dockside. It seemed the rescuer had also imbibed and the two of them had been picked up by the Panamanian police who wanted to put them in jail, but they had put up quite a fight and insisted on being returned to the ship before it sailed off without them. It was a very noisy delivery. You wouldn't have known at breakfast though, Armando was there in his usual impeccable attire, looking none the worse for what must have been a very bad hangover.

After breakfast, we had to board a train to take us across by land to Balboa, where it had been arranged for us to have a meal at the USO building. The torrential rains had continued during the night, and halfway through our trip there was a landslide which derailed the train. We had to wait about four hours while the train was set back on the single line tracks, and by this time we were covered in mud.

Arriving in Balboa, we discovered that the USO had given up on us (no communication system). Fortunately the mayor of the town had come to meet us and took us to his brother's restaurant. This was a beautiful horseshoe shaped building, overlooking the entire canal and we could see our ship heading through the locks as we started eating our delicious three-course meal.

Unfortunately, we couldn't eat much. We had been so used to very small rations for the previous six years, and had to give up after just a few mouthfuls. As our ship exited the canal, it was an amazing sight. When the telephone in the restaurant rang, the maitre'd asked if anyone spoke Norwegian. My father, being of Norwegian extraction, took the call. It was from the Captain of the Trondanger, advising that we should proceed to the pier immediately, and board the ship while it was in progress. Otherwise, as before, if he stopped, he would have to pay freight charges.

When we arrived at the pier, we were met by the most beautiful lady I'd ever seen. I was sure she must be a movie star. She was dressed in a powder blue outfit, wearing a large straw hat over shiny silver curls, and carrying an enormous bouquet of flowers. Behind her stood very handsome identical twin men in white suits, and behind them was a large launch. This lovely lady was to be a new passenger on the Trondanger. The twins were her sons, there to see her off, and the launch was theirs. She invited us to join her and they took us out to board the ship, which at this point, had slowed to a speed of just three knots, but was some distance out in the open sea.

When we arrived we could see a rope ladder hanging down the side of the Trondanger and we were expected to climb aboard, up this rope ladder. The lady, whose name was Mrs. Englekey or 'little angel', went first and my Dad followed, helping her up by edging his shoulder under her behind, and taking the weight, as she hoisted herself onto the next rung. Mum followed, and I did the same behind her, also taking charge of the flowers, and we made it safely to the top.

The flowers were for the Captain's wife, who showed Mrs. Englekey to her cabin, up another flight of stairs amidship, and we went to ours, a very large cabin, but below decks. At some point on our trip, Mrs. Englekey also met with my parents and asked them if I could accompany her on a trip around the world for a year, but they declined that offer too. Such a pity, it would have been a wonderful experience, certainly better than Armando's offer. Oh well, it was on to Canada.

Actually it wasn't, as we developed engine trouble, and found ourselves making slow progress into Astoria, Oregon, where we stayed on the ship for a day while they decided if we could continue on to Vancouver by ship, or would have to disembark and continue by train. While we were awaiting the decision, we heard loud sirens, just like the ones we had been hearing constantly during the war in England, heralding an air raid. Mum and I were scared this was another air raid and dove under the table, where Dad found us a few minutes later. He told us we were docked under Times Bridge, and a police car had driven across the bridge with it's sirens blaring. I must say, it was several years before I could hear a siren without cringing.

As it happened, we had to finish our journey by train, and upon arriving at the CPR Station in Vancouver, were met by both my grandparents and Dad's half brother, Alan. Alan and I had been stationed together at Honeybourne. He was a Wireless/Navigator in the RCAF at that time. We had become good friends so when I saw him again, he was the first person I rushed to and gave a hug.

My grandparents had been divorced when my Dad was just 9 years old, and were not exactly on good terms, so this action brought a scowl from my grandmother, whom I was meeting for the first time. I guess I didn't make a very good impression, as she withdrew when I tried to give her a hug too. My Grandfather, on the other hand, was very warm and huggable. I really liked him.

After all the introductions were made and a promise to see more of my Grandfather and Alan, we were herded into a taxi and driven to my Grandmother's house, high on Hollyburn Mountain, with a beautiful view of the Straits of Georgia. This was the highest house on the side of the mountain at that time (1945), and the pine forest was immediately at the back door.

We arrived just a few days before Christmas and Dad and I were instructed to go and find ourselves a Christmas tree, so off we went into the woods. I had only taken a few steps, when I suddenly dropped about three feet into a hole. It turned out to be a bear trap, fortunately not the metal jaw kind. I was too surprised to yell, but Dad soon realized I wasn't behind him. He came back to find my head sticking up through the fallen leaves. HE thought it was funny, I wasn't so sure. After extricating myself, and brushing off the wet leaves, we continued our search for a special tree. We never told my Grandmother what happened, I'm sure she would have thought it funny too, but in a different way.

She and I never did become friends, and after realizing I was very much in the way, I moved out of her house into the YWCA in Vancouver, where I made friends with a couple of girls who had been in the Canadian air force. They knew their way around Vancouver, and with them, I was soon beginning to have a social life and enjoying myself.

I had to find a job now that I had decided to be independent, and started work at the Royal Bank of Canada on Hastings Street. Seems my middle name was still Trouble, no matter how hard I tried I couldn't shake it. At the bank, we were supposed to work every other Saturday morning, but I could never get the days straight and would forget, and sleep in. Then I'd shoot out of bed at the last minute and arrive at the bank just as the boss was drawing the line on the sign-in sheet. Anyone signing in below the line was LATE and docked an hour's pay. This was not a good thing. I knew I wouldn't last long at this job, so I left the bank and went to work for the Hudson's Bay Company on Granville Street, Vancouver.

Rationing was still in effect in Great Britain. Food parcels were being sent by friends and relatives from Canada to supplement the food allowance, and afford them a few treats. My job was to take their orders and type them up, and I was kept very busy doing this. Not only was I meeting lots of people, which I enjoyed, but I really liked working for The Bay and hoped to stay for quite a while.

While I was there I celebrated my 21st birthday, and having moved out of the YWCA into a rooming house on Huron Street, it was decided by the other roomers that we would have a beach party. My friends from the Y, and some I'd met at the Bay, were also invited. Everyone was bringing his boy or girlfriend; however, at the last minute I found myself without a date. Someone decided the library was a good place to meet people, and found a nerdy-looking guy to even out the numbers. Not exactly my type, but I wasn't complaining.

My grandmother had promised to supply the cake. It turned out to be two cakes joined together like a figure 8, smothered in icing with the appropriate greetings. We arrived at the beach and found a flat rock, setting the cake on it for later, and proceeded to build a bonfire, roast weenies, and party. We were in a beautiful spot in Stanley Park, one of the biggest and prettiest parks anywhere, with gorgeous sandy beaches, ideal for beach parties, and we were ready to celebrate.

Everything was going fine. We were having fun, and just getting ready to cut the cake, when a totally nude figure came bounding across the rocks, and stepped right into the middle of the cake. I was horrified, but this character had the nerve to sit down and proceed to wipe the cake off his foot.

Someone threw him a towel to cover himself, and we divided what was left of the cake among those who would eat it, sand and all, and the mystery nude left as quickly as he'd arrived, never to be seen again - thank goodness. Not the way I expected to spend my 21st, but certainly unforgettable!!

5

HOME ON THE RANGE

Dad wasn't having much luck finding work. Although he was a returning Canadian, he had not served in the Canadian military, and those who had were first in line when it came to getting employment. He and Mum were running out of money fast and the situation was getting desperate. With my grandmother's financial assistance, they purchased a Dude Ranch in the Cariboo Country of British Columbia, beside a beautiful lake 2 miles wide x 24 miles long, dotted with many small islands which were either animal or bird sanctuaries.

When they first saw it, the road to the property was under several feet of snow so they had to drive over the lake which was frozen, and even in it's wintry state they fell in love with it. Mum had a knack for seeing the potential in things that to others looked hopeless, and she could see that this place would be beautiful in spring and summer.

They moved into the ranch house, which was a large log cabin, in the Spring of 1946, and proceeded to stock the underground larder and refurbish the 14 cabins, as well as get some chickens, a cow, and a horse, but it wasn't long before they realized that there was too much work for two people and they needed help. Although they advertised for young men, no-one was willing to leave city life for the unknown, so it came down to me. At their request, I gave up my job at the Bay and headed for the hills.

The train ride to Lone Butte was very interesting. Travelling on a single line track, which wound around lakes and through mountains, amid some of the most beautiful scenery I have ever seen, stopping occasionally to let the few passengers take pictures. This was such a far cry from the scenes of war I had left behind in England just a few months earlier, I didn't want the journey to end.

I arrived at Lone Butte very late in the evening and had to stay overnight, as there was nothing available (no car or buggy), to take me out to the ranch, 33 miles away at Bridge Lake. There was only one building in Lone Butte which contained the post office, general store and hotel, with a very primitive bathroom, and this is where I spent my first night in the Cariboo. The next day the proprietor of the hotel enlisted the services of an old Studebaker car and a driver to drive me out to the ranch. It was all over unpaved dirt tracks, and I got car sick long before we reached our destination, much to the consternation of my driver, who had to keep stopping at my request.

I fell in love with the ranch the moment I saw it. Breathing the clean air, and smelling the earth, trees, horses, nature in general, was wonderful, I knew I was going to be happy here. It's hard to believe I was born right in the heart of London, one of the biggest cities in the world, and yet I'm much happier and more relaxed when I'm in the country. Think there must be a bit of the 'farmer' in me!

I was soon put to work getting the cabins ready for potential visitors, churning

Veronica feeds the chickens at the Dude Ranch

butter and cheese, taking care of the chickens, grooming the horse and all sorts of other odd jobs which kept me really busy. The weather was absolutely gorgeous, and after all my chores were done, I'd either get one of the boats out and do some fishing or take a swim in the fresh water lake. The war was the farthest thing from my mind, I was in heaven. Sometimes I'd have to pinch myself to make sure it was all real.

Across the lake was another ranch-house where two girls about my age lived, and we became friends. Either they would row their boat over to visit with me, or I would row our boat over to visit them, and sometimes we would arrange to meet at the end of the road, on horseback, and just ride wherever the fancy took us. The last time I had ridden a horse was many years before on the farm in Somerset where I spent some of my school vacations. Everything was fine as long as the horse didn't decide to gallop, that was something I never did master.

I worked really hard keeping the 14 cabins clean, washing sheets by hand, and hanging them on the line to dry (no washers and driers), learning to bake bread, and making fruit pies, using a huge wood burning stove to cook everything on. Our guests might stay for a week or a month, fishing, or hunting, or just relaxing by the lake, and we had to feed them. Once a week, I would head to the other end of the lake in the outboard motor boat to do the grocery shopping, fill three or four burlap sacks, put them in the boat, and then return home. It usually ended up being a full day's trip, not only was the putt-putt very slow, but I would always stop and socialize for a while and have lunch with the family who ran the store.

This family also had a huge barn in which they held dances once a month. The dance would start on Friday night, and continue through to Sunday morning, when they served a huge breakfast of pancakes with lots of maple syrup, sausages, eggs and just about anything else you could ask for. I would meet up with my two friends from across the lake, and we rode our horses over the plateau to the barn, which by land took us almost two hours.

People who came to the dances were mostly cowboys and ranch-hands who worked on ranches scattered throughout the Cariboo. Some would have ridden for a couple of days, spending nights wherever they came across a building. They'd arrive wearing their chaps and spurs, which they didn't remove. The jingle of spurs could be heard in time to the music, which was provided by other ranch hands, and their fiddles. Definitely toe-tapping music, you had be lively to keep up with them.

During daylight hours on the Saturday, there would be a huge barbeque. Although the fiddlers still played their music, most people relaxed waiting for the sun to go down so they could return to the barn and start dancing again, by which time there would be visitors from neighbouring campsites and dude ranches joining in. They really were fun times and the people we met were wonderful.

We three girls managed to stay over, dancing the nights away until after breakfast on Sunday morning, then take the opposite route home, riding around the lake, watching the animals stirring from their sanctuaries, making their way to the shore for a day of hunting. It was a magnificent sight. We would take off our shoes, and cross our feet over the pommel on our saddles, and just jog along at a slow pace, enjoying the morning air. Dad had recently given me my own horse, which was a beautiful Arabian with a white blaze down its nose, and I named him Little Baldy.

Veronica on Little Baldy, ready for a day in the saddle

Some time during the summer, a pack of as many as a hundred wild horses travelled across the hills, and could be heard whinnying from far off. Little Baldy also heard them and got very agitated. He managed to break out of his stall and took off after them. I had to go look for him on a borrowed horse, across the ranges with nothing in sight for miles, definitely not any horses, but plenty of moose and deer, as well as an occasional black bear. I had been warned that if a bear looked like it was going to approach me, **DON'T PANIC**. HUH! Easier said than done, but fortunately, I didn't need to follow that advice.

I must have ridden quite a few miles away from home, and with really no idea where I was, the sun was beginning to set. Just about the time I was thinking I might be lost, I saw a cowboy rounding up a herd of cattle. From the other side of the herd, he waved for me to come to where he was. After waiting until all the cows were in the dairy barn, I approached, and was surprised when he addressed me by name, he knew where I had come from. The bush telegraph must have been busy. I was invited into the farmhouse, where his mother asked me to stay for supper, then he very kindly drove me back in his pickup truck, to Bridge Lake and home, and returned my borrowed horse the next day.

Little Baldy was still missing, and I was a wee bit too sore to spend another day in the saddle, so Dad enlisted the help of a horsewoman from Vancouver. It took her three days, but she finally found my wayward steed near the railway station in Lone Butte, and brought him in. After a good rubdown and a meal, he was back in his stall, safe and sound. I was really enjoying living and working on the dude ranch, not missing city life at all, although by the time winter set in, I'd probably be changing my mind about that.

It cost quite a lot to purchase sufficient supplies, not only for the animals, but for the guests we anticipated arriving to fill the cabins, which never happened. In fact, our visitors were very few and far between despite heavy advertising in Vancouver papers, which was also very costly. Our food supply was stored in an underground 'cave' beside the lake, but it wasn't waterproof, which caused the food to rot very quickly. Since we were storing far more food than was being eaten, we were wasting precious dollars, and it soon became apparent that we couldn't continue this way, especially as the off-season was approaching when there would not be any visitors for at least three months, and possibly more if it turned out to be a long winter.

It was a very distressing time for Mum, and she was beginning to show signs from all the stress, experiencing bad headaches and losing some of her hair. While Dad was out hunting one day (he would bring home venison which we bottled and it supplemented our food supply), Mum and I had a heart-to-heart talk about the situation.

Dad and Mum had both worked for the same company in London, and had stayed friendly with the President, actually he was my Godfather. It was the practice to hold a job open for the duration of the war, should an employee wish to return to his old job. Of course, in Dad's case, his job was filled by someone else when he decided to return to Canada, but the friendly relationship remained. I suggested that Mum write a letter to Uncle Peter, letting him know the situation, without making it a sob story.

Uncle Peter, bless his heart, took the bait, and instead of responding to the address at the ranch, the letter was redirected to Dad from my grandmother's house. In it, he wrote about the post-war situation at the company in London, and general subjects of interest without acknowledging that he had heard from Mum, adding a PS: 'Should you ever think of returning to England, we can always find a job for you'.

This was just the incentive that Dad needed to take the next step, and very soon sold the ranch for a song, and returned to England. Uncle Peter was as good as his word and made Dad the manager of a new branch office in Leeds, Yorkshire. They only received enough money on the sale of the ranch to pay their own fares back to England, and I had to return to Vancouver alone. I hated having to let Little Baldy go, but one of the girls from across the lake took him, so I knew he was in good hands. I was also not looking forward to living and working back in the city, but at that point I really had no choice.

When I returned to Vancouver I was fortunate to be able to rent a room in the same house I had lived in before on Huron Street, and got a job at the War Assets Corporation, this time typing lists of surplus war materials that were being stored, or dismantled for parts. Not a bad job, but a bit boring. I made up for it though, and together with my friends from the days at the YWCA, spent most evenings dancing at the Service Club, which had opened up on Burrard Street. I loved ballroom dancing and the bands that played at the service club were really good.

One of the bands I recognized had entertained the Canadians at Honeybourne when I was stationed there, and I made myself known to the leader. He asked me one day if I could sing, and what was my favourite song. At the time it was *The Gypsy*, one that Doris Day had made popular. I started singing and the band followed on, with each instrument picking up the tune. It sounded so good that they asked me to sing it during the dance, and then another song, and another, until I found myself singing with them during their radio show on Wednesday afternoons, as well as at all the dances. Wow! I didn't know I could do THAT.

Being a 'service' club, the dances were attended mostly by ex-servicemen from all three services. I met one who had been with the Signals Corps in Byfleet, and had actually assisted with the search for my brother at the Blue Lagoon. This formed a bond between us and we became good friends, but he already had a girlfriend, so as much as I would liked to have known him better, I didn't stand a chance.

Almost every letter Dad wrote was asking me to go back to join them in England. Not only did I not want to leave Canada, but as the saying goes 'If it only cost $10 to leave town, I couldn't afford to cross the street'. Dad was so insistent though, that he finally sent some money and expected me to arrive in Southampton on the ocean liner, Queen Mary. That was news to me as I was planning to take the train across Canada to Saint John, New Brunswick, and sail back to England on a freighter, which was actually all that the money he sent would allow.

I left Vancouver by Canadian Pacific Railway on New Year's Day 1947, and spent the next four days marvelling at the different scenery as we passed through each province, finally arriving in Saint John, anticipating the next stage of my journey back to England. With everything ready to go, and with my bags on board, I was informed that we couldn't leave. Engine trouble had developed, and it would be a couple of weeks before it was repaired. They would call me.

But where were they going to call me? I had no Canadian money and nowhere to go! I went to the nearest bank to try changing my small amount of English money back to Canadian, only to be told they couldn't do that. Just about the time tears started welling up in my eyes and I was on the verge of making a fool of myself with a panic attack, the bank manager appeared and offered to help. First, he offered me a place to stay at his home (with his family of course), but I declined that offer. He may have been the bank manager, but I didn't know him from Adam, and wasn't about to take a chance.

From a drawer in his desk, he took out a cigar box and counted out sixteen Canadian dollars, for which I exchanged my meagre four English pounds. It wasn't much, but it was enough to get me to Halifax, where I checked into the YWCA. I had chosen to go to Halifax because I had met a sailor on the train trip across Canada who was going to be stationed there at Dartmouth Naval Air Station. I thought I'd at least know one person in a strange city, although I didn't expect to be in Halifax for long.

However, the two weeks it was supposed to take for the ship's engine to be repaired, stretched into three and then I found that the ship had actually returned but left again without me, and my money was practically all gone. My sailor friend had been shipped out and I was on my own. The only thing to do was get a job, and I was in luck for once.

War Assets Corporation had a branch right near the Y. They didn't have a job available, but after I told the manager my predicament, he agreed to let me do the filing for as long as it took for the ship to return, and he would pay me the going rate. At least I could pay my rent at the Y, but didn't have much left for food. I solved that problem by taking a short evening shift job at a restaurant almost next door to the Y, where they gave me a good dinner, breakfast I had to pay for.

This lasted almost three months, during one of the worst winters Halifax had experienced. It was bitterly cold, with the wind so strong it would blow me off my feet. The restaurant was warm though, and I found myself spending more and more time there right up to the time I made a phone call, and found out that the ship had returned to Saint John, so I had to make a hasty departure. The two Chinese men who owned the restaurant (Charlie Night and Charlie Day as I called them), helped me pack and sent me on my way back to Saint John, hopefully, to board the ship this time.

All was well, and we left Canada during a heavy snowfall. The trip wasn't nearly as comfortable on this freighter as we had been on the Trondanger. I was sharing a cabin with a young woman who was going to England to meet her fiancé. She had the bottom bunk, I had the top, but I was suffering from an awful case of neuralgia and was in so much pain I couldn't sleep.

I found myself pacing the companionways, drinking gallons of strong tea from the galley, where the crew congregated before changing watch. At some point, someone suggested if I drank enough rum I would kill the pain. I don't know about killing the pain, it almost killed me. Somehow, I had found my way, or been placed in my top bunk, when I felt I was going to throw up. Forgetting I was on the top bunk, I stepped out, and down with a crash, hitting my head on the washbasin, but not hard enough to knock me out.

Rather than try climbing back up to the top bunk, I crawled in beside my lower bunk mate and like spoons, we wedged ourselves in, and with the motion of the ship, finally slept. The ship's doctor started dosing me with morphine to ease the pain, but it didn't have much effect and I spent a miserable 14 days before we reached land.

As we were approaching England and hearing about how the lovers were going be re-united dockside, I began to wish I had someone coming to meet me, and asked the radio operator on the ship to send a telegram to Mum and Dad letting them know where we would be docking, and when.

They were there to meet me, but did not appear happy to see me. I learned they had previously driven all the way to Southampton to meet the Queen Mary several weeks earlier, only to discover I had never been booked to sail on it. I had a lot of explaining to do but it would have to wait, I was still in too much pain, and tried to feign sleep until we arrived at their home in Leeds.

Leeds is not the prettiest place in the world, a far cry from the openness and fresh air of the dude ranch in the Cariboo. Home was just four rooms, two up and two down, with the toilet at the end of the street, one of a row of toilets that smelled like whitewash. We did have our own toilet key though.

For a few days I lay low and had my neuralgia taken care of. It turned out to be an abscessed tooth. Once the offending tooth was removed, the pain soon subsided and I was feeling well enough to answer all their questions. They couldn't understand why I had chosen to travel on a dirty old freighter, instead of the luxury of the Queen Mary. The answer was really quite simple, they hadn't sent me enough money and I didn't have enough to make up the balance to pay what it would cost to travel by liner, as opposed to freighter. That was the truth of the matter.

I came to the conclusion I did not like Leeds, and did not want to find a job there, so decided to rejoin the WAAF. Instead of rejoining at the recruit station in Leeds, I wrote to RAF Headquarters in London, and received a reply almost by return mail, with orders to report to Innsworth, Gloucester. I was back in uniform once again, on familiar territory. Unlike the first time I was at Innsworth though, it wasn't raining and I didn't get lost trying to find the canteen.

6

A WAAF ONCE MORE

With the cessation of the war two years earlier, my beloved Wellingtons had become obsolete, being replaced by jet-propelled aircraft, about which I knew absolutely nothing, and the air force was not prepared to train me on them, so I had to select a new trade. I'd always enjoyed precision drilling, so chose to become a drill instructor.

My training took place in several phases at different stations, and I passed with flying colours, receiving two stripes with the rank of corporal after a few short weeks. My next posting was to a recruit training station, Wilmslow, in Cheshire, and my new quarters were in the familiar long wooden hut. The little room near the door was mine this time. About 15 young women, all raw recruits, occupied the big room. Of course it had the usual coal stove in the middle, and a table with benches on either side, but this time there were single beds, rather than the two-tier bunks we had in wartime. The adjacent hut also accommodated 15 recruits for whom I was responsible, making up my squad of 30.

Later that year what had been the Women's Auxiliary Air Force, became the Women's Royal Air Force and we no longer wore the 'A' badge under the albatross on our uniform sleeves.

I had to teach the new entries how to mark their kit and lay it out for inspection, as well as making up the bed, cleaning their buttons and shoes, how to tie a necktie with the correct knot, and I was enjoying my new responsibilities. Reveille was just the same raucous noise over the tannoy that it had been way back when. It still brought the same groans from those who weren't ready to get out of bed.

There were lectures to be given, drill to be taught, and inspections to be made, nothing changes. We had just six weeks with our new recruits to whip them into shape, all in step, arms swinging just so, head high, chest out, and all following a change in order at the same time.

The first week or two were rather frustrating. So many of the women seemed to have two left feet, or tried swinging the same arm as the leg, or turned right instead of left. There would be as many as 120 airwomen on the parade square at the same time with thirty women in each squad, and each squad with an instructor yelling orders. At times, half my squad followed someone else's orders and ended up in a bunch at the other end of the parade ground, while the other half stood its ground, giggling at the sight. With so many bodies marching in different directions, it was hard to tell which squad belonged to whom. The next two weeks would see some improvement, you could tell that their pride was showing. The final two weeks would be positively amazing, it was all taking shape, and our day for the Passing Out Parade was fast approaching. Extra care was taken with shining buttons and shoes the night before, uniforms were pressed. We were ready.

Veronica as a Drill Instructor at Wilmslow 1947

Each instructor, either a corporal or sergeant, marched her squad of 30 airwomen onto the Parade ground, positioning themselves in front of the reviewing stand, on which stood several officers, including the station commander (usually a Wing Commander) and our own WAAF Commanding Officer (a Flying Officer) and her Adjutant. The Air Force Band would be playing some rousing Souza Marches, and the air was electric as the reviewing of the drill began. All 120 women performed the same drill on command from one of the sergeants, and we corporals would each be in front of our own squad, following the commands.

While we all stood at attention facing the reviewing stand, the officers walked along the ranks, sometimes stopping to speak to an airwoman. Then, with the inspection over, came the command for us to Right Turn and, By the Centre, Quick March, at which time the band would strike up a resounding Air Force March. We marched as one past the reviewing stand, eyes right, with chests out and arms swinging to the waist of the woman in front of us, past the Commanding Officer on the stand taking the salute, eyes front again, until we marched off the Parade Ground. When we reached an area where we were given the order to Halt and Stand at Ease, you could hear the breath let go from being held in for so long. When the order to Dismiss was given, there were cheers and hugging all around for a job they knew they had done well.

Next came the assembly, where the postings were handed out. I knew how they were feeling parting company with friendships they had so recently formed. They were now airwomen and about to start learning a trade on a base somewhere in England. Some may be lucky enough to be posted near their home town, but most would be venturing into the unknown. Some of them were leaving immediately, their kit-bags put into a garry and deposited at the nearest railway station, others would have to wait a few hours, but by the end of the day they would all be gone. No rest for the wicked though, our new recruits were coming in as the others were going out, and the process started all over again for another six weeks. There was never a shortage of recruits.

Usually two corporals had to travel with the kit bags in the back of the garry and supervise the unloading at the station, making sure all our squad left safely. On one such occasion, there were three of us returning to camp after seeing our squad off. Our driver stopped at the back gate to check in at the picket hut, and we decided to get out here and walk back to our quarters. We had taken out the pin that holds the tailgate up and were just about to let it down, when the driver took off with a jerk and the tailgate went down with a crash.

The other corporal fell out and rolled, but when I fell out my foot caught between the floorboard and the tailgate, and I was being dragged along suspended that way. The third corporal was standing near the window of the cab and started yelling for the driver to stop, and she stopped so suddenly that I was jerked free, and landed heavily on both legs. I was sure something was broken or that I was covered in blood, but was more concerned that my skirt was up, and the first thing I said was, 'Please pull my skirt down'.

I didn't want to see what damage I had incurred, as they took me into the picket hut and laid me on the desk, so I had my eyes shut very tight. Then I felt someone trying to take my shoes off, but I was protesting loudly, 'Why?' they asked, 'Because I have a hole in my stocking', I said (remember what your Mother told you?).

Someone had phoned the station hospital for the ambulance. I could hear the siren as it approached. Still with my eyes closed tight, I heard a voice whisper in my ear, 'Put your arms around my neck'. I opened one eye a little bit and saw a very handsome young man leaning over me. Oh yes, I put both arms around his neck, and he carried me into the back of the ambulance. Now I had both eyes open, as the other corporal and I were being transported to the hospital. On the way there we were singing, 'Cigareets and Whuskey and Wild Wild Wummin', a silly song of the day, and the orderlies in the ambulance thought we must have suffered some brain damage.

Fortunately my injuries were not severe, thank goodness, although I did have difficulty walking, since the tendons in both thighs were twisted. No marching for me for a while. I was sent home for a three week sick leave, and spent it exercising and taking hot baths to unlock the muscles. During the third week of leave I attended a dance at the local dance hall and discovered my legs felt fine. I was ready to go back to being a drill instructor when my leave was over. I love dancing so much I think I would have danced whether my legs hurt or not, but this was a good test that I passed OK.

When I returned to Wilmslow, there was a new posting waiting for me. I was going to Bridgenorth (the same station I was demobbed from in 1945) which was now an advanced recruit training station. When I arrived at Bridgenorth and was shown to my new 'room' in the billet, I was also told that I was being promoted to Sergeant, but it had not yet come through on orders, and until it did I was unable to wear the three stripes. I also learned that the Adjutant was on leave, and as she would not be back for a week, I was expected to take care of things in the Administration office until her return, as well as lectures and procedures with the squadron.

I was kept very busy, mostly getting ready for a major inspection by some high-ranking officers. When that day arrived, every button and shoe had been polished 'til you could see your face in it, tunics pressed, kit spotlessly clean and laid out as prescribed, billets cleaned and re-cleaned, no dust bunnies under OUR beds, coal dusted and fire buckets painted, not to mention the ablutions which had received a thorough scrubbing. All was ready to be inspected. I joined the long line of inspectors which started with the Group Commander, Group Medical Officer, Station Commander, Medical Officer, Warrant Officer and Sergeant; this was just the male contingent.

Then came the female officers, four of them, then little old Corporal me. Everything was fine so far, we had inspected everything but the ablutions, they came next. The Senior officer leading the procession was pushing open the door of each stall, when he suddenly stopped, turned and looked down the long line to me, beckoning me forward with his index finger.

I marched forward and saluted as I came to a halt in front of him. He then pointed his long bony finger into the stall, indicating a small puddle in which reposed a toilet roll. With a dead straight face he said, 'Corporal, have you ever tried using a piece of WET toilet paper - it's virtually impossible?'. I know I turned a bright red but had to respond, 'No sir, I'll take care of it immediately'. Mortified, I returned to my position at the end of the line. I do believe that was my most embarrassing moment ever, I wasn't sure whether to laugh or to cry. You can be sure though, that my squadron heard about it, and although it really wasn't a laughing matter, we couldn't help but see the funny side. We learned a valuable lesson though, making sure there were no more puddles on the ablution floor from then on.

A couple of days later, after the Inspection, the Adjutant returned from leave and had the monumental task of opening and reading all the mail that had accumulated in her absence. I had not touched any of it, other than to place it on her desk in chronological order. One of the pieces of official mail she opened was the order promoting me to the rank of Sergeant. She told me I could pick up the three stripes immediately and sew them on.

Unfortunately for me, a few minutes later she opened an order for me to be returned to Wilmslow with the rank of Corporal, so I never did get to sew on my new stripes. I don't think it had anything to do with the puddle in the ablutions though, they were just short of Corporal drill instructors at Wilmslow and needed me there. So back I went, and soon fell into the old routine of training new recruits until they were sure they knew their left foot from their right. Nothing had changed.

At the end of one course when everyone had departed for the railway station, I was left alone in the canteen with one of the recruits. It so happened this young lady had had a lot of trouble responding to certain drill commands, the Change Step in particular, and I must admit it was a little tricky. I showed her how to kick the instep of her right foot into the heel of her left foot and step forward with the left foot. To me it was easy, I'd been doing it for three years, but she just couldn't get the hang of it, and kept trying.

Suddenly she went down, having kicked the foot from under her and losing her balance. She landed on the hard concrete on the point of her chin and I saw a pool of blood begin to spread out around her head. When I knelt down to see the damage, I could tell she had split the skin under her chin almost from ear to ear, and the blood was pouring out. I took off my tie and tied it around her head to hold the wound together to stop the blood flow, then ran to get help.

The poor girl ended up in hospital, receiving several stitches, and missed out on her posting, but did get three week's sick leave once she left the hospital. I also went home on leave that day and by the time I returned to Wilmslow, she had already been released. I never saw her again, but I thought about her whenever I was teaching the Change Step to other recruits and hoped she fully recovered. All over a silly procedure, which is like the Latin I learned in the convent - totally unnecessary.

7

THE CORPORALS' CLUB

We had a Corporals' Club on our station, where we could socialize with our male counterparts in the evenings, drinking coffee or tea and swapping funny stories of the day.

One day, two strangers arrived at the Club. Both were very tall and good looking, wearing colourful flashes on their air force uniforms. We, being a friendly group of about twelve corporals who always sat together, invited them to join us, and we learned the flashes signified that they had been with the Occupation Forces in Japan. The war with Japan had ended with the dropping of the Atomic Bombs on Hiroshima and Nagasaki in early August of 1945. Actually August 14th was considered V.J Day, but there was a lot of 'cleanup' work to be done there and several American and British troops stayed behind to take care of this, including these two. We discovered that they were Armament Fitters, but Wilmslow was a recruit training camp, we had no guns or ammunition here; however, not too far away, all the surplus army tanks had been stored and had to be dismantled, that was what they had been sent to do, using our camp only as living quarters.

Some evenings our group would venture out to the local pub for a few beers, or my favourite shandy, which was a light beer with ginger ale mixed half and half (very refreshing), and a game of darts and a sing-along by way of a change of scenery. On one such occasion which coincided with a Domestic Night, I was held back to redo the billet (someone found some dust bunnies under a bed!!) and arrived at the Corporals Club rather late. The only one there was one of the two 'good looking guys' who had been elected to wait for me. We were supposed to join up with the others at the pub, but when we got to the pub nobody from our group was there. Funny thing was, we didn't even notice that fact, we were enjoying each other's company and having so much fun. We later found out they had deliberately gone to another pub and set the whole thing up so we could be alone to get to know each other better.

It worked, this was the beginning of falling in love, but he, Tommy was his name, had applied to go to New Zealand to join the New Zealand Air Force. He had decided, that if he was not accepted, he would ask me to marry him, and that's exactly what happened. We were married in the little church in Wilmslow just six weeks later, on January 15, 1949, with my squad of recruits and friends from the club providing an honour guard as we left the church.

My grandmother had sent me one of her evening gowns which was a white, two-piece Brussels lace sheath with a blousey jacket. Although beautiful, it was a bit old fashioned so I decided to have it altered. One night I dreamt about the dress and how I would like it to look. The following day I took it into the village to a dressmaker who redesigned the whole thing with the aid of a sketch I provided and transformed it into a lovely one-piece wedding dress.

Since the dress was entirely lace, I needed a long slip which Mum provided. It was an ivory satin evening dress of hers and was perfect. To complete the ensemble I was loaned a beautiful veil, a pair of white sandals and a six penny piece to carry in my shoe - an old English tradition.

My best friend, Pauline was my bridesmaid whose only dress available was a white satin, not exactly appropriate, so we came up with the bright idea of dyeing it by soaking it in a basin full of water to which we added two bottles of blue ink, and hanging it to dry overnight in the ablutions. The result was a lovely pale blue, just what was wanted, and she too looked perfect.

They say if it rains on your wedding day, that's good luck and you'll be rich. That doesn't happen on air force pay, but it sure did rain. We boarded a train for our honeymoon in Newquay, Cornwall and a beautiful hotel overlooking the ocean. By Sunday morning, the rain had stopped and a wintery sun was trying to shine. We were having breakfast enjoying the view from the hotel dining room, when Tommy opened the newspaper, and there in bold print saw that the New Zealand Air Force was looking for Armament Fitters - SINGLE ONLY NEED APPLY! I don't think he ever recovered from the fact that he'd missed by one day, the opportunity of going to New Zealand, compliments of the New Zealand Air Force. Although we were married for 18 years, it was never mentioned and we never did go there.

On our return to Wilmslow, after our two week honeymoon, Tommy had to go to his quarters and I to mine. As far as the air force was concerned, we were not legally married until it had appeared on Personnel Occurrence Records which are posted for everyone to see. We did manage to spend weekends together at a little bed and breakfast in the village and six weeks later I learned I was pregnant. I received my discharge from the air force three months later and went to stay with my parents in their two up and two down house in Leeds (the one with the whitewashed toilets!).

Having completed his mission with the disarmament of the tanks, Tommy was then posted to Upper Heyford. He found a place for us to live in a very nice little house, where we rented two rooms until it was time for me to have our baby, a beautiful daughter who was born at Cross Houses Hospital, near Shrewsbury, Shropshire on February 5th, 1950. We christened her Vivienne Sheila, and decided to move into larger quarters.

Our new home was a suite in an old country mansion. The dining room was so huge it took me two days to clean it, and the dining table so big I had to kneel on it and polish it as if I were polishing a floor. When we had Vivienne's christening party, I had the table pushed up against one wall and was still able to seat fourteen people comfortably on three sides.

The original enormous kitchen had been divided into several kitchens as there were quite a few suites in the mansion. Meal times were a big get together of swapping recipes and getting, as well as giving advice on cooking, something I definitely needed. Our bedroom was up a very ornate staircase and was as large as the living room, with a huge picture window showing off the view of the surrounding farmland and gardens, which were beautiful.

The rent for such a lovely home was quite steep, so to supplement I offered to keep the entry hall clean. That entailed polishing the hardwood floor and antique tables and chests, as well as all the brasses and crossed swords hanging over a magnificent archway. It was quite an achievement to keep this area spotless, but I thoroughly enjoyed the task and was amply rewarded.

Vivienne was just a few months old, and spending many hours in her pram on the gravel drive outside our living room window. The owners of the mansion had a very large pet goose who took it upon itself to guard Vivienne's pram. The goose would stand for hours with it's beak resting on the side of the pram, daring anyone to come near. If that should happen, there was a great hissing and flapping of wings. I couldn't have asked for a better guardian. There was also a big St. Bernard dog who would take over the duties if the goose should wander away or not show up, and it was obvious there was some friendly rivalry. The dog would stay at a safe distance until it was his turn to take over, then he too would stand with his nose resting on the side of the pram, eyes darting all around, daring anyone to approach. Even I had trouble getting near sometimes, and usually remembered to have a treat in my hand to coax him away from the pram.

As I mentioned, there were several suites in the mansion occupied by other young couples, some civilian and some from an air force station nearby. One of these couples was leaving on vacation one day and had their car packed to the uppers. Everyone was outside to wave them off, and away they went.

Suddenly, there was an awful noise which none of us recognized but soon found out, when the couple came walking back looking very glum - they had run over, and killed the poor old goose! I had lost my baby's bodyguard, but the lovely big dog came to the rescue and never left the pram from then on. No, we didn't have the goose for dinner, it would probably have been a tough old bird, but we had a funeral and buried him in the rose garden.

My parents were just about to vacate the house in Leeds and move into a very nice semi-detached house with a big garden in a cul-de-sac a short distance away. The owner of the house they were vacating was leaving on an extended cycling tour around the world. He had invented a motorized bicycle which he had patented and called an Otto Cycle (actually an auto-cycle). As he was going to be away indefinitely, it was suggested that Tommy, Vivienne and I could take over the rental, and so we did, even though I still didn't like Leeds.

It was quite different living in our own place. There were seven houses on either side of the road all joined together, each with two steps up to the front door, and one window which was in the kitchen-dining room. I soon found out that I was expected to polish my steps and window sill with Cardinal Red polish, and scrub my area of pavement with a special stone, as well as keep the toilet at the end of the street newly whitewashed.

It became apparent if I didn't do this, because we were fairly near the coal mines and there was always coal dust in the air. It settled and made everything grey very quickly. I had a clothesline strung from my house, across the street to the opposite house, and hung Vivienne's diapers and the rest of my washing out there to dry. No mod cons, like washer and dryer. Needless to say, anything white soon became grey and stayed that way for as long as we lived in this house.

Just as Vivienne was about to have her first birthday she started to lose weight and wouldn't eat. I rushed her to the doctor up the hill, sitting her on the bump that was the new baby I was expecting. The doctor could not diagnose a specific problem and told me to feed her a spoonful of glucose, but it didn't work and the liquid would go straight through her. I couldn't even put a diaper on her, and as she lay in her crib, I was sure I was losing her. I managed to convey a message to my mother who, at this time, was secretary to seven physicians at Leeds Infirmary, one of whom was a Pediatric specialist.

As soon as she saw her grand-daughter she contacted the hospital and Vivienne was admitted immediately, on her birthday, having been diagnosed with gastroenteritis. She had dropped to less than her birth weight of six and a half pounds and was skin and bones, when only six months earlier, she had won first prize in a Bonnie Baby contest. I was scared.

I visited the hospital every day and in just two weeks, my little one was standing up in her crib and looking much better. I was able to take her home, although I had to be careful not to get her excited or she would throw up, and I was warned that her digestive system would take a few years to settle down. Unfortunately, in my dash to get her to the doctor up the hill, I had caused the baby I was carrying to drop, and a few weeks later she was stillborn with the cord wrapped around her neck.

Vivienne, age 10 months

It was almost too much to handle by myself. Tommy was still stationed at Upper Heyford, which was in another part of the country. He was able to get special leave though, and came home for a few days until I was able to function by myself. My folks were a big help too, although they were still both working full-time jobs. Mum would stop by to feed Vivienne, and make a meal for me.

When things got back to normal, more or less, I'd put Vivienne in her big Swan pram and go to where the coal was dumped to pick up as much as I could for our fireplace, loading it all in the bottom of the pram. These prams had leather straps instead of springs, and as I was easing the pram down a rather high curb, one of the straps broke, over went the pram and out fell baby and coal. Fortunately, Vivienne was not hurt, but I got quite a few glares from people passing by who could see I had an illicit load of coal on board. I quickly piled baby and coal back into the pram, but it was a bumpy, lop-sided ride, which Vivienne thought was fun and giggled all the way home.

Money was extremely tight. I was supposed to receive a marriage allowance from the air force, but Tommy was not aware of it, and had not applied. He was sending me just enough to pay the rent and little else. Most days I would go to the bakery and buy day old bread and meat pies. The underside of the top pastry on the meat pies was usually mouldy and I'd have to throw that away, but eat the rest. Occasionally I'd buy whale meat which, if you cook it with enough onions, is OK. But usually I didn't have onions, and it would make me sick. Sometimes I'd take Vivienne for a walk and stop by my parent's house, where a cup of tea and piece of cake, was probably the only thing I'd have to eat that day. Those were rough days until Tommy found out about the marriage allowance and I started to receive it on a regular basis. The situation improved somewhat after that, and we survived.

8

A HOME OF OUR OWN

One Christmas my cousin April, a trapeze artist who was performing at Earls Court with the circus, invited us to visit and see the show. She was living in a very nice mobile home which, in England, was called a caravan. I was so taken with the convenience and layout that I suggested we might consider buying one. After looking at several different types we finally settled on one that was 18 ft long by 7 ft, 6 ins. wide. It was moved into a new park in the village of Boreham Wood in Hertfordshire, where there were about thirty other caravans of various sizes.

Our new home consisted of a very narrow kitchen with a small sink about a foot square, a stove and a cupboard for food. The living space had a drop-down bed against one wall, the under-side of which had a drop-down table. The shelf the bed rested on, when it was down, was also the seat at the dining table. Along one wall was a small clothes closet beside a very tiny stove, which burned very tiny coal, called Pithers Peas, a built-in china cabinet completed that wall. Along the other end of the living area was a couch which could also be pulled out for a bigger bed and beside that was the front door. It was really cozy, I loved it even though it was small.

There was no running water or bathroom in the caravan, so all the men who lived in the park got together and laid pipes from the main house, down the road and installed taps at the junction between the homes. It necessitated filling very large water cans from these taps two or three times a day. There was also a building with laundry facilities and a bath-house with a toilet for everyone's use, no charge.

Each lot was about 33 ft square, with plenty of area to make a nice flower garden on one side and a vegetable garden in the back. It was close to the railway tracks where the steam train passed by four times a day, and it actually slowed down so people could enjoy the view of all the pretty gardens. The air was clean and fresh, and my laundry was white! Life was good and we couldn't have been happier.

The village was about a mile and a half away, a nice walk with a variety of shops and the usual pubs. It was also the centre of the film industry, with United Artists, Associated British Pictures, Metro Goldwyn Mayer and Douglas Fairbanks studios. We saw many of the famous movie stars of the day, like Clark Gable, Gregory Peck,

Loretta Young, Anna Neagle, and many others who worked at the studios and lived in the area.

The movie *Ivanhoe* was filmed on one of the farms and the castle they built for the set remained long after the film was finished. The Dam Busters, the famous raid on the dams in Germany led by Wing Commander Guy Gibson of 617 Squadron which I mentioned earlier, was also filmed there. The interesting thing about that film was seeing all the extras dressed in WAAF uniform. I had to laugh at them, because they had not learned the trick that we did of keeping their hats flat, and the crowns stood up like 'out of work chefs'. When I was a WAAF we used to wet the crown of the hat and insert a ring of wire to keep it taut and flat. I wanted to say something to them but never did.

Tommy was demobbed soon after we moved to Boreham Wood and went to work at the DeHavilland aircraft factory, some distance away. We each bought bicycles and cycled to our jobs. I had started work at Hunting Aerosurveys, which made topographical maps. Vivienne rode in a little seat on the back of my bike, and I dropped her off at a day nursery on the way to work, picking her up on my return home. I enjoyed my job, and we were settling into a very nice routine. I loved our little home, the pretty garden we planted, as well as appreciating all the fresh veggies we grew and, for the first time, we didn't have money problems.

Hunting Aerosurveys had a cricket team and Tommy was invited to join. I learned how to keep score and we spent our Saturday afternoons at the cricket field, followed by a few rounds of brew and a game of darts in the clubhouse after the cricket match. When the cricket season finished, it would be soccer matches on the same field. I was elected in charge of refreshments and made a big urn of tea and the sandwiches for half time, followed by the usual brew and darts after the match. I enjoyed these times and the camaraderie, and making friends with other wives, swapping recipes and ideas. Vivienne had other children to play with also. She was growing fast and had totally recovered from her bout with gastroenteritis.

While Tommy was working during the day at DeHavillands, he was also attending night school to become a draftsman. When he had finished the course and graduated, he left DeHavillands and got a job in the drawing office at Adhesive Tapes. This, as the name implies, was the factory where rolls of Sellotape were made. There were nearly 800 employees, a lot of them related, from grandparents down to the a younger generation, and there was a wonderful feeling of family.

When my job at Hunting Aerosurveys was terminated, I too went to work at Adhesive Tapes in the Home Office, typing invoices for deliveries of Sellotape to everywhere in Great Britain. There were several women in this office on the fourth floor who typed either invoices for overseas deliveries or other kinds of correspondence. Every afternoon at 3:30 pm, we stopped for a tea break. During our break we were usually visited by a young man by the name of David, from the accounting department. He was quite a character, telling us jokes and had us laughing our heads off. Our boss, who was a rather stern man seated at one end of the room always had a hard time settling us down and getting us back to work. David was definitely a welcome diversion in an otherwise humdrum day.

Although I loved working at Sticky Tapes, the work I did was actually rather boring because I was typing a variation of the same thing over and over again, and I would find my eyes drooping. One day I couldn't stay awake and my head dropped onto the typewriter, but although I expected to get into trouble, I was surprised when I was given permission to take a 20-minute nap every day, and it certainly helped. After

Vivienne, age 4, with a parrot at Bognor Regis

all, when I was falling asleep I would make typing errors, so it was to their, and my advantage to let me nod off and rejuvenate. I was really surprised that I could actually go into a deep sleep for that twenty minutes.

After I went to work at Adhesive Tapes, fondly called Sticky Tapes, I joined their theatre group, known as The Curtain Club, where we put on several very good plays. I had the lead in a couple and found I thoroughly enjoyed acting, being a ham at heart. I had visions there could be a talent scout from the film studios in the audience and I'd be picked to star in a film, but that never happened - just wishful thinking I guess, but I did get some excellent reviews.

David (of the jokes) was also a member of the theatre group as well as another David. They decided one year that the three of us would put on a skit during the Christmas party, with Vivienne dressed up as Rudolph the Red Nosed Reindeer. We rehearsed and were ready for our big night, but right at the last minute our little reindeer decided she didn't want any part of that, and no amount of cajoling helped. But the show must go on, as they say, so on we went and we really hammed it up. From then on we were an acting threesome, David P, David G and me.

Sticky Tapes also had a cricket team, and when I started work there, Tommy and I both switched our allegiance. We often found ourselves playing against our old team of Hunting Aerosurveys, but we were all good friends and there was no real rivalry. I still did the scoring and made the tea and sandwiches, that routine didn't change.

At Boreham Wood in 1954, left to right, Olive Porter, Tommy, Mum, Veronica and Vivienne

In 1953, when we had been in Boreham Wood for about a year, our beloved King George VI died. His daughter Princess Elizabeth, who succeeded him as Queen, was on vacation with her husband Prince Philip in Africa when she received the sad news, and they rushed back to England for the funeral. I think the whole country turned out to pay their respects, and the route of the funeral procession from Buckingham Palace to Westminster Abbey was packed with mourners from around the world. King George was very popular and he was sadly missed. His wife, Queen Elizabeth then became the Queen Mother, and the following year Princess Elizabeth was crowned our new Queen.

My grandmother came over from Canada, my parents came to Boreham Wood from Leeds and we all listened to the ceremony together on the radio, it was very moving. Our new Queen was so young we wondered how she would cope with running the country. I guess she must have done a good job because she is still at it some 50 years later.

Each year Sticky Tapes closed down for a two week's summer vacation with every one heading for parts unknown, except it didn't matter where you went for your vacation, you were sure to run into someone you knew.

In 1955 we went to Torquay, a beautiful seaside town on the south coast of England, and because the weather forecaster had said it was going to be a really hot two weeks, it seemed everyone and his relatives from Sticky Tapes was in Torquay. We stayed at a funny little hotel on Daddyhole Plain, overlooking the English Channel, it was beautiful. There were actually palm trees and tropical flowers growing along the promenade. We even walked on the beach at midnight without a sweater, it was so warm - not what one expects to do in England in August, it seemed more like we must have been transported to some tropical island and we thoroughly enjoyed it. As events unfolded, that turned out to be our last holiday in England.

9

THE BIG MOVE

When I accepted Tommy's proposal, I had mentioned that I didn't want to spend the rest of my life in England and hoped to return to Canada some day, and he had agreed that we would work towards that end. As coincidence would have it, my girlfriend, Anna was leaving Sticky Tapes to join her brother who lived in Toronto, and we went with her to London's Victoria station to see her off. There was so much luggage with Canadian addresses on the platform and so many people leaving, I suggested that now might be a good time for us to do the same thing.

Immediately after the train pulled out of the station and my friend was on her way, we went to the Emigration office on Green Street in London, where you filled in all the paperwork to emigrate. After all the necessary medicals and inoculations were completed, my wish was fulfilled, six weeks later we were also heading for Toronto, where Anna had promised to find us a place to live. I couldn't wait to be on my way to the country that I had fallen in love with.

After the long train ride from Victoria Station to Barry Docks in Cardiff, Wales, the same docks I had previously left from with my parents in 1945, we boarded the ship that would take us to New York. Now it was ten years later, but we were not on a freighter this time. Our ship was the Maasdam, a passenger ship with a lovely dining room and lounge, nightly shows, swimming pool, cinema and a very comfortable cabin, our home away from home for the next two weeks.

Of the 800 passengers on board, there were only a dozen British and about twenty Americans, the rest were all more or less refugees from European countries which had not yet recovered from the Second World War. Most of them were going to work at mediocre jobs in America, which to them was the land of plenty. They were not very good sailors, and only a few of them managed to appear at mealtimes, looking very pale, although we had a reasonably smooth crossing this time, with only a day or two of rough seas.

Vivienne was an excellent sailor and, although only five years old, managed to communicate with the European children, and taught them how to play a game of cards called Down the River. She and her playmates spent hours together playing this game and I always knew I could find her in the card room. We met up with the other Britishers in the lounge after dinner, and enjoyed their company. Most of them were young single men and women emigrating to Canada or the United States. Some of the women were going to join their boyfriends whom they had met during, and kept in touch with after the war, hoping romance was still on the agenda, while the young men were just hoping to get good jobs, and didn't have any specific destination. We told them we were going to Toronto, but hoped to eventually make our way to British Columbia, expecting that to take a year or two.

When we docked at Hoboken, New Jersey, we had to find our way to Penn Station in New York, so after being cleared through customs, passing all the other inspections and saying goodbye to our new friends, we hailed a taxi. Our driver was a big burly Irishman who was smoking an equally big cigar leaning the arm with the hand holding it along the back of the passenger seat so the smoke was drifting over and choking us, and to this day I hate the smell of cigars.

Christmas was just a few days away, and everything was decorated for the occasion. At one point the driver asked us what we thought of the decorations, and in unison we said, 'Not much'. I thought we were going to be thrown out of the cab, but it was the truth. We had come from London, which for years since the war ended, had the most gorgeous Christmas decorations along Oxford Street, Regents Street and Piccadilly Circus, pictures of which had been printed in newspapers around the world, and New York's didn't even come close. We managed to smooth things over by making some other complimentary comment, but our driver didn't say another word until we reached our destination.

Our plan was to take a train to Toronto and meet up with Anna there. Tommy realized we didn't have enough American or Canadian currency to pay for the trip, so he made a phone call to Cooks Travel Office and was told that they were about to close for the day but would wait for him if he would take a cab to their address. He made a dash across Penn Station, which is enormous, holding his hand out to open the door as he arrived at the exit, but it was an automatic door and he went flying through it. It had also snowed and was slippery as he landed flat on his face in the slush out on the sidewalk. Welcome to America!!!

I didn't know about this incident until he returned with the cash and we saw how wet he was all down the front of his raincoat. Vivienne and I couldn't help laughing, he was quite a sight, but of course, he didn't think it was particularly funny.

Since the train for Toronto was not leaving for another couple of hours we went into a drug store which had a lunch counter and ordered our very first hamburger. I couldn't believe the size of it and wasn't quite sure how it was supposed to be eaten

- with a knife and fork, or not - so I looked about at others and saw what they were doing, and assumed this must be the correct (?) way. You put your elbows on the counter, pick up the hamburger with both hands and take a big bite. I tried that and immediately most of the ingredients fell back onto the plate. I carefully re-packed the burger and tried again, a few times, before I finally managed to get it eaten. What a messy process, but it was good!

The train ride to Toronto was fairly long and we managed to sleep most of the way, arriving there in time for breakfast. It was twelve degrees below freezing, with a very cold wind blowing off Lake Ontario and all we had on were our English top coats, which were not very warm. Anna was nowhere in sight and we stood in the cold for some time, before a car pulled up and a good looking redheaded fellow came towards us. I had not seen Roger for several years but he hadn't changed much, just added a few pounds. I recognized him right away as my girlfriend's brother. Apparently Anna had other plans and had sent him to pick us up. We were certainly very glad to see him.

We also learned that she had been unable to find a place for us to live, so Roger drove us around the residential areas, looking for 'For Rent' signs, until we found a place to suit. It turned out to be the top floor of a three-storey house on Huron Street (seems I was destined to live on streets named Huron). It was furnished quite adequately and the three rooms were large and comfortable, so we decided this would be our home for the next little while. The only problem was, we still didn't have enough money to pay the first and last month's rent, as well as a security deposit, which were requirements at that time.

Fast talking by Roger assured the landlady that we were respectable people and would be able to find jobs and pay her in full if she let us move in, and she agreed. Fortunately, as it was fully furnished we didn't need anything but our clothes, but they had gone astray somewhere between Penn Station and Toronto. It was a couple of days after Christmas before they were delivered to us.

We celebrated our first Christmas and New Years in fine style since there was no chance of looking for work until after the festivities. Roger and Anna were living nearby in a very large house that was divided into bed-sitting rooms. On the main floor was a huge dining room where everyone congregated at meal time, sometimes bringing in their own food, other times taking a turn at cooking for everyone. This Christmas, Roger cooked the dinner for everyone and we were invited to join the party, also again on New Years' Day. This was indeed a life saver, as we had no food of our own yet.

Instead of the traditional Christmas Pudding, Roger had made one of his famous jelly rolls and hid threepenny 'Joeys' in the dough. These Joeys are little silver coins from England, the equivalent of three pennies, as well as little silver boots, which were always hidden in Christmas puddings, and the children loved this special treat. There was a huge Christmas tree loaded with ornaments and lights, and gifts for everyone. It was a wonderful party and we didn't have time to feel 'homesick' at all. I'm sure we wouldn't have had this much fun in our little caravan in Boreham Wood.

Once into the New Year we had to enroll Vivienne in school and look for jobs. I soon found one as a secretary in the Canada Trust Company in Toronto, but Tommy was not so fortunate. There wasn't much call for draftsmen, and all he could find was a consignment job that didn't pay very much. But at least we had something to keep us going. Our main aim was to get to Victoria, British Columbia eventually, where my grandmother was now living.

School for Vivienne was not far from our new home and she was able to walk there with the children of our downstairs neighbour, a boy and a girl who were rather unruly, to say the least. When I came home from work one day, Vivienne was nowhere to be found. I assumed she was downstairs playing, but when I asked the children they said they hadn't seen her, and she hadn't come home from school with them. I was frantic, and started knocking on doors up and down the street, asking if anyone had seen my little girl, but all answers were negative. I panicked.

I was ready to call the police, when I heard giggling, and found that the neighbour children had hidden Vivienne under their bed. She was covered in dust and dirt (guess those folks were not very good housekeepers). I immediately put her in a bath of soapy water, fully clothed, to get her, and her clothes clean.

On my way downstairs to have a few words with their mother, I slipped on the polished wood and went down two flights of stairs on my bottom. My tail bone was hurt, and by the time I reached the last step I was in no mood for a fight, so retreated back upstairs. Maybe I'd have another chance later, but never did. Fortunately this incident was never repeated and the children behaved. I suspect Vivienne must have told them about being dunked in the bathtub fully clothed (it could happen to them!).

Vivienne's teacher called me one day to tell me that Vivienne was unable to read and was well behind the rest of the class. I couldn't understand this as she had already been in kindergarten and grade one in England, and was able to read the newspaper before we left there. I told the teacher this, and she said she would send all nine (very skinny) books home with Vivienne, marking the point the rest of the class had reached, and I was to have her read to that point.

No problem, when Viv brought the books home she read through them all, past the marker to the end of the last book. I was puzzled, how could the teacher possibly say she was unable to read? I quizzed Vivienne, and eventually it came to light that the teacher had a funny accent which Viv couldn't understand. They were ready to put her back a grade until I put my foot down and insisted that she was probably AHEAD of the class, rather than BEHIND them, so she stayed put, but with no apologies.

Happily, things took a major turn for the better. After enduring a very cold winter of snow and ice, and each of us suffering with the 'flu and bronchitis, our luck was about to change. In the Sunday newspaper was a very large ad asking for draftsmen to apply for jobs with the BC Power Commission in Victoria, BC, fortunately NOT 'Single Only' this time. There was to be an interview held at the Royal York Hotel on Yonge Street at 11:00 am the following Monday and Tuesday. Needless to say, Tommy was all spruced up and ready to be first in line.

The deal was, that if you were accepted, the fare would be paid for the entire family, plus all belongings, to Victoria and BC Power would assist in finding a place for you to live. A contract had to be signed agreeing that you would work for them for four years without having to pay back anything, however, if you quit before four years was up, all monies had to be repaid. It all sounded too good to be true, but fortunately, it was true. We received a call two weeks after the interview to say Tommy was accepted, and two weeks after that we were heading for Victoria. We had been in Toronto just ten months and could hardly believe we were going to be realizing our dream so soon.

There was no hurry for us to get to Victoria as the job wasn't due to start for a couple of weeks, so we decided to take the bus across Canada and see some of the country. Anna accompanied us, and on August 4th, 1956 we headed west. The whole trip took five days and four nights, stopping every four hours (no toilets on board), changing busses and drivers frequently.

Leaving Toronto, we headed south west through Detroit and Chicago, then back into Canada, spending an overnight in a hotel in Winnipeg, which gave us the opportunity to have a hot bath and a good night's sleep. Off again through the prairies and stretches and stretches of flat land, with nothing to see in any direction.

Soon we were heading for Saskatchewan, the scenery was changing and becoming more interesting. On into Alberta, cowboy country, and the beginning of the Rocky Mountains. From here on the scenery was spectacular, we were sitting up and taking notice, and lots of pictures.

Our bus kept going all night and we were able to get some sleep, waking up in the morning when we stopped at a roadside restaurant for breakfast. Our stops usually lasted about 20 minutes, which gave us a chance to have a quick wash and clean our teeth. At this point there were not many passengers left and we were able to stretch out on a seat, which was a bit more comfortable.

On one occasion we had left Vivienne asleep stretched out on the back seat, while we went into the restaurant and had breakfast. When we came out of the restaurant, to our horror, the bus was nowhere in sight. I started screaming that my baby had been kidnapped. All my yelling brought the driver from around the corner of the building and he informed me that everything was alright, the bus had gone to be washed, and my little boy was still asleep on the back seat! My panic quickly subsided, but I became quite indignant that he had called my little girl a boy; I was also very relieved that she was OK. Vivienne was still asleep when we boarded our newly-washed bus, totally unaware of what had happened. We made sure not to leave her behind after that episode.

After this stop we crossed the border again into the United States and made a loop through Idaho, back into British Columbia and into the mountains. At one point, we were travelling along a very narrow road high above the Thompson River, when we were stopped and informed that the road ahead of us was about to be dynamited. A few second later there was an almighty explosion and the side of the mountain blew out, with dust and rocks flying everywhere. We sat for the next four hours watching Caterpillar tractors (which looked like ants) clear a surface for traffic to proceed. There was a lot of it lined up at both ends of the area that had been blasted from the mountainside.

The first vehicle to cross the cleared section of road was a tall furniture van. We watched it approach and were holding our collective breath as the van rocked precariously from side to side. There was only room for one vehicle at a time, and it was our turn next. As we bumped over the rocks and saw big boulders going over the steep side into the river below, we were not at all sure we would make it across. Not a sound could be heard in the bus. Our driver was white knuckled as he hung onto the steering wheel chomping down on his chewing gum, proceeding at a snail's pace. When we did finally reach the other side safely, spontaneous applause erupted and we all started singing 'For He's a Jolly Good Fellow' - he certainly was!

It was soon discovered, however, that there had been some damage done to the underside of the engine, we were losing oil, so the last few miles into Hope, British Columbia were taken very slowly and we missed our scheduled dinner at the restaurant there. They had given up on us and closed for the night (sounds like a repeat of our trip across Panama when the train was derailed!). All of us were covered with dust, hungry and tired, but thankful we had made it this far.

Our driver had to contact his office in Vancouver for them to send out another bus to pick us up, but it would be another two or three hours before its arrival. When the new bus did eventually arrive with a relief driver, it was nearly 10 pm and we were anxious to get moving. Anna and I sat behind our new driver, who was a cute young Australian who loved to whistle. We asked him to whistle a certain tune and we would sing the words. Soon everyone on the bus was joining in, so the two hours it took us to get to Vancouver passed quickly and we were all in good spirits when we arrived at midnight.

Because it was too late for any of us to get to our final destinations, we were given rooms at the Devonshire Hotel in downtown Vancouver. Room service came to our rescue with hot chocolate and sandwiches. In our dusty, dirty state we made quite a rough looking group, receiving strange looks from the guests who were leaving a function in all their finery as we checked in. We four were fortunate to get a large suite of rooms with complete laundry facilities, of which I took full advantage. So, freshly bathed, hair washed, and clothes ironed after a good night's sleep, we showed up for a late breakfast looking very respectable and unrecognizable as the hoboes of the night before.

10

VICTORIA AT LAST

We were now ready for the last leg of our long journey, taking the ferry Princess Marguerite, from the dock at the bottom of Burrard Street to Victoria on Vancouver Island, and my grandmother's house. It had been raining as we stood on the deck admiring the scenery, while the ferry wove its way through all the little islands in the Georgia Straits, and the air smelled so fresh and clean. We were looking forward to our new home in this lovely part of the world.

A taxi took us to my grand-mother's house where we were greeted warmly and stayed for a few weeks until Tommy settled into his new job. She fell in love with Tommy and Vivienne and was very generous toward my girlfriend, but I may as well have been invisible. I didn't mind as long as she treated my family well, I had no complaints, but I was glad when we were able to move out. She made us promise

Veronica, left, Vivienne and Anna on the Princess Marguerite en route to Victoria 1956

to have dinner with her once a week though, and was most upset each time we happened to have other plans.

The advance Tommy received from his employer enabled us to move into our own apartment, and furnish it ourselves. We also bought a 1949 Chevrolet and began to explore this beautiful island. I hadn't been here when I lived in BC years earlier, so everything was new to me too. We found lovely beaches and places to picnic, including parks with streams where we could watch the annual salmon run, fighting their way upstream to spawn. The weather was perfect after such a cold winter in Toronto. We were really thankful that things had worked out so well.

Our new apartment was quite near a school for Vivienne and once again she made friends with two young girls next door who were older and well behaved, so she had someone to walk to and from school and play with, and she was in good hands until Tommy and I arrived home from work. We were all happy, relaxing in our new environment.

Soon after Tommy started work in the drafting office of the BC Power Commission, Anna and I also started work there, she in the accounting office and I became secretary to the personnel officer. This was rather like working at Sticky Tapes - one big happy family. I really enjoyed my job, interviewing prospective employees, giving them aptitude tests, answering the phone and keeping the files in good order. I became quite good at finding the right person for the job. When my boss told me there was a vacancy, I would remember we had recently interviewed someone with the required qualifications and pull up their file, calling them in for a second interview. Nine times out of ten they would be hired. It worked out well.

I wrote and told my parents nothing but good news, and they immediately started making plans to join us, but it would be a couple more years before Dad could leave his job, and they could leave England. They too had settled into their new jobs and bought a nice house, so it wasn't as easy for them to make sudden moves.

Soon after moving from my grandmother's house, Tommy and I joined the Territorial Army at Bay Street Armouries where we met in full uniform (khaki this time) once a week. When it was learned that I had been a drill instructor, I was given three stripes (and this time I actually stitched them on my uniform) and drilled both the men and women, which was quite a challenge.

The first year we paraded on Armistice Day, November 11th, we found ourselves standing in about two inches of snow at the Parliament Buildings for what seemed like an eternity, while wreaths were laid at the cenotaph and a short sermon was delivered. When it came time to come to attention and march off, we could barely move, we seemed frozen on the spot. Fortunately we were taken back to the armouries by transport and given hot rum toddies to warm us up, we certainly deserved them.

Having joined the militia, it brought us in contact with a number of very interesting and fun people and we thoroughly enjoyed the dinners and dances both with our own regiment and the Canadian Scottish Regiment. They invited us to their New Year's Party which they celebrated in true Scottish fashion with bagpipes, haggis and much swirling of kilts. We were definitely enjoying our new life.

I noticed in the newspaper one day that the Victoria Theatre Guild was holding auditions for the upcoming season and on the spur of the moment, decided to try out. I was fortunate in being cast in the first play of the new season and was in my element.

From that performance and some very nice write-ups, I was cast in several subsequent plays. Among them was *Love in Albania*, *Separate Tables* and others, the names of which I've forgotten, but not the wonderful people I met or the flubs and ad-libbing that happened no matter how much you rehearsed. It was a lot of hard work, and I loved every minute of it.

We had not been in our apartment very long before Anna met a wonderful young man and they started dating, soon we were planning a wedding. Roger, Anna's brother, together with their best-man-to-be drove out from Toronto in a spiffy new Edsel, nicknamed 'Ford's Folly'. There were only a few of these cars built, it really was quite ugly. This monster caused quite a stir in the neighbourhood, but became the centre of attention when we decorated it for the big day with the usual tin cans and ribbons and 'Just Married' across the back window. When the happy couple returned from their brief honeymoon (he was in the Navy and only had 7 days leave), they moved into an apartment near the Navy base in Esquimalt and settled down to married life.

Home seemed very quiet without Anna, however that was short lived too. The wonderfully funny young man from Sticky Tapes who kept us so amused during our afternoon tea breaks, had decided he too was going to emigrate to Canada, and soon David arrived on our doorstep, but it was a different doorstep. We had moved again, into a bigger and much nicer duplex, which gave us more privacy and a lovely garden. Being from England, of course we appreciated being able to putter among the flower beds. We were glad to have David stay with us, he was so much fun to have around, and he and Vivienne had a great time together. However, his was only a brief stay too. He soon got a job that took him away from us again, and also found love and settled down to married life in Sidney. We could not have been happier for him.

After Tommy had worked for the BC Power Commission for about three years there was talk of a merger with BC Hydro, which meant a lot of people would not be required, particularly draftsmen. That was scary news as there was no other industry on the island that employed draftsmen. I left when the personnel office was moved to Vancouver, finding a job as secretary in a real estate office. Tommy was moved with others into a room over a tailor shop and had nothing to do. Staff was being eliminated at random, their names being pulled out of a hat, and they were given their pink slip immediately.

Rather than wait for this to happen to us, I had typed up several resumés and mailed them across Canada and into the United States, but almost all of them came back telling us they did not employ sight unseen, and 'if ever you are in the vicinity.........' which wasn't a lot of help in our situation. Then came a letter from Hawaii, which was actually the same resumé I sent to them, with a scribbled message across one corner, 'Call this number when you get here'. Tommy had been reading in the National Geographic that Hawaii was enjoying a twenty year building boom and was in need of all sorts of tradesmen, especially draftsmen. It sounded promising.

This meant applying for immigration to the United States for all three of us, so we went to the American Consulate in Vancouver to pick up the necessary application forms. The forms were quite extensive, and all in triplicate. Then came medicals and inoculations, and we went back and forth to Vancouver several times before all the necessary paperwork and requirements were met. It would be six months before we learned we were accepted, in fact our visas arrived Christmas Eve 1959, a most welcome Christmas present. Our luck once more, was changing for the better. Tommy had phoned the number scribbled on the resumé and was assured that there would be a job waiting for him when he arrived in Hawaii.

11

PARADISE FOUND ??

Tommy flew to Honolulu, Hawaii, three weeks later on January 15th 1960 (our 11th wedding anniversary). He was met by a gentleman who signed him up, and he started work right away with a structural engineering company. Seems there was indeed a building boom. Tommy was so busy at work and finding a place for us to live that I didn't hear from him immediately and I had no idea what was happening. I went ahead with our plans anyway, and sold the car, the furniture, and anything else I thought we wouldn't need in Hawaii.

When information arrived three weeks later, it was just a post-card with an address and Tommy's phone number, so I phoned and told him we were ready to leave. On February 5th, Vivienne and I left Victoria during a freezing rainstorm, on our way to Honolulu, celebrating her 10th birthday on the plane. When the plane touched down at Honolulu Airport and the doors opened, we felt like we had been hit in the face with a bucket of warm water, soon discarding the heavy rain coats and scarves we had needed when leaving Victoria.

Tommy had found a little (very little) apartment for us, and as he was working full time, we had to move in by ourselves. I was hoping this apartment was just a temporary stopover until we could find something bigger and better. Not only were we very cramped, the place was full of cockroaches and ghekkos. Fortunately, he had only signed a six-month lease, so we had time to find a much larger and cleaner home.

Our first night in Honolulu, Tommy took us out to celebrate with dinner at a very nice restaurant in Waikiki. Then we strolled along Kalakaua Avenue, which at that time had only five hotels, including the famous Moana-Surfrider with the huge banyan tree in the ocean-side courtyard. The surroundings

Vivienne, at age 10

were absolutely beautiful, and the fragrance of the plumeria blossoms everywhere was heavenly.

After a while we stopped at the Royal Hawaiian Hotel, also known as *The Pink Palace*, Henry J. Kaiser's magnificent property, and walked through to the Monarch Room. As we appeared in the doorway, the pianist, who was seated at a grand piano on the other side of the huge ballroom, began playing 'Maybe It's Because I'm a Londoner'. Who should it turn out to be but a friend of ours who had worked at BC Power in Victoria. I had no idea he was in Waikiki. When he left Victoria he was supposed to be heading for Australia, seems he had a 'stop-over' en route and changed his mind about continuing on to Australia. Hawaii has that effect on people.

We arrived in Hawaii just a few months after it had received statehood to become the 50th of the United States of America. Celebrations were ongoing with a parade almost every weekend of beautifully decorated floats, all with real flowers, of course, Hawaiians in their muumuus of every colour, not to mention fire-dancers, hula dancers and Hawaiian music everywhere. It truly was *Paradise*. The Hawaiian people were so friendly we found ourselves invited to many of their impromptu parties. They have no inhibitions and are multi-talented, singing, dancing and playing the ukulele. Quite often we were the only 'haoles'(white people) present. Being 'malihines' (new-comers), they made us extremely welcome.

After a few weeks of being totally lazy, lying on the beach and getting thoroughly tanned, I decided it was about time I started looking for a job, and found one as secretary to a very dour Scotsman, president of an insurance company. Unfortunately no-one, especially me, could get along with this man, so after a few frustrating months, I left and went to work at the Sugar Planters' Association, within walking distance of the much larger and nicer apartment we had moved into. This was certainly a happier atmosphere than the insurance company.

We also became regular church goers, and Tommy and Vivienne sang in the choir. The church was a very old, rather small and picturesque one that I enjoyed attending. I also volunteered at the pot luck dinners and other functions. Our circle of friends was expanding.

Something else we enjoyed was the cricket matches held in Kapiolani Park every weekend. Tommy soon became a member and I was enlisted as scorer, and again making the tea and sandwiches. He then became president of the Athletic Association, arranging not only cricket matches but also soccer matches held in another area of the park. Our opposing team was usually made up from the crew of a visiting ship, either passenger liners of the P & O Line, who were just in port for the day, or British Navy ships, as well as airmen of the Royal Air Force stationed at Hickam Air Force Base.

After both the cricket and soccer matches, everyone congregated at The Queen's Surf, a bar and restaurant across from the park on Kalakaua Avenue in Waikiki, or the crew invited us back to their quarters on the ship for a game of darts accompanied by a few beers. Sometimes we missed the announcement, 'All passengers ashore', when the ship was due to sail and we'd find ourselves scrambling to get off the gangplank just as they were removing it, amidst cheers and catcalling from the crew whom we had probably just beaten at their own game - darts, but it was all in good fun.

During the month of April every year, Naval ships from many different countries converged in the waters off the Island of Oahu, Hawaii for what was known as the *Pacific War Games.* Honolulu would be crowded with young sailors off duty. There were times when they'd get themselves into trouble wandering into the wrong district. Most of them were below drinking age, which at that time was 21, and there was very little they could find to entertain themselves other than lying on the beach. As a group, the Athletic Association thought it would be a good idea to have some organized activities such as dances, group outings, picnics and entertaining the sailors in our homes to keep them off the streets, so to speak.

A meeting was held and it was decided we would call ourselves *The British Commonwealth Club.* Tommy and I, as the lone members from Canada were asked to contact Naval Headquarters in Esquimalt, British Columbia for information regarding the number of personnel we could expect ashore at any one time so that we would know approximately how many to cater for.

I wrote a letter to the Commanding Officer; however, before I received a reply, two suited men came to the office where I was working at the Sugar Planter's Association and requested my presence in the boss's office. Immediately they flashed a badge at me and informed me this was an official inquiry into my activities. It seems my interest had been misconstrued as a subversive act. I was asking for secret information for unknown reasons, which was ridiculous since the names of ships and their country of origin would be listed in the newspaper well in advance of their arrival.

I couldn't believe my ears, and was horrified that our good idea and intentions were being twisted in this manner. As a result we were not allowed to go ahead with our plans, Tommy and I were also blacklisted from the VIP group which was invited to all the official functions through the British Consulate in Hawaii. However, that didn't stop Vivienne from inviting visiting sailors home for dinner, and as with Mum's house during the war, word spread and we soon had quite a number of repeat young visitors each year the *war games* were held.

About the third year we were in Hawaii, we moved into a large house on Diamond Head Road owned by a couple who were going to be cruising around the world for a year. The idea was, we would be house sitting in their absence. Since the house was so close to the park, it became the party place after the games and we didn't bother with the Queen's Surf, although a visit to crew's quarters was always fun.

The Moana-Surfrider Hotel had a very large bar with a huge grand piano on which a Canadian from Victoria, Jack Pitman, entertained nightly. This also became a favourite place for us to migrate to after the games. Sometimes as many as forty of we cricket and soccer players (cleaned up of course) would completely take over the room, while tourists and other folk lined up outside waiting for someone to leave. No such luck, we would be there until closing time, much to their chagrin.

On one such occasion, while 'The Gang' as we called them, were celebrating at the Moana-Surfrider, there was a tsunami warning. Our house was only a block back from the beach, and the police with their bull horns were telling us we had to evacuate to higher ground. I had returned home immediately after the cricket match, but Tommy had joined the others and I didn't want to leave home without him. I suspected they had not heard the warning, it was usually extremely noisy in the bar, so I phoned and spoke (or rather yelled) at the hostess to ask Tommy to get home as soon as possible, but he found all roads were blocked off and the police would not let him through. It took a lot of persuading but he finally made it.

I had everything we needed ready to pack into the car, blankets, flashlight, water, battery operated radio, the canary and Vivienne, off we headed for higher ground as instructed. Fortunately, no tsunami materialized, but we had many such warnings on a regular basis, which always seemed to come at weekends when there was a cruise ship in port. Although we were beginning to think it was a hoax, we didn't dare chance it in case wolf was cried once too often, and we would certainly have been in harm's way.

We moved into the house we were to be 'house-sitting' soon after the episode with the 'suits' at the Sugar Planter's Association and I decided that I preferred retail work to the humdrum repetitious work I was doing. They say that a Gemini (which I am) gets bored very quickly doing the same thing over and over again. That is certainly true in my case. So once again I was fortunate to be employed in an absolutely gorgeous department store in the cosmetics department. I represented two well known cosmetic lines, and make-up artists from Hollywood came to Hawaii to train me in the use and application of them, in order for me to be able to know how to sell what to whom. This was my niche and I loved it, meeting people from all over the world in Hawaii on vacation, as well as the locals.

Some of my customers were female impersonators from the *Glades* nightclub. These young men would come to my counter, wearing VERY short shorts, their legs shaved and shiny, tapered finger nails with bright red nail polish, arched and plucked eyebrows and mascara. At first I was a bit embarrassed serving them, but had no choice as the other assistants pretended to be busy when they saw them approaching and I was too naive to do the same. After a while though, I enjoyed showing them new items and colours, they became my 'regulars', and were fun to work with.

Every Friday was 'Aloha Day' and we wore muumuus and flower leis to work. Vivienne and I collected the plumeria from the trees in our garden and made our own leis. Besides plumeria, we also had many different colours and type of hibiscus. Those blossoms only last for a day, so each morning I picked a bag full of buds to disperse on our counters in the store. They opened up during the day, adding a colourful display, and quite often a customer would decide to wear one in her hair. The tradition is, if you wear the flower over your right ear, you are 'looking', over your left ear, you are 'taken', and in the middle of the back of your head you are 'undecided', though I think the last one is just a joke.

In October of 1963, Queen Elizabeth II and her husband Prince Philip touched down at Honolulu Airport en route to a State visit in Australia. When her entourage returned to board the plane after a brief walkabout, they were wearing flower leis. The Queen was quite upset that she had not received a lei (and that made the daily papers). So when they were to touch down again in Honolulu on their return flight, my girlfriend and I decided to make sure Her Majesty received a lei. We each purchased a huge red carnation lei and carried them in long gold-coloured boxes. Fighting our way through the throng at the airport, some idiot yelled out, 'Lookout, she's got a bomb'.

Immediately we and our gold boxes were grabbed and escorted hastily to the security office, where our beautiful leis were torn to pieces. Of course there was no bomb and we were released - with an apology. Our friend Rowan Waddy who was responsible for protocol, and had been waiting for us to arrive with our leis in the VIP Lounge, quickly came to our rescue and replaced our gifts with new ones from one of the stands in the airport, and they were duly presented to Her Majesty. A few months later, my girlfriend and I each received letters from Windsor Castle, signed by Queen Elizabeth, thanking us for our "Garland of Flowers".

The following year, Vivienne and I sailed up to Victoria on one of the P&O ships for her school vacation. As I was only a part-time employee I was able to take that time off work without pay, starting again when I returned. Tommy stayed behind, claiming he had a big job to do and couldn't get away. My parents had arrived back in Canada from England just before we left to move to Hawaii, and although they came and spent a few months with us each year, I always felt I should reciprocate and spend

Uncle Henry's "Sou'Easter" at rest

time with them. Besides we really loved Vancouver Island, it was so peaceful and we always had a chance to spend time out on the water in Dad's or Uncle Henry's boats.

Dad and his uncle Henry had built a home for my parents right by the water in Sidney, a lovely seaside resort town with many quaint little shops and beautiful scenery. They couldn't understand why we had left Canada so soon after they returned, when we loved it so much, so of course, I had to explain about BC Power merging with BC Hydro and putting us out of work, so we really had no choice but to leave.

The Sprite

Dad's uncle had a flourishing boat building business nearby and a personal 44-ft cabin cruiser which we went out in often, with Dad as first mate. We also had a little runabout we called 'Vivette', a combination of Viv/ienne, Ve/ronica and T/ommy T/homas, as well as a Sprite sailboat at our disposal. Several beautiful days of our vacation were spent sailing around, visiting a lot of the islands in the Georgia Straits, between Vancouver Island and the mainland, thoroughly enjoying the peace and quiet of being out on the water with no phones or television, just the sound of the water lapping against the sides of the boat. It was wonderful.

This was the 'hippy' era, and most of the smaller islands were home to 'communes' of young men and women who preferred to live without the rules and regulations of society. They built little shacks for themselves which were painted in psychedelic patterns and colours. Being very artistic, their paintings, pottery, beadwork and fashions became popular, with the women in their long 'broom-stick' skirts and loose blouses, braless of course, usually wearing several strands of colourful beads and earrings, all of which they had made themselves. They also had flowers in their hair, chosen from the beautiful gardens they planted.

They were very well educated, interesting to talk to and extremely friendly, their motto being, 'All you need is love'. Dad made friends with several of the young men and women, whom he employed as models in his photography. They certainly were photogenic, and a number of his photographs were prize winners.

Some time during this particular vacation, Vivienne got very sick with whooping cough and pneumonia, and was hospitalized. Our six weeks extended into several more, which gave my grandmother the opportunity she was looking for, to take over what we were going to do about Viv's schooling. I had told Mum that Viv was having trouble with some of the students at her school in Hawaii. Apparently she had repeated this information to Grandmother who also happened to have plenty of money, and we know money talks.

So Grandma decided that Vivienne would attend private school in Duncan, a town further north on Vancouver Island. She had already paid the first year's tuition, there was nothing I could do or say to stop her. The uniform was purchased and had to be marked just as I did my WAAF uniform, making sure she had everything needed to start school with the next semester. Poor Viv, she wasn't sure what was happening, but she did like being with her grandparents who became her guardians for that year.

Vivienne then discovered she was going to be a boarder and only home on weekends. That didn't go over too well with either of us, remembering my days as a boarder. We agreed that the school in Hawaii was not helping her very much academically, some of the students there were very disruptive. The fact that Vivienne was from England was cause for much teasing also, they thought she talked funny!! So I convinced her she would be better off in a more compatible environment. When the time came for me to leave for Honolulu, she felt I was deserting her. I really didn't want to be without her for a whole year, she would certainly be missed. However my hands were tied. Grandmother had won!

My return trip to Hawaii was on the maiden voyage of the P & O ship 'Canberra' with most of the passengers being students returning to Australia from studies in Europe. I shared a cabin with three very nice young ladies and we became friends during our five day voyage. They tried to persuade me to go on to Australia with them. I would have loved to, but couldn't, I was married and couldn't very well ignore that fact. I knew Tommy was going to be dockside to meet me, besides I was sure when everyone returned to their homes and friends, I would find myself on my own in a strange country, so reluctantly declined their invitations.

One of the young ladies with whom I shared the cabin, being Australian, did not have to go through customs, as I did, before disembarking for the day, so I sent her dockside to introduce herself to Tommy. She had told me she wanted to go to Ala Moana Centre, and as it was on our way home I said we could take her. During the drive, Tommy announced that he had to go back to work after dropping me off at home, so I suggested that Sheila and I spend the afternoon together, I was still in vacation mode.

However, once we arrived at the house Tommy changed his mind about going back to work. After discovering a salad in the fridge big enough for all of us, we had lunch then spent the afternoon together at the beach, picking up my best friend, Gladys who worked at the front desk of the Reef Hotel. While Sheila and I were enjoying a swim, she remarked that Tommy and Gladys, who were sitting on the beach together, seemed particularly cosy, but I thought nothing of it at the time. How naive could I be?

It soon became apparent in the following days though, that things were not what they seemed to be, but I didn't find out until too late. When I'd walked into my house on my return from Victoria, I was greeted by the most beautiful sight of flowers everywhere. Hibiscus and plumeria from our garden as well as gardenia floating in glass bowls, and the fragrance was intoxicating, I was very impressed. I was sure I had been missed and after a romantic homecoming, found out a few weeks later that I was pregnant again. When I told Tommy the news, the response I got showed it had obviously not been what he wanted to hear.

I had discovered a few things in the house which did not belong to me, and when I questioned their presence I was stunned by the news that my best friend had moved in with my husband while I was away. Actually, this was not the first time other women had come into the picture. I had turned a blind eye to several other affairs, but this time was different. Now that I was pregnant, I really wasn't sure what course of action I should take.

It was obvious he wasn't about to give her up, any more than she was willing to give him up, and life became pretty miserable, although I tried to put on a brave face, carrying on as before. I still did the scoring at all the cricket matches and held the after game parties at my house, with the sincere hope that once our baby was born, things would right themselves. But leopards don't change their spots overnight, do they?

Although I could have gone back to work at the cosmetic counter in Liberty House, I decided to stay closer to home and get a full time job which paid more, and started work at a travel agency within a few weeks of my return, before learning that I was pregnant. I needed to know I could be independent if the need arose. However, as soon as they were aware I was pregnant, I was fired. I wasn't going to be able to find another job in my 'condition', and added to that, the fact I had a slipped disc in my back which was causing a lot of pain as my pregnancy advanced, made it a very unhappy nine months.

Since I was unable to move around very much without hurting, most of my days were spent being extremely lazy, something I am definitely not used to, my tolerance for boredom being very short, so I decided I was going to do a little housecleaning. As I reached for the mop which was outside the kitchen door, an enormous tarantula flew out of the mop head onto my bare foot. I mentioned before that spiders were something I cannot stand. I let out a scream which was probably heard from one end of Waikiki to the other.

Throwing the mop away from me, I rushed into the house and phoned Tommy who, of course, could do nothing but try to calm me down. Meanwhile, the radio which had been playing music cut in with a bulletin .... President John F. Kennedy had been shot. My fright forgotten, I repeated this terrible news to Tommy, then in stunned silence I hung up the phone.

The President and Mrs. Kennedy had been in a motorcade in Dallas, Texas when a shot was fired from a window high up in a building. The President was hit in the head by a single bullet, and died a short while later. This was a very sad day for America, JFK was very popular. The date was November 22nd, 1963. His killer was caught and about to be brought to justice, when he too was murdered outside the courthouse, which still leaves the case unsolved as to why, and who ordered the killing. The investigation is still ongoing, but it seems unlikely that it will be solved.

The day my baby was born, which also happened to be my 39th birthday, I almost gave birth on the freeway, and made it to the hospital with little time to spare, only to find that he too was born with the cord wrapped around his neck just like his sister, 15 years earlier. Tommy was nowhere to be found as I received the news that my baby had succumbed after just two hours, despite the efforts of the doctors and nursing staff to keep him alive. I was devastated.

I stayed in the hospital for some time, as I had lost an awful lot of blood, and was still very weak by the time I went home. Tommy was supposed to take care of things like getting meals ready and cleaning, but he wasn't much help, using the excuse that he was working overtime. I think I knew otherwise. Moral support was sorely lacking also. At one point Tommy said he was, 'glad the baby died, he hadn't wanted to be married and have kids in the first place'. I had no response other than to say, 'Now's a fine time to tell me that, 16 years and 3 babies later', but my world stood still and I'm sure my heart stopped beating for a few seconds; however, I did rally and managed to survive, turning the other cheek and pretending everything was fine, when in fact it was just the opposite.

We settled into a sort of working arrangement, but some time during the following year things really came to a head and I announced that we should divorce, life was too short to go on this way. The afternoon I made that announcement, Tommy broke his kneecap while playing cricket and wore a cast from ankle to hip. This meant he couldn't drive, walked with crutches and had to rely on me. Of course, the 'other woman' was conspicuous by her absence when it came to taking care of him. The divorce was put on hold for another year and his affair continued once he was able to fend for himself again.

Finally, I could stand it no longer. He was served on the day that my parents were arriving for their annual Christmas visit. He drove me to the airport to pick them up and deposit them at the hotel, drove me to the courthouse to get the divorce, then drove me back to where my folks were staying in Waikiki, all very amicable (but weird). Having my parents there to spend Christmas was a very welcome diversion, but it was strange being alone when their vacation was over and they returned to Canada.

By the time this all took place we had moved out of the house we had been house sitting as the couple had returned from their trip around the world, and into a very nice two storey duplex high up on Maunalani Heights overlooking the Palolo Valley. The unobstructed view of the ocean and beaches from Coco Head all the way round to Barbers Point was spectacular and nothing could be built in front of us. It was brand new and spotless (no bugs), and we were finally able to have our own furniture, and even though things between us were tenuous to say the least, I was still hopeful that we could make our marriage work, but that was just a pipe dream.

After the divorce Tommy moved out, but not with his girlfriend as one would expect. She had apparently become tired of waiting, found herself an army officer, and moved with him to Texas. So be it !!

12

VIVIENNE'S RETURN

Vivienne, now 16 years old, had returned to Hawaii and was attending Roosevelt High School in Honolulu. She had also been chosen to participate in the Duke Kahanamoku Surfing Championships at Makaha, having been discovered a few months earlier on Kuhio Beach, Waikiki, by a scout looking for prospective contestants.

She was spending several afternoons a week after school practising balancing on a surfboard on the sand, then standing on a young man's shoulders in various poses, prior to attempting these same manoeuvres on the waves. Her instructor, who was actually the Phys Ed professor at the University of

Vivienne training for tandem surfing, Waikiki

Hawaii, said she was a natural for tandem surfing, with perfect poise and balance. She was a very good swimmer, but I wasn't at all sure about surfing, let alone tandem surfing. It seemed rather precarious to me.

The time came for her to start practising at Makaha on the North shore of Oahu where, during the months of November and December, the waves can get as high as 50 feet. She and her tandem partner stayed at a friend's house in the village of Makaha, while they practised. The waves were indeed getting bigger as the 'storm season' and the time for the Surfing Championship approached.

The third week in December the championship meet had started, and during that week, several events had been won by young men and women surfers. After the end of each day's meet, those who had not yet competed would go out and practise some more. The day before Vivienne and her partner were to compete, they caught a huge wave, and just as she was ready to stand up, her hands slipped off the rails and the board smacked her in the mouth.

Her two front teeth went through her bottom lip, one breaking off and embedding in the board, the other one breaking in half, she was covered in blood and unable to get up. Fortunately someone with binoculars on shore had seen the mishap and drove his car down to the water's edge. Her partner brought her in, and wrapped in a towel, they rushed her to Queen's Hospital in Honolulu, a 45 minute drive from Makaha. The hole left by the missing tooth was plugged and the other tooth capped, and she received several stitches to her bottom lip. Then they sent her home, heavily sedated.

When I had recovered from losing my baby, I went back to work at my cosmetic counter in Liberty House, on Fort Street in Honolulu and, although my boss was listening to the surfing contest on the radio, she did not tell me what was going on and I was oblivious to the accident. Tommy came to pick me up from work that evening (we were not yet divorced), and warned me of what I would see when I got home. Poor Viv. She still had a lot of congealed blood in her hair and around her face, which was extremely swollen, but with the pain pills they had given her, she was sleeping soundly. Tommy said she couldn't possibly go to the competition the next day, but I told him it would have to be her decision. If we stopped her, she would never know if she could do it.

I didn't sleep much that night and heard Viv getting up about 6 am. She washed her hair and face the best she could, and was making up her beautiful almond shaped eyes with their half inch long lashes (where did she get them from). I was sure she must be very hungry since she had been unable to eat any lunch or dinner the day before. I had no idea what to give her, and tried some warm milk. Unfortunately she couldn't move her mouth, and gave up. Then a thought occurred to me and I asked her, 'How are you going to smile for the camera when you win your trophy?'. I could see the wheels turning, and then without saying anything, she gave me the biggest wink. That would have to do.

The time came and went for her partner to pick her up, but he was very late and we were concerned they wouldn't reach Makaha before the meet started. Finally he arrived with no excuse or apology, and they were on their way. As soon as they left I called the meet coordinator to let him know, and asked, 'Please don't start their part of the meet without them', and reluctantly left for work. I was extremely busy all day and unable to listen to the radio to learn how the surfing championship was progressing, not even knowing if Vivienne and her partner had made it in time to compete.

The day seemed endless, but eventually I arrived home and learned that, on the way to Makaha, they had a flat tire and needed to take the back seat out of the car to get to the spare. No-one would stop to help them, everyone was in too much of a hurry to get a good spot on the beach from which to view the surfers. In their confusion and anxiety, Vivienne had lost her pain pills and they arrived just in time to hear the claxon sound, letting the contestants for the tandem surfing heat know it was time to hit the water. They grabbed their surf board, paddled out and waited for the right wave.

The waves were extremely high that day and they managed to perform several of the required positions, when suddenly the straps on Viv's bikini top broke and she became topless. Her partner quickly took off his T-shirt with the letter 'O' emblazoned on the front, but it was several sizes too big and flapped in the breeze as they continued to compete, becoming more hindrance than help.

Unfortunately, the pain in Viv's mouth was beginning to bother her and when it was time for the final balancing act on his shoulders, which was extremely daring and quite spectacular, she was unable to muster the energy to perform, and fell off into the whitewater. Whitewater has no substance, being just froth, and she was unable to swim in it. Her partner had stayed on the surfboard and made it back to the beach, not realizing she was in trouble, but thankfully there were always people watching through binoculars, and again someone went to her rescue.

As she sat on the beach recovering, the winners were being announced. Starting with the fifth place, the fourth, the third, and it was their names that were called. Vivienne and her partner were representing Hawaii, and the second and first place winners were from Australia and California. This meant that despite the accident of the day before, and the mishaps getting there on time, and losing her bikini top, they had actually come first for Hawaii. I was so proud of her.

A couple of weeks later she and her father went back to Makaha for the presentation of the trophy, and once again I missed it because I was working. They didn't arrive home until after midnight that night. When I went out to the car to meet them, Vivienne was fast asleep in the passenger seat with her head buried in beautiful flower leis and clutching her trophy, a surfer on a surfboard with a huge monkeypod wave curling over her and a little plaque reading, *3rd place Hawaii, Tandem Surfing, 1966.* There was quite a writeup in the local newspaper and the surfing magazine about 'The plucky little English girl who lost two front teeth......'

Pictures in the newspaper showed the surfers standing beside their boards. In Viv's case, when the photos were being taken, she and her partner stood with the board between them, each with their head down. The photographer had asked them to hold their heads up and smile, and when they did, they each showed a big gap where their two front teeth should have been, her partner having suffered the same mishap in an earlier competition, but she managed the big wink, as promised.

Vivienne, waiting for her escort to the Prom

The following year Vivienne was seventeen, and graduated from high school. Her father and I had been divorced for about six months, but he attended the graduation ceremonies, then took a group of us out for dinner. I had planned a big party for Viv and her friends that evening, so after dinner it was back to the house to begin celebrating. We had not sent out invitations, Vivienne had mentioned it at school and the word had circulated.

Before long there must have been fifty or more noisy teenagers who had graduated that day, crammed into our living room. All of them had received, and were wearing several flower leis. Very soon the carpet was covered with petals and gyrating bodies, dancing to the Beatles and singing at the tops of their voices. They were really enjoying themselves, and the noise was deafening. It's a good job our house was the only one on the hillside.

About 9 pm the phone rang, but it was impossible to hear. I had no idea who was calling, so I said, 'If you're a friend, HELP!' and hung up. Within an hour the 'friend' arrived and we managed to keep things under control. Although I was not providing any liquor, it was inevitable that someone would, and it was obvious as the evening wore on that a few were feeling the effects. I had collected everyone's car keys as they arrived and would not hand them back if I thought the person was too intoxicated to drive. Instead I phoned their parents and told them their offspring would be spending the night at my house, or called a taxi to take them home if they insisted.

About thirteen bodies managed to sleep it off on my living room floor and were still there in the morning to help clean up the mess, then we all went out for breakfast, my treat. This was the first graduation party I had been a part of, we didn't celebrate that way in England when I graduated. It certainly was an experience and I wouldn't have missed it for the world!

13

ON THE MOVE AGAIN!

It soon became apparent that we were not going to be able to afford to stay in our hillside home with the fabulous view. Once Tommy moved out, I had all the bills to pay, and the alimony I received hardly covered the weekly groceries. Vivienne was not yet working, and was undecided what exactly she wanted to do, so we sold everything that Tommy hadn't taken, and with the money we received, opted for a trip to Sidney, on Vancouver Island, and we would make it an extended vacation.

Since we were expecting to stay on the island for a while, we needed to find temporary work in order to be able to eat. That also meant living in Victoria rather than with my parents in Sidney, so we rented a very nice studio apartment on the 7th floor of a high-rise in James Bay, one of the oldest neighbourhoods in Victoria, with lots of heritage homes. We scoured the second hand stores and found a few nice pieces with which to furnish our little home, and each took a part-time job at Eaton's Department store within walking distance, just to help make ends meet.

Vivienne with her Grandmother
at Butchart's Gardens, Victoria

The beautiful view we had from our 7th floor picture windows of the mountains and ocean with all the passing ships and sailboats, only caused us to be homesick for the islands and after just a few months, we packed up and moved back to Honolulu. We were both going through a changeable and unpredictable period in our lives, me being newly single and Viv not having school, we really didn't know what we wanted, and of course, all this moving to and fro was eating into our meagre savings.

We arrived back in Honolulu, and I was fortunate in being able to go back to work at the new Liberty House in Ala Moana Centre, this time as a secretary to the merchandising manager. Viv got a job as a telephone operator with the Hawaiian

Telephone Company, and a friend offered us a place to stay until a colleague at Liberty House suggested we share a condominium. Together we found a very nice fully furnished, two bedroom unit on the 16th floor of a high-rise, with all linens, dishes etc, provided. It also included laundry facilities and a swimming pool.

Splitting the rent three ways made it affordable, except that Vivienne decided now that she was 18, she could use the money she had inherited from her Great-grandmother, who had died two years earlier. She had started dating a young marine who was about to become a civilian and return to his home in Washington, DC and had invited her to go with him. It was not something I approved of, but she was no longer a minor so, after being back in Hawaii just a few months, off she went.

It was almost a year before she returned (having broken up with the young man some time earlier, but enjoying her independence and discovering the Capital of the USA). She had certainly grown into a beautiful young lady. When I picked her up at the airport, she looked like she had just stepped off the cover of Vogue fashion magazine. Of course she moved back into the condo with us, and went to work at the telephone company where they were glad to have her back.

The woman with whom we were sharing the condo took a dislike to Vivienne, I have no idea why, and friction started. Their arguments became frequent and heated, and on one occasion the woman raised her hand to strike Viv. I intervened and caught her arm with mine, causing a bruise to appear on her wrist.

I couldn't believe it when she actually summoned the police and informed them that Vivienne had attacked her. This woman had been calling Vivienne, and her father (whom she thought she knew), some pretty ugly names, using a lot of four letter words, but when the policeman asked what provoked the attack, she remained silent and sat with her hands in her lap and head down, trying to look innocent.

Finally, I insisted that she repeat what she had said. Stuttering, stammering and turning bright red, she repeated every word. Vivienne and I could hardly refrain from giggling at her discomfort, and I could see the policeman had a twinkle in his eye, but he looked very sternly at Viv and said, 'I'll see you outside, young lady'. After they left and closed the door behind them, they really started laughing. It was some time before they could come back into the room with straight faces. He gave us all a warning and finally left, but things went from bad to worse after that incident. I had no option but to ask the woman to move out, even though she had been the one to sign the lease in the first place.

Not long after she left I discovered that my silver cutlery service had disappeared, plus a few other personal items. I called the (friendly) policeman, who suggested I change the lock on the front door and then call my former roommate to return my possessions, holding the clothes she had left in her closet as collateral. Much heated discussion followed before she gave in. When she finally arrived, I opened the door only as far as the chain would allow. She handed me the silver cutlery and other items, which I made sure were all there, before I handed her clothes to her, one piece at a time, through the small opening.

Viv had moved out soon after the 'incident' and joined a group of young people who were protesting the war in Vietnam. Most of the time I had no idea where she was, and since these groups of protesters were always getting into trouble with the law, I was afraid for her safety. I had asked her father to track her down and see if he could talk some sense into her, but he seemed to be disinterested and reluctant to get involved. I also asked our friendly policeman to help, but he said he could do nothing unless she was actually breaking the law, and of course, as a typical teenager, she didn't want to hear anything I had to say.

It was obvious that I would have to leave the condo as I couldn't afford the rent payments on my own, so once more I had to find an affordable place in which to live. As luck would have it, the former roommate and I were no longer working in the same store together. I had been at the new store in Ala Moana Centre, while she was transferred back to the original store in town. For a little while life remained fairly calm and uneventful, although that too was about to change.

I had found a really nice cottage to share with two young sisters who were attending university. The cottage was adjacent to and part of a very large house, which was being run as a boarding house, occupied by several young women who were either working or attending University. Once a week we were all invited to dinner in the main dining room of the house and the landlady would also invite officers from the nearby marine base, but there was something about this woman that aroused the suspicion of a couple of us, and we decided to do some investigating.

Her story was that she was the daughter of an Australian politician, and 55 years of age, among a few other facts of her life which she made sound very interesting. However, by coincidence, the two young ladies I shared the cottage with were getting married (a double wedding), and we were all invited. Who should be one of the 'special' guests but the Australian politician who was amazed when we confronted him with his 55 year old 'daughter', obviously there was some mistake. As he said, 'I must have been a very precocious *two year old* to have become her father!'

This disclosure prompted further investigation. We discovered this lady was not such a lady after all, in fact after insisting that we all join her for an evening at the Marine officers' club, I received a phone call from the sergeant on duty upon returning home. He happened to be a friend of mine, and asked me what I was doing with 'that woman'. Seems she had a reputation as a 'Madam' and we were supposed to be her 'chicks'. Soon after this revelation, the young women residents started moving out of the house. Since I had the cottage to myself after the sisters married and moved, I felt I could distance myself from any further invitations, but as it happened I didn't have to worry about that.

I came home from a late date one evening to find all the lights on in the cottage, and the owner of the property standing in the doorway. When he saw me getting out of my car I heard him say, 'Oh, Oh, here comes the red-head, now we're in trouble', and I soon found out what he meant.

The cottage was totally devoid of any furniture and all my belongings were in the middle of the bedroom floor wrapped in my bedding, the main house had also been stripped, every room was totally bare. We had no idea where Elizabeth was or what she had done with the furniture, but the owner asked if I would stay on as 'caretaker' for a couple of months rent free and I agreed. I spent a very uncomfortable night sleeping on the floor, but the next day he brought a bed and a few other pieces of furniture, and I did my best to make it comfortable, although it was pretty spooky with no-one else around.

One Saturday morning, which was my time for housecleaning and hair washing, I was dressed in a rather gaudy penoir set, a Christmas present from Mum. The doorbell rang and when I answered, hair in rollers and no makeup, I was confronted by two FBI men (shades of the confrontation at the Sugar Planter's Association a few years earlier). It seems they were looking for Elizabeth and a friend of hers (thank goodness it wasn't me this time). The car that she had been using was found abandoned at the airport, and subsequently the furniture was found in a warehouse. Unfortunately, the owner couldn't identify it so couldn't get it back. The car which was also his, had been disabled by removal of the distributor cap and the culprits long gone.

The FBI became involved when a claim was made against the American Automobile Association for the loss of $40,000.00 worth of travellers' cheques in the Virgin Islands under a name they recognized from an earlier claim for the same amount from the New Hebrides. I wasn't able to give them any useful information and they left, with a promise that they 'would get their woman'. I heard no more about it, but I hope they did.

During the short time I spent in the cottage by myself a major event in history took place. NASA had launched a space shuttle on a mission headed for the moon. I watched as this was being shown on television and was amazed to see the shuttle actually land on the moon, the doors open and an astronaut step out. What was making it even more astonishing was that I could see the moon through my window. It didn't seem possible that, at that very moment, the first man to set foot on the moon, astronaut Neil Armstrong, was saying the now famous words, *'One small step for man, one giant step for mankind'* which were being heard all over the world. It was Apollo 17 and the date was July 20, (21 GMT) 1969, the beginning of the 'Space Age'.

Since Tommy and I had divorced, my parents had not visited Hawaii again. Instead they had started spending several winter months in Palm Springs, California, having purchased a mobile home in a very nice park. After learning of my latest situation, they invited me to join them, and never one to shirk an opportunity, I accepted their invitation.

14

PALM SPRINGS

A couple of months previously, I had managed to convince Vivienne to leave the bad situation she had been involved in with the war protestors. She was sharing an apartment with a girl friend she had known since they went to school together, and whom I trusted to be a better influence. I decided it was OK to leave Hawaii, at least there would be no harm in spending some time in Palm Springs and, hopefully if all went well, I would have Vivienne join me later.

I flew back to Victoria and spent a week with my parents who were preparing for the trip south in their Volkswagen van. This was my first time heading south by road. I was very impressed with the scenery along the coast road. Starting off by ferry from Victoria to Port Angeles in Washington State, we soon arrived in Oregon and spent the first night in a very nice motel.

Dad was all for getting on the road again as early as possible to avoid the traffic heading for work in the city, and we made good time as we headed for California. I had no idea that California was such a big State, it took another day and a half of driving before we reached Palm Springs and their mobile home. Actually it wasn't any bigger than the 'caravan' we had in Boreham Wood, but certainly adequate for a vacation.

The date was October 2nd, 1969, the temperature was 98 degrees Fahrenheit when we arrived in the desert community and the air was extremely dry. We were almost afraid to touch anything for fear of causing a spark, it was HOT. Although their mobile home was very small and I had to sleep on the sofa in the 'living room', it was cute and the park itself was beautiful.

Besides an Olympic sized swimming pool, there was a large clubhouse where activities were almost constant. Most of the 150 mobile homes were only occupied during the 'season' which officially started on November 1st and ended about May 1st by snowbirds who came from all across the United States, as well as from Canada and a few other countries, to get away from freezing winters and shovelling snow. Everyone knew everyone else, it was like old home week by the time they had all arrived in November.

After a couple of days doing nothing, I decided it was time I explored my new surroundings, and although it was hot and getting hotter, I walked the length of Palm Canyon Drive, up one side of the street and back down the other, hardly meeting a soul or any traffic. Most of the stores were closed with their windows covered in foil sheeting. I did find a little restaurant open and stopped for a quick cold drink before continuing my exploration. This was definitely not the tourist season, the snowbirds would not start arriving for another month, we were early 'birds' it seemed.

As I approached the centre of Palm Springs, lights were on and I saw someone moving in the large Bullocks Wilshire Department store. I was surprised to see that it was actually open for business. Since I always enjoy browsing the big, glamorous stores, I walked in and took advantage of the air-conditioning and a chance to cool down. It was indeed a beautiful store. As I walked up the ornate curved staircase to the washroom and a water fountain for another much-needed cold drink, I passed the office. Just out of curiosity, I asked if they were hiring, and was immediately ushered into the managers' office.

Although I was hardly dressed for an interview in shorts and tank top, they were delighted I was so experienced. I was offered a job in their cosmetics department, and he wanted me to start the following Monday. As I had only just arrived in Palm Springs, I said I would like to have a two week vacation first, and was rather surprised when he agreed. I couldn't wait to get back to the mobile home park and tell my parents I had a job. I guess that meant I'd be staying in Palm Springs for a while, but little did I realize at the time that I'd be in the area for almost 22 years.

I was so excited to think I had found a job in a beautiful store that I decided to use my excess energy to clean the little mobile home inside and out, sending Mum and Dad to the pool out of my way. I donned my bathing suit, and set to work immediately. After a while my parents returned from the pool, and with them were their neighbours and son, to whom I was introduced. He was tall, well-built, nice looking and about my age.

I must have looked quite a sight by this time, with my hair in rollers tied back with a scarf and perspiration pouring down my face in streaks. We shook hands, smiled and he surprised me by asking if he could take me out for dinner that evening. Of course I accepted, it was certainly the second best offer I'd had all day and I was in the mood to celebrate. I had a feeling though that our parents had a hand in this. We started spending a lot of time together after that first date; however, it was the parents who were deciding how we were going to spend it.

Chuck had a new Mustang convertible in which we did a lot of sightseeing, driving up into the San Jacinto Mountains to the lovely little alpine village of Idylwild, or to Lake Hemet, where we swam and picnicked, arriving home in time to change for an evening on the town. There was a really swinging night club called 'That Johns' which we visited frequently, dancing the night away for the two weeks of my vacation. I was having more fun than I'd had in a very long time.

Chuck's parents had made up their minds that we were definitely a couple. After my Mum and Dad left to return to Canada, they moved one of their mobile homes (they had several in different areas of California) into another nearby park for us to live in together. I was not at all sure this was a good idea. I knew that he had recently been through a rather nasty divorce, and had three children, a boy and two girls who were not yet teenagers. I also found that, besides being a heavy drinker, he was also a womanizer.

The drinking I observed during our evenings out, but the womanizing I found out about later, and having already been married to a man like that, was not about to commit myself to the same again. After a very ugly scene one day, I moved out and found myself a small studio in a nice apartment block in Palm Springs within walking distance of my job which, now that the season had started again, was bringing in lots of interesting customers.

Palm Springs and La Quinta, as well as Palm Desert and Indian Wells, were home to many movie stars who were regular customers at Bullocks and I thoroughly enjoyed serving them and talking to them, finding out they were just plain folk like me. Red Skelton, Dinah Shore, Phil Harris and his wife Alice Faye, Liberace, Lucille Ball and her mother Mrs. Magilicuddy, as well as her daughter, plus many more were either shopping in Bullocks or lunching in the deli next door where I had lunch. And of course, Elvis Presley who would close the Woolworth's store at Christmas time and spend thousands of dollars buying up all the toys to be given away to the children.

Other frequent customers at one of my favourite Italian restaurants was the entire Gabor family, Eva, Magda, Sza Sza and their Mother, a Princess from Yugoslavia (but I forget her name). There was never a dull moment, always someone new and interesting to meet in Palm Springs.

Chuck decided he wanted me back, and would not take 'No' for an answer. He started harassing me at home and at work, and of course my boss was not too happy with these disruptions. Once more I was at a disadvantage. The only thing I could do was get away, either back to Canada or Hawaii. The year was 1970, and as soon as the tourist season was over in Palm Springs, Bullocks started laying people off, me included.

Since there is absolutely nothing happening during the off season in Palm Springs, finding another job there was not an option, so that was when I moved back to Hawaii.

Vivienne had met a young man several months earlier who seemed to have a steady job and good intentions and they had moved into a large two bedroom condominium together. They invited me to stay with them, which I did, and found a job almost immediately, thank goodness.

Back to being a secretary, this time to the City Architect, a very interesting job. The pay was excellent and I was anticipating that, after Christmas I would have saved enough money to be able to move into an apartment by myself. Christmas was wonderful. Vivienne cooked an excellent dinner, and they invited several friends in to share in the festivities. We had decorated the condo, including a big tree, opened lots of presents and had a really lovely day, our first Christmas together for a few years. I was certainly glad I had returned to Hawaii instead of going back to Canada. New Year's was also a celebration we enjoyed together, staying home and watching the ball drop in Times Square on TV, popping the champagne cork at midnight and realizing how much we had missed each other.

One week later, on Jan. 7th, 1971, I had just arrived at work when I received a call from the Honolulu Police Department with the devastating news that my daughter had been murdered. I had left for work not knowing that she had not returned home from her night out with friends from the telephone company the night before. I thought she was still sleeping so had crept out without disturbing anyone. I was beside myself with grief, but had to call her father to tell him, and we met together back at Vivienne's apartment.

Arrangements had to be made, and like a zombie, I went through the motions. Two days later her funeral was held in the same church where she and her father had sung in the choir for so many years, and her ashes were interred in the Chapel of Peace there. I hadn't realized she had so many friends. All those school friends who had been at her graduation party, as well as some of the war protesters, and many more, filled the church and the huge carnation leis and wreaths were overwhelming. Her special friend sang The Lords Prayer, it was beautiful.

Tommy had remarried just two weeks earlier, and although I needed his support at that time, and to share my grief, I had to let him go back to his new wife. He had married a woman who claimed he was the father of her 6-month old son, despite the fact he had told me when our son died at birth that he had never wanted to be married and have kids. Life has a way of getting it's own back sometimes.

I went to stay with a girlfriend, unable to face going to Vivienne's apartment. I was a basket case and couldn't go back to work for the architect, or for anyone else for quite a while. It was about six months later that I felt strong enough, both mentally and physically, and found a secretarial job with a travel company. All was well until

Christmas came around again and the anniversary of her death brought all the pain back. I didn't think my life was worth living at this point.

It seemed everyone, and everything I loved had been taken from me, I was totally alone. The detective who had contacted me with the news of Viv's death, had called me just after her funeral and informed me that a suspect had been arrested and charged with her murder. He was actually charged with manslaughter, instead of 1st or 2nd degree murder and he confessed to the crime.

After being incarcerated in the Honolulu Jail until the following October, he went on trial and received the mandatory ten year sentence for manslaughter, but served only three years. The course of my life was changed for ever, yet he was able to resume his former activities in the military, even receiving his back pay and former rank. I was not at all happy about this, but there was absolutely nothing I could do. Justice had definitely not been served.

I behaved badly, and did a lot of very uncharacteristic things for several months, having lost my purpose in life I didn't give a damn about anything. Jumping from one job to another, one boyfriend to another. No matter what I did, it certainly wasn't making me happy, only creating more problems.

At this time, I was fortunate enough to be sharing a very nice condominium with a young woman, Sarah, a Baptist Missionary, who taught at a local school. I have to credit her with bringing back my sanity when I was very close to losing it all. She didn't preach, just talked about everything and anything, making me realize that everything does happen for a reason, even though we can't see that at the time, and I certainly couldn't see any reason for my beloved Vivienne being killed.

One of my former friends resurfaced when he heard my sad news and we became friends again. He was going to Arizona to visit his mother, and suggested I might like to go with him for a change of scenery. Seemed like an excellent idea, so I accepted and spent a very nice quiet two weeks at his mother's home in Phoenix, giving me time to focus on where my life was going.

Just before leaving for Phoenix I had met with two of Vivienne's girlfriends who had been with her the night she was killed. For the first time I heard what had happened. Apparently the three girls, who worked together at the telephone company, had been in Waikiki for a Girl's Night Out. Vivienne was walking in the middle when a couple of marines approached them. As one walked between Viv and her friend he grabbed her purse off her shoulder. She had just cashed her paycheck and wasn't about to let him get away with it, chasing him as he ran into a hotel. The two girls and the other marine also gave chase but lost sight of them, eventually giving up, not suspecting that she would come to any harm.

Vivienne's body was found in the stairwell of the hotel next morning - she had been strangled. The second marine turned his buddy in when he returned to base with scratches down his face, and was acting suspiciously. He was picked up by the police immediately. This was as much as I was ever going to learn about that night. It didn't answer the question 'Why?' and didn't ease the pain, but at least I knew something.

15

LIFE DOES GO ON

I didn't go back to Hawaii, there was nothing there that I needed, so I decided that since I had enjoyed living in the desert in Palm Springs, I would go there to be close to my parents who were back in their little mobile home for the winter. Before I left Arizona I phoned the apartment manager in Palm Springs where I had lived before and found there was a studio available, so I asked him to hold it for me. I boarded a little puddle jumper and flew into Palm Springs from Phoenix, ready to start life anew.

All I owned was in one small suitcase which I deposited in my new home, then went across the street and bought a bicycle which was to be my transportation, since I couldn't afford a car. You know the expression 'as easy as riding a bike'? Well, that's not necessarily true. I had ridden a bike in England with no problem, but as soon as I got on this one, I fell off and received a bruised ego.

Mum and Veronica in Palm Springs

I had made an appointment for a job interview at one of the hotels and was anticipating cycling to it, but evidently that wasn't going to happen, so I parked the bike in my apartment, and walked (quite a long way) to keep my appointment. I had a very successful interview, and was to start work the next day as secretary to the Catering Director. He asked me where I was parked, and when I told him I walked all the way to the hotel, he very kindly drove me back to my apartment, which I really appreciated since the temperature was at least 90 degrees, not exactly 'walking' weather.

I had to master the bike and soon discovered that straightening the handlebars and lining up the saddle made a big difference, and rode it all the way to the airport and back safely - now I had a job and wheels. It was a good start, and it felt good to be back in familiar surroundings.

The following morning I was up bright and early, hopped on my bike and headed for the hotel ready to start work, calling it my next adventure. I shared an office, converted from one of the suites at the Riviera Hotel, with a very nice gentleman, and for almost a year we had an excellent working relationship. The hotel was always full during the season with conventions and groups. One of the conventions was called Desert Roundup, which was Alcoholics Anonymous. I was surprised at how many very well known people were members (but whose names I won't disclose). Besides their 11 step lectures there were also stage shows with performers such as Dean Martin, Frank Sinatra, Sammy Davis, Jr and the Big Band Sounds of Les Brown and his Band of Renown.

At that time I was dating the hotel engineer whose job required him to be in attendance at all the shows, and he would sneak me in with him to watch. Actually this entailed climbing a steep ladder to a trap door in the ceiling of the men's toilet to the attic where the stage lighting controls were, and viewing the show through the projectionist's window. Exiting was even more precarious, as the men's room became very busy once the show was over.

One day there was a raid by the border patrol police which managed to eliminate most of the kitchen and housekeeping staff, by rounding up all the Mexicans who had entered the country illegally. This left us so shorthanded at meal times that my boss found himself working in the kitchen, and I was filling in as a waitress in the dining room. Conventions and group reservations were cancelled, and soon the hotel went into receivership with staff being laid off - me included, once again. A couple of months earlier I had married the hotel engineer, which outwardly appeared like a good thing, but was anything but. Seemed I was still making bad choices.

This man I married could have been brilliant. He had a very sharp mind, the problem was that half the time it was pickled. He was a bonafide alcoholic, the bar was too handy for him. Despite the fact that he set up all the arrangements for the Desert Roundup and was present at all their meetings, he wasn't learning anything from them, spending our wages and time with his drinking buddy, who happened to be another woman! I sure knew how to pick 'em didn't I? Well it wasn't long before the same judge who had performed the marriage, was performing the divorce. I was back to square one, with no job, plus the no good so and so had cleaned out my bank account (what little I had).

The police department was advertising in the local newspaper for a dispatcher. This sounded interesting, so I applied and was hired. They loved my British accent.

I started work right away, but wasn't able to use the same monotone that you hear in the movies on the police radios, and always ended my communications with the patrol cars with a 'please' or 'thank you'. It was a habit I just couldn't change. Dispatching was not for me; however, they didn't want to lose me, so they put me to work in the records department typing up cases, filing reports, and answering the phone. That was good, no problems there.

Elsewhere in the building, fourteen detectives shared a large office we called the Bull Pen (for obvious reasons), a really crazy bunch of guys, with one secretary who was about to retire. I was asked if I would like her job, and jumped at the chance. Policemen, like firemen are a special breed, I loved working with them. Each had a little speaker on his desk which only he could hear, and I'd be busy typing when suddenly they would rush en masse out of the room putting on their helmets and stuffing their batons into the holster, as well as their guns. I would have no idea what just happened and waited, not too patiently, for their return.

One by one they would straggle back in and usually there would be a funny side to whatever just went down. On one such occasion I noticed one of the detectives was nursing his little finger suspecting it may be broken, and amid much laughter and nose holding (at his expense) I found out that they had been tailing a suspect in a home invasion, when this particular detective fell over backwards into a garbage can, and was unable to extricate himself. It took two other officers to dislodge him, covered in garbage of course. Needless to say the suspect got away, but they did catch up with him eventually. They were a great group and I looked forward to going to work every day, not knowing what mischief they would get up to.

One afternoon I came back from lunch and the bullpen was empty. I thought they had probably been called out, but noticed a very odd odour as I walked into the room. Those devils had filled a dish with marijuana (from the confiscated evidence locker) and set it smouldering in the middle of my desk, I could hardly take a breath it was so pungent, but managed to dispose of it outside before the Chief came to investigate, and it took a long time for the smell to dissipate. When they all came out of hiding (from the interrogation room) they expected me to be 'high' but I don't really think I was, was I?

Two years after I had divorced my second husband (the alcoholic) and was working at the police department, one of my jobs was to take large files across the street to city hall where they had a binding machine that binds the files to form a book (some crime files get very thick!). On one such occasion I was greeted by a tall skinny chap, wearing a shiny black suit, pants about four inches above his ankles and a silly grin. He thought he was being really funny, making smart-alecky remarks and trying to make a date with me, but I thought he was a jerk and brushed him off.

A week or two later the City Hall, which included the Police Department, was having its annual Credit Union Christmas party. I had asked a neighbour to go with me. He told me he was going with a friend so I said, 'Fine, bring your friend and his date to my apartment, we can have a cocktail before we go'. Who should the friend turn out to be but the jerk from city hall, with a girl young enough to be his daughter - I groaned! After a (very) quick cocktail, we all piled into his (the jerk's) yellow Volkswagen and went to the hotel where the party was being held.

The girlfriend managed to find someone at the party more her own age (thank goodness), and my neighbour also found other company. The evening ended with me being driven home alone by the jerk in the yellow bug much against my better judgement. However, since he and I had to work together from time to time, I decided to at least be friends.

Just about this time Palm Springs elected a new Mayor, and despite his funny voice and mannerisms, Sonny Bono (of Sonny and Cher fame) won in a landslide over the previous Mayor who had been in office for so many years he held the title of 'Mr. Palm Springs', but it was time for a change, and he had to retire.

Sonny's office was right across the aisle from 'the jerks' office in City Hall, and they became good friends. He, along with most of the employees from City Hall and the Police Department, were invited to Sonny and his new wife's beautiful home for Christmas. He was an extremely generous man with great foresight, and in the years he was in office, Sonny brought a lot of good things to Palm Springs, such as the Classic Film Festival, Grand Prix Cycle Race, a lovely new building for senior citizens, and many other activities. He also gave the main streets a face lift which they had badly needed for some time. It was a very sad day when he died in a skiing accident on the mountains he loved above Palm Springs, but his legacy continues.

I soon found myself spending more and more time with the jerk, whose name was Frank. I called him Frankenstein. He seemed to be a pretty decent fellow, and with a little coaxing from me, was dressing better too, and we started dating. Then he popped the question. Oh no, not again, I had already been bitten twice and I was somewhat gun shy, so continued to put him off. We still went out occasionally and he still kept proposing, but it would be months later before I finally said 'yes', despite the efforts of my boss, the Police Chief advising me not to, and jumped right out of the frying pan into the fire!

This marriage lasted seven years, during which we parted company several times. The only reason I kept going back was that I had found out something that made me afraid of him. While we were separated he would leave threatening notes on my car, or stuck in my front door. The angry phone calls were constant both at home and at work, and were causing a lot of problems, especially at work.

It got so bad at one point that I called the District Attorney. Apparently the DA could do nothing unless I was physically attacked, which I was pretty sure was inevitable. I had done it again - what was wrong with me that I attracted these types, or was attracted to the wrong types? Eventually, I couldn't take any more and told him I wanted a divorce. Even then the harassment continued until he found another woman to harass, and married her soon after our divorce was final.

Too bad ex-wives don't get a chance to warn their successors!

Maybe I could start an Ex-Wives Club? Though with my luck I'd probably have the FBI after me again for 'subversive activities'.

16

LIFE IMPROVES

When Frank and I were first married I had moved into his home in Cathedral City, but when HE decided to divorce ME, he moved out just before my parents arrived to spend Christmas and the 'season' with us, having sold their little mobile home in Palm Springs the previous year. On Christmas Eve Frank announced that he was selling his house and we would have to move out. This created a rather embarrassing situation, but fortunately, the police chief's secretary came to our rescue and offered us her house in which to stay while she was away. At the end of the month, when my parents decided to cut their vacation short, they convinced me to return to Victoria with them. Dad drove Mum home in the camper, then returned to Palm Springs, and he and I drove my car back to Victoria, this time with a trailer containing all my possessions.

A couple of weeks later I had a bad case of the 'flu and as I lay in my sick bed I was mulling over my situation. It occurred to me that maybe I was giving up on my marriage too soon, so as soon as I was feeling better I phoned Frank, who seemed delighted to hear from me, and was on the next plane north. We drove back to Palm Desert together to a rented apartment and divorce proceedings were cancelled, for a small fee. I was determined we would work things out.

A new hotel had been built in Rancho Mirage earlier that year and I secured a job there as secretary in the Sales Department. This was a beautiful hotel built in the Spanish style with lots of archways, red tile, mosaic and dark wood beams. My office was on the mezzanine overlooking the huge foyer where the gift shop, restaurant and front office were located. My job was to correspond with companies planning groups and conventions in our area, to convince them to stay at our hotel, describing all the amenities available as well as the sightseeing advantages, such as the Palm Springs Tram which travelled a mile up to the top of the San Jacinto Mountains with a panoramic view of the desert floor. The temperature would be several degrees cooler at that altitude, and in winter would be covered in snow, with cross country skiing available.

*The Sales staff prtraying the Wizard of Oz,
Veronica at front right*

I was enjoying my job very much. Although we worked hard, we were one big happy family and shared a lot of fun times. Every Hallowe'en the entire hotel staff dressed in costume, each department adopting a different theme. One year the Sales staff became the characters from 'The Wizard of Oz'. I was a Munchkin, my boss was the Mayor, and there was a wonderful Tin Man, the Cowardly Lion, and of course Dorothy and the Wicked Witch, plus as many characters as the rest of the staff could fill. Our Manager's name was Mr. Small which was most appropriate, and we covered the floor with yellow bricks (paper ones), with lollypops on the railings along the corridor to his office and "Smallville".

*Raggedy Ann and Andy with Darth
Vader, Veronica at front left*

Another year we chose a cartoon character and my friend and I were Raggedy Ann and Andy, and we mustn't forget the year all the females in the Sales Department became Saloon girls while the men were dressed as Bart Maverick, that was hilarious. Each of these occasions ended with a party after work at someone's house, still in costume. I don't know what our clients thought, but I know we thoroughly enjoyed ourselves.

There was a formal dance held in the hotel ballroom every New Year's Eve for which I volunteered to collect the tickets as guests arrived. By 11 pm the doors were closed and I could join the party and bring in the New Year with the rest of the revellers. That was an event I always looked forward to.

While my working days were enjoyable, my marriage was anything but. Despite the fact that I had returned to Frank with good intentions, we were not getting along well at all. We had vacated the rental apartment and purchased a beautiful triple-wide mobile home situated in a very nice park on Highway 74, the road leading into the mountains and the little village of Idylwild. I spent most of the two years we lived there making stained glass windows which filled in the top of the windows across the front of the home. By the end of the second year we knew a divorce was inevitable and this time I was the one to move out. Frank sold the beautiful home and the stained glass windows went with it. All I received was half the furniture.

I wasn't worried about being on my own again though, I knew I could manage and found myself a nice little apartment in a complex that had been a motel, complete with swimming pool. I picked up a gorgeous ginger Persian cat, whom I christened 'Princess' and breathed a sigh of relief to be out of another bad situation; however, I was still being harassed by my ex. He was leaving obscene and threatening notes on my car, and phoning me constantly at work, but my friends at the police department were aware of the situation and kept in touch with me on a daily basis.

When I arrived home from work one day, my Princess who was usually standing on the roof above my front door waiting for me, was nowhere to be seen and did not respond when I called her name. I could hear a faint cry coming from the bushes and there she was. Although her eyes were open and I could see she was alive, she didn't come to me, and I could tell something was terribly wrong. When I tried to pick her up she let out a howl, and was obviously in pain.

I called the vet who told me to pick her up in a pillowcase and take her in to the pet hospital. I managed to do as he said, all the time she was crying in pain but didn't fight me, she was too weak. When the vet examined her he found that she had been shot with a pellet gun and there was a fairly large hole in her side. I had a feeling I knew who was responsible for this vicious attack, but had no way of proving it. Thankfully, after a couple of days in the pet hospital and then lots of TLC at home, Princess recovered and suffered no ill effects.

During the months from November to June the area was alive with people and vehicles bumper to bumper along Palm Canyon Drive, the main thoroughfare through Palm Springs, but after June 1st almost everything was deserted when the temperature reached over 100 degrees, and you could shoot a cannon down Palm Canyon Drive without hitting anything. However, work at the hotel still continued, and it was the busiest of times for secretaries in the Sales Department.

After I'd been working at the hotel for a few years, I was given the opportunity of transferring to their hotel in Scottsdale, Arizona. I had really liked Arizona when I spent two weeks there some time before. Being on my own with nobody to answer to, it seemed like yet another adventure about to unfold.

I decided to sell my furniture and advertised in the newspaper. One of the responses was from my ex-husband of all people, who was actually willing to BUY the sofa and easy chair back, even though he had paid for it in the first place. It seems he forgot that fact though, and I certainly wasn't going to remind him. I was just glad to get rid of it (and him), and a few other items I no longer needed.

I bought a 1969 Mustang hatchback, and was ready to go. My girlfriend, Carol, decided she would move to Arizona with me and we would rent a nice condo, sharing expenses. She had also been working at one of the hotels in Palm Desert and was confident she would have no trouble finding another job.

Since the temperature during the day was liable to be above 100 degrees Fahrenheit, we planned to leave Palm Desert at 3 am while it was fairly cool and arrive in Arizona before it got too hot. Its about a 2½ hour drive on the I-10 freeway. It wasn't long before the hunger pangs started, so we decided to have breakfast at a truck stop where we'd be sure to get a good helping of biscuits and gravy, with lots of hot coffee to keep us awake. The dawn was beautiful, and we were enjoying the drive, but realized that we were not going to arrive before the heat.

My cat, Princess had been in a special cardboard carrier on the passenger seat, but had decided to chew her way out of it. At one point I put my hand on her head to coax her back in the box and she bit on my finger instead of the cardboard. Her sharp teeth went right through my fingernail and finger, and blood was shooting out everywhere. For a minute I couldn't see for the pain and swerved across to the other side of the road.

Fortunately, there was a gap in the previously continuous flow of semi-trailers and I was able to get back into my own lane before there was a collision, but had to stop and tie a handkerchief around my finger before continuing the drive. Princess had eventually made her way out of the box and spent the rest of the drive sitting on the back of my seat, gasping for a drink. Although I had a tub with water in the car, she didn't want to budge from her perch. Afraid she might try to jump out of a window I had to keep them closed, and my air conditioning was working overtime without doing much good.

I couldn't wait to arrive at our destination, and by the time we found our new address we were drenched in perspiration and my finger was throbbing with pain. As soon as we were inside, we put Princess in the coolest room in the house, the bathroom, with plenty of water, found a band-aid for my finger and set about unloading the car. It took us until dinner time to put things away and clean ourselves up. Tired and starving we found the nearest steak house and feasted on enormous and delicious steaks. I wasn't due to start my new job for a couple of days, so we spent them enjoying a well earned rest, while making our mark on our new home.

The hotel in Scottsdale where I was to work was absolutely beautiful, set in a circle around a magnificent pool area with beautiful terraced landscaping against a backdrop of Camelback Mountain. Everything about it felt right, I was sure I was going to be very happy here. My boss was a gentleman who had been at the previous hotel in

Rancho Mirage and he was the one responsible for getting me transferred, so I knew I was welcome.

There were three other secretaries in the Sales Department each working for their own Sales Manager, and we were kept very busy typing contracts for conventions, and other groups, as I had been doing in Rancho Mirage. I also had an added responsibility which entailed using a computer, something I had never done before. I thoroughly enjoyed learning about it, mostly by trial and error, since no one else had a clue either.

The weather was perfect for the first couple of months, although it was very hot, but then the monsoon season came, and along with the rains there was heavy thunder and a terrific amount of lightning. Sometimes it rained so hard it was impossible to see to drive. I would have to pull off the road and wait it out, which could be for quite some time.

I don't think I have ever seen such spectacular lightning displays, it would be chasing in all directions across the sky, and was constant throughout a storm. I'd hear it hit a puddle and hiss, or a transformer and shower sparks, but everything was grounded because these storms happened frequently. Unfortunately though, people were not grounded and an unsuspecting golfer would get a shock which usually proved fatal.

Carol, in the meantime, was acting as housekeeper and having dinner ready when I arrived home. Which was all very nice, but she had not yet found a job, so I was paying all the bills, including the rent on our very nice townhouse in the beautiful 5th Avenue area of Scottsdale. I was beginning to get concerned that this is the way it was going to stay. It seemed she couldn't be bothered looking for work. I was making it too easy for her, so I had to issue an ultimatum, then she found a job as a switchboard operator at the Hilton Hotel. Certainly it was not a very high paying job, but better than nothing, and little by little she was repaying me what she owed.

The year was 1983, and I was prepared to make Scottsdale my home from then on, but as luck (or rather, misfortune) would have it, my father was diagnosed with cancer that November, and my mother phoned and asked me if I would go back to Canada to take care of them. Mum was now 89 years old, Dad ten years younger. He had actually been doing everything for her up to this point, not that she couldn't, just didn't. He had always enjoyed cooking and trying new recipes, as well as baking special cakes and decorating them, so Mum had just let him go ahead and do his thing. She did hers, which was usually knitting and playing bridge, and they were each happy with their choice of activity.

Actually, when Mum phoned, she only told me that Dad was tired of doing everything and would I please come home and help him. Not being aware that he was sick,

I procrastinated until the following May, but was feeling guilty, so of course I told them I would be happy to take care of them. By that time I had been working at the hotel in Scottsdale for just over a year. My birthday fell on the last day of May, which was also going to be my last day of work, and the Sales and Catering departments each gave a party for me with cake and gifts and a fond farewell. This was most unexpected, I was very sorry to leave and hoped I'd be able to return in the future.

Since my last divorce I hadn't dated anyone, not that I hadn't had the opportunity. I spent a couple of nights a week at a dance club enjoying mixing and mingling with a lot of different dance partners and I was asked out on dates, but always declined. I wasn't ready to become involved again, so it was easy to leave Arizona with no broken hearts.

Carol and I drove my Mustang north as far as Olympia, Washington State together, along the beautiful coast road. We stopped at Monterey for a meal and Carmel for the night, also Solvang, the little Dutch village full of windmills and souvenir shops. We also visited Hearst Castle, home of Randolph Hearst the newspaper baron, and enjoyed the drive. But then the rains started, and it continued to rain heavily through the rest of California and into Oregon and Washington State.

At one point I found myself driving down a steep hill in Washington State with a 30 mph sign at the bottom. I was afraid to apply my brakes too hard on the wet road and was probably a couple of miles over the speed limit. Of course there was a wily policeman waiting for me and he slapped me with a ticket and a very heavy fine, which I certainly didn't need. I don't think he had a sense of humour either, he didn't laugh at my retort!

When we arrived at Olympia soon after that unfortunate episode, Carol and I parted company. She was met there by her brother with whom she was going to visit for a couple of weeks before returning to Scottsdale. I drove on, choosing the route alongside the Hood Canal to Port Angeles to board the Coho Ferry, which would take me across the Strait of Juan de Fuca, to arrive in Victoria about an hour and a half later. This trip is not quite as spectacular as the one between Vancouver, Canada and Vancouver Island as there are fewer islands and much more open sea en route, but I was glad to relax and breath in some fresh air after all the driving I'd done for the previous week. I was anxious to see my parents and find out what was really going on.

17

VICTORIA ONCE MORE

I don't know what I was expecting to find when I arrived at my parent's house in Oak Bay. Since I had not been told that either one of them was sick I had mixed emotions about why I had been summoned, but I soon found out that I was expected to take over the cooking, shopping and cleaning house. However, Dad was not prepared to give up his jobs, so all I did was peel potatoes as my contribution to the cooking. I was given a shopping list with strict instructions of 'no substitutes and no extras', and had to drive Dad's car which I didn't like driving and called the 'old folks car'. It felt like I was sitting in a straight back chair, I much preferred my little Mustang, which I had driven up from Arizona with all my worldly possessions packed tightly inside, and had no intentions of getting rid of. Alas, without my beautiful Persian Princess though, she had been hit by a car and killed in Scottsdale the previous Christmas Eve.

I found that my parents had a very strict timetable when it came to meals. Breakfast at 9 am, coffee at 10:30 am, lunch at noon, tea at 3 pm and dinner at 5:30 pm, and every night before bed, a cup of tea and a cookie at 10:30 pm. I was expected to be present at all these events, so if I wanted to go out anywhere it was a mad dash to get back in time. I felt very constricted, and very bored. I took up knitting, which I hadn't done for several years, living in the desert one didn't need woolly sweaters very often. I made about five sweaters in different colours all in the same pattern, but then some of my mother's friends decided I could knit for them too. I made a little extra pocket money doing that, but the boredom was taking its toll. I was beginning to resent the fact that I had left my great job in Scottsdale for no apparent reason - or so it seemed.

Since I had so much time on my hands I felt it would be a good idea if I got a part-time job maybe a couple of days a week, or even a morning or afternoon, which would give me some kind of an income, which at present I didn't have. I soon found though, that jobs of any description were few and far between in Victoria, although I did manage a brief spell at one place where I was setting up the board room for meetings and serving tea, and washing up afterwards. But that didn't last long enough for me to appreciate the few extra dollars I received.

Dad decided to pay me $200 a month which hardly covered my expenses. There was car insurance, gas and maintenance, as well as clothing and the other necessities of life. Although I appreciated having a roof over my head and food on the table, I felt that I had lost my independence and, after so many years on my own, this was not good.

Veronica, with Mum and Dad at Uncle Henry's place in Sidney 1986

Dad's Uncle Henry, with whom we had spent so many wonderful outings in his cruiser, had died a couple of years earlier and his wife, Aunt Lil had followed shortly after, so we didn't have anyone to go sailing with. Uncle Henry's daughter Irene, my Dad's cousin, was still living on the property in Sidney. I would drive my parents out there on a Sunday afternoon for tea once a month, and Irene's daughter and two grandchildren would join us. I always enjoyed these visits, when Dad and his cousin reminisced about their young days together. I learned things about the family that I would never have known otherwise.

On one of the outings on my own I discovered a brochure advertising a dance club, and since I love to dance, decided this was worth investigating. So the following Friday, I got dressed in one of my nicest outfits, and headed out for the dance, making sure Mum and Dad knew where I was going to be for the next three hours or so, as they insisted I leave a phone number where I could be reached whenever I went anywhere.

At that time the dances were held in the ballroom of the beautiful Crystal Gardens on Douglas Street in Victoria, with live music. There could be as many as 100 to 200 people from 20 to 90 years young enjoying a wonderful evening of ballroom dancing. I was invited to dance almost every dance and had a fabulous time, the very best in a long while. I started making friends among both the men and women, and looking forward to Friday nights.

A group was in the habit of going to a local restaurant after the dance for coffee and a chance to chat, which it was almost impossible to do during the dance. I hesitated accepting their invitation to join them, and decided I would let my folks know I'd be joining them the next time if I was asked again. Soon I had met several people who were inviting me to go here or there, and I started to enjoy other company, but I also felt a bit guilty because I couldn't always be on hand to make the tea or run an errand for my folks, but life went on, and nobody complained, at least not too much.

One of the men I met at the dance and danced with frequently, was a farmer who lived some distance out of Victoria. He claimed he had known my parents when they built their house in Sidney, so I invited him for dinner one evening to reacquaint, but they didn't remember him and felt it was just his way of 'getting his foot in the door', so to speak. Then one day he announced that he was going to Vancouver to see the lighting of the Lion's Gate Bridge, which was part of the opening of Expo '86 in that city, and he asked me to go with him. I was quite sure my parents would say definitely NOT, so was very surprised when they said OK. Actually, my mother insisted, and I was excited to be going somewhere and doing something interesting, if only for a weekend.

The ceremony was quite spectacular as the beautiful bridge which spans across the Burrard Inlet from the North Shore to the city of Vancouver at Stanley Park, came alive with millions of twinkling lights, and the ceremony was followed by a brilliant fireworks display. A marquee had been set up at the North Shore end of the bridge, for a cocktail party attended by government dignitaries, and members of the cabinet, plus the Premier of BC.

Evidently we were invited also, as I found myself being introduced to the Premier, Bill Bennett who just happened to have the same surname as mine. It was a wonderful party that went on for hours, and it was midnight by the time we departed.

I awoke early next morning to learn that I was not going home, and not even for a short drive around Vancouver, but on to the Coquihalla Highway, a brand new highway connecting Vancouver to a point in the interior of BC, which was being opened and christened by the Premier. To my surprise we joined the procession, and were fourth in line behind Mr. Bennett's limousine.

What a fantastic view and a fabulous ride as we wound our way through the city of Vancouver and out onto the open road. The new highway and the surrounding forest of pines was covered with snow resembling a winter wonderland, under brilliant sunshine and a clear blue sky. I hadn't taken my camera with me, which was a pity as there would have been some spectacular pictures to show my Dad, who was a photographer, among his other accomplishments.

We stopped in the beautiful little town of Hope, the same place where the bus dropped us off after the oil sump was cracked on our trip across the mountains so many years earlier. Not too much had changed here, except for the addition of magnificent wood carvings on nearly every corner. One carving was an enormous Royal

Canadian Mounted Policeman. Every detail of his uniform was perfect, including the embossing on his buttons. There was a huge grizzly bear, a moose, elk, beaver and other small animals, all looking extremely lifelike.

The procession of cars gathered in a small park in the centre of Hope and the Premier made a moving speech about how we were all connected now by this great new highway, but that this was only a small start to what was to become the Trans-Canada highway. That accomplishment took a few more years, but eventually was finished. It is now possible to drive from the west coast to the east coast and back on one main highway. It still takes many days and nights, but it's definitely worth the time. The ever changing scenery from mountains through prairies, small towns, past rivers and lakes, from the old to the new, is an experience that is priceless, and if you ever have the opportunity to make the trip, don't let it pass you by.

Because we were travelling in a camper we didn't have to worry about finding accommodation since everywhere was packed solid, even the restaurants had long waiting lines and we were starving. We arrived very late in the day at Wells Gray Provincial Park, with lots of camping sites and hookups for trailers. We were fortunate enough to get one of the last sites available, right beside the magnificent waterfall. The roar of the water rushing over the falls was like thunder. It was also a soothing sound and I was soon lulled to sleep, only to be awakened very early by the sound of other campers preparing breakfast over campfires and shouting greetings to each other.

After sharing a bacon and egg breakfast with the camper family next to us, we decided to explore the terrain and discovered the North Thompson River running by in another area. From our vantage point high above, it looked like a narrow stream with a waterfall making a beautiful rainbow far below us. There were pine trees, Douglas fir, and berry trees everywhere, covered in snow. Even though this was my first taste of winter weather in several years, I found it quite invigorating.

We met up with several other campers and stopped to chat. It was very interesting to find that some of the people had come from as far away as Japan and China as well as Great Britain, the southern States of the USA, and many other parts of Canada to witness the events of the previous day. They all gave rave reviews.

Soon we were off again, where we were going I had no idea, but for the next sixteen days we drove through the interior of British Columbia, even to Bridge Lake. I had a look at the place where Mum, Dad and I had spent a summer being dude ranchers, forty years earlier. That seemed a whole lifetime ago, and a pang of nostalgia swept over me remembering how much I had loved it there. The surrounding country was still mostly forest, and we travelled mainly on logging roads which seemed to stretch for miles with no end in sight.

I saw more animals than people. There was a mother bear with four cubs, and as the camper approached she stood on her hind legs and made noises, telling her babies to go and hide somewhere. She was huge and could easily have attacked us, so we kept the windows closed and crawled past her safely. When I looked back, she had returned to standing on all fours with the cubs running around her feet, watching us to make sure we left. She was beautiful and the cubs were so cute, but it could have been dangerous.

We stopped to watch a great big moose by the roadside having a meal. He didn't care, just kept on eating until we drove off. We saw lots of meerkats, or prairie dogs, first one would pop up out of a hole, then another and another and just sit there, then one by one they'd disappear back into the hole. They were funny to watch as you didn't know where the hole was until a little face suddenly appeared. We had a small dog with us that we let out to play with them, but he was going crazy trying to find them, they disappeared so quickly.

Houses were very few and far between, and we travelled many miles before spotting smoke coming from a chimney in the distance. We would stop to visit with the people and usually end up sharing a meal with them. They didn't have visitors very often, and although we met as strangers, we always parted as friends. Everyone knew everyone else, they were wonderful people.

One farmhouse we stopped at was situated at the base of a mountain, on top of which were Scotch Caps. These are pillars of stone with a rock sitting on the top like a 'tam o'shanter' or Scotch cap. We decided to see how near we could get to these pillars, but the terrain was very muddy. The farmer lent us each a pair of boots, which actually fitted, and we started the climb a bit awkwardly in the boots, but made fairly good progress.

The dog came with us, and at one point decided he was quite high enough, so I stopped and the dog and I sat on a fallen log watching as his master continued to the top. The view from up there was fantastic and we enjoyed the fresh air for a while, then came the climb down, which actually became a slide most of the way. We certainly descended quicker than we went up. The farmer stood at the bottom laughing his head off at us, as we were on our bottoms with legs flying in all directions. We did suffer a bruise or two, but no major damage was done.

There was one innovation the people in this part of the world had that my parents hadn't had at Bridge Lake, and that was the Forestry Service, brought into the area by float plane. Besides the lumbermen felling trees, there were other people checking to make sure that anyone living in the area was doing just that - living!

They also had phone service, and in an emergency, could call for help and a float plane would be sent in with a medic if needed, or supplies, and if necessary, airlift them out to hospital. The logging roads were very good, though a bit rough in some areas. It was possible to travel for hundreds of miles not having to bother about stop signs or traffic lights. A whole day would go by without seeing another vehicle.

We also visited one of the largest cattle ranches in the country at Riskey Creek, once again stopping to visit, though these people were friends of ours whom we had met in Victoria months before. After sharing a delicious meal with them, we were directed about two miles away to the Lookout Post for the night. There are a great many of these posts all over the Interior where lookouts serve as checkers to spot any smoke which may be the start of a forest fire.

Each one is manned by a government employee, there for about three months at a time, then another person takes over from him. It was very cozy, although quite a climb up the ladder to get to the one room shack. It had two bunk beds, table, chairs, and a little wood stove for cooking and heating. The sink was used for bathing as well as washing dishes. The outhouse was as implied, outside, and it was VERY cold and somewhat primitive, definitely an experience. I wouldn't want that fellow's job.

As I said, this was an extremely large ranch, which required the rancher to fly his own plane to round up his herd. We were awakened very early the following morning by the sound of the roundup. It was quite a sight. Hundreds of cattle were moving across the fields towards the corrals and sheds which we could see in the distance, there were also men on horseback and dogs to assist. We had not seen any cattle when we arrived the day before, and learned that the herd goes into the forest at night. Since its easier to see the cattle from the air, the plane is used to flush them out into the open.

Our host in the lookout tower made us a huge breakfast of pancakes, maple syrup and very strong coffee, and we set off again on the next leg of our journey. It was a very long drive over ranch land high above the Fraser River before we finally left the ranch without seeing another building or person for hours. It was huge.

I was beginning to be concerned that I was away from my parents for so long. They really had no idea where I was and neither did I. Guilt was taking over. After all, I had left my job in Arizona to take care of them, not to be gallivanting all over the country in a Volkswagen camper with a virtual stranger. I was sure they were getting a bit anxious to hear from me to say the least, but when I suggested we should be getting home, I soon found out that we were only half way through our trip and had a long way to go yet, so made a mental note to use the next available phone and call home.

British Columbia really is the most beautiful country anywhere, and I have lived in a lot of nice places. As our journey continued by lakes, through and around mountains, along river banks and over rickety bridges, seeing more bear and moose, bald eagles, elk and deer, I must admit I had to relax and enjoy it. After all, as the saying goes, 'If you can't fight 'em, join 'em' and, since I couldn't alter the situation, I might as well make the most of it.

Eventually though, after two weeks of sightseeing we left the logging roads and joined the highway again, stopping at a little town still fast asleep on a beautiful Sunday morning. We picked up a newspaper, the first in 16 days, and found a little coffee shop in which to have breakfast. The headlines in bold print read 'Premier Quits'. This after only just meeting him at the cocktail party. Was it something I said? I had whispered in his ear, "Mum says, 'Shape up, you're giving the family a bad name' " (remember, he had the same last name as my folks). Of course I was only joking, and he had laughed heartily so, Nah, he must be quitting for some other reason - and of course he was, but I never did found out what that reason was.

Just one more day on the road and then we'd be catching the ferry back to Sidney on Vancouver Island. The only reason I was glad to be getting home was to have a nice hot bath and sleep in my comfortable bed again. That's not to say I wasn't grateful for having seen all I had seen, and been to so many beautiful places. Although I had managed to keep my clothes fairly clean, considering I had been expecting to only be away for a weekend and had just two changes of clothes, an extra change would have been more than welcome.

Nothing bad had happened while I was away, no emergencies or problems. The folks were certainly glad I was home and it didn't take long to find myself back into the old routine. They were very interested in hearing about my travels, where I went and whom I'd seen, until I mentioned seeing the ranch at Bridge Lake, and that did not go over very well, especially since I really couldn't tell them anything good about it.

What I'd had in my memory as a large log cabin ranch house, was actually very much smaller and run down, to the point of being derelict and overgrown with weeds. The 14 cabins, that I had taken such good care of had been moved onto small parcels of land and were occupied by families or young couples who looked like hippies. Of course I didn't tell the folks all this, but I think they could tell I was disappointed by what I'd seen. I know they had loved being on the dude ranch as much as I had, and I'm sure they regretted having to leave it.

I soon found myself catering to them again and trying to make up for being away so long. Dad still insisted on doing the cooking (and I peeled potatoes). Of course the house hadn't been cleaned in my absence, so that took up a couple of days, as well as the laundry, the ironing and other odd jobs. Oh yes, mowing the lawn and washing the windows were added to my chores, but I managed to get to the dance on time, thank goodness!

Not long after the trip through the BC Interior, my third cousin (Uncle Henry's grand-daughter) and her daughter were going to Hawaii to stay in their timeshare condominium, and invited me to go with them, but how could I go away and leave my parents again? To my surprise though, they once again insisted I go, and Mum even offered to pay my fare. Seemed like she was the one feeling guilty, trying to make up for taking me away from my previous lifestyle, although I wasn't complaining (at least not aloud). My cousin's girlfriend who was to make up the foursome became ill at the last minute and was unable to make the trip, so my companion with the camper invited himself along to take her place, much to my dismay. I was looking forward to we 'girls' having fun and also to playing tour guide, since I knew my way around the island.

We had to leave on separate planes at different times of the day, and met up again at the condo in Waikiki. It wasn't really a very good arrangement, one man and three women, but we managed. Some time during that trip I must have had a couple of mai-tais too many as I found myself accepting his proposal, and returned home wearing an engagement ring. Was I crazy? For some strange reason, my parents were delighted with my engagement and I had the impression they were pleased I was going to be moving out to the farm. Was I not wanted after all? Had I given up my job at the beautiful hotel in Arizona for nothing? Why was I here?

It was decided (by my fiancé) that we would be married in England, so after we had been engaged about three months we were off to England and Scotland. In all the years I had lived in England I had never visited Scotland and was very pleasantly surprised at all the wonderful history. I visited several ruins of castles from Edinburgh to Ayr, as well as churches and grave sites of many historical figures, including Robbie Burns birthplace, and found it all fascinating. We paid a visit to Gretna Green, where not so many years ago young couples, below the minimum age, would run away from home and get married. That was put a stop to, and now it's just another tourist attraction, with souvenirs of course.

The intention was for us to be married in the oldest church in England, in the little village of Hexham, just below the border between England and Scotland, but as it turned out, we were several days short of the three weeks notice the church required to 'Call the bans'. We had been delayed by the main road being closed due to a huge apartment fire in Glasgow, and had to spend the first night in a Bed & Breakfast there, not arriving until late on Friday night at our destination.

We learned from the church warden that the Registrar was only available for half an hour on Tuesday of the following week. When we arrived in time to see her, we then had to file papers which had to be sent to London. This would take another week or more, by which time we'd be on our way back to Canada, so we gave up on that idea and decided to enjoy our 'honeymoon' anyway.

Actually all this worked to my advantage because, although I was once again enjoying places I would never have seen otherwise, our trip was anything but congenial. By the time we arrived back in Victoria, I knew I'd be making another big mistake if I married this man, and I called everything off. I don't think he was exactly devastated by my decision either. I was sorry to be leaving the farm though, the farmhouse was situated on top of a hill which sloped down one side towards the sea, the other side spread over farmland, with a fabulous view in all directions. It was really very lovely. I could have been very happy in such a peaceful setting, but it was obviously not meant to be.

So it was back once more to the old routine with Mum and Dad: breakfast at .... coffee at .... lunch at.... you get the picture! Thank goodness for the weekends and the dances at the Crystal Gardens. They were certainly a welcome relief and most enjoyable. Although my ex-fiancé showed up a few times, I managed to avoid having to dance with him and it wasn't long before he found another partner. So life went on.

Soon after our return from the trip to Hawaii, an Hawaiian Theme dance had been arranged. I knew about this before we left for the island and had brought back several items: Pikake perfume, Monkeypod bowls and a few other souvenirs to give away as door prizes. Dressed as Hilo Hattie, a well known entertainer in Waikiki, with muumuu, straw hat and lots of flower leis I acted the part of Emcee. Having lived in Hawaii for so many years, I really hammed it up the Hawaiian way. It was a lot of fun and everyone seemed to enjoy themselves. I know I did.

18

MAJOR CHANGES

Not long after I'd moved from the farm, and back in with my parents, the atmosphere at home changed. I found the relationship that had always been so good between my father and me was now one of aggression and argumentative, although I noticed on the days when my mother was out playing bridge at a friend's house, and Dad and I were alone, we were getting along fine. We'd talk about our days in the RAF and sing some of the silly songs from the 'good old days', but the minute Mum reappeared his attitude did an about face. I could never understand the change, and since I was still unaware that he was so sick (he certainly wasn't showing any signs of how sick he was), I took his actions personally and things went from bad to worse.

We were sitting at the dining table having our afternoon tea one day when, out of the blue, Mum told me it would be best if I found another place to live. The reason she gave was that I was upsetting my father, but I think that was just an excuse. I really think she was jealous of my presence, although she had been the one to request it in the first place, and I don't think she was too happy that I wasn't going to be married after all.

I tried very hard to find a full time job, but I was either too old, or too experienced. The market was closed to me. The $200 a month Dad was giving me ceased when I moved out, and I wasn't in any position to rent an apartment. There was only one recourse, to apply for welfare, something I never would have believed could happen to me.

To say that my spirits were at their lowest ebb at this point would be putting it mildly. Again I was wondering why I'd left my well paying job and life in Arizona. However, there was no other road for me to take at this point in time, so I bit the bullet and applied for welfare. I really hated having to answer all the questions, and felt like it was the end of the road for me. I had to remind myself that I'm a survivor and things definitely could be worse. Having lived by the air force motto, Per Ardua Ad Astra, which means *Through Adversity to the Stars*, in wartime, I adopted that attitude again, and somehow or other was determined to come out a winner.

I was fortunate enough to get a nice top floor, corner bed-sitting room in a low income building, just a block away from where my parents lived in Oak Bay, and furnished it with bits and pieces of furniture from their basement. The saving grace was the beautiful view I had from the top floor, I could see over the tops of all the buildings right out to the ocean looking west, so I had the added advantage of beautiful sunsets. I still felt responsible for my parents, and continued to clean house and do their shopping as well as being on call to drive them wherever they wanted to go, but I was not included in their plans, which in a way was a good thing, as it allowed me to pursue other interests.

The recreation centre was just across the street from my apartment and I spent a few hours a week ice skating, something I hadn't done for many years, in fact not since just before the war when I was a teenager in England. Needless to say I was very wobbly, but it was like riding my new bike, fall off once and get a bruised ego, but get back up and try again. The swimming pool was something else I enjoyed and found myself joining an exercise group twice a week, also making some new friends. Life wasn't so bad after all.

A few months after I moved out, Mum and Dad decided to sell their house and buy a condominium. I wanted to help them sort things out and pack, but they clearly did not want me around, except when it came to the garage sale, and then I was enlisted to spend a few hours bargaining with potential buyers and keeping the coffee pot full. A lot of the things they were selling were things I thought of as family heirlooms and would like to have kept, and each time someone bought something, a little piece of me went with them.

The house sold quickly with the help of a realtor who drove them around to find the right condo. They looked at several, before deciding on one on the third floor of a building overlooking Beacon Hill Park and the lawn bowling greens. It had two bedrooms, two bathrooms, galley kitchen, L-shaped living/dining room which was quite large, and a patio that ran the full width of the suite on the park side, and it was really very nice. I thought that now would be a good time to bury the hatchet and move back with them, but I thought wrong and continued to live in my tiny bed sitting room. Fortunately, with the rent being subsidized and a little left over, I was managing OK.

At one point I was able to have a decent conversation with Dad, and learned that the reason he sold the house and moved into the condo was because he would not be around for much longer and didn't want Mum to have the responsibility of taking care of and selling the house when he was gone. This really unsettled me, but he still wouldn't tell me what his problem was, so I took it upon myself to call his doctor whom I'd met when I drove Dad to his appointments. He was quite shocked that no-one had told me that Dad had prostate cancer, and although he'd had an operation and was in remission for a while, the prognosis was not good. I asked the doctor how long my father had to live and he said he would make it through Christmas, but not long after that. I felt terrible, if only I'd known. I asked myself, 'What could I have done differently?', plenty I'm sure.

Christmas was just a couple of weeks away and I had been invited to dinner with my parents, actually to cook dinner, and stayed to eat with them. We managed to make it quite festive and exchanged gifts, and I made sure I gave them a hug and told them I loved them before I left, but my heart was heavy knowing this was the last Christmas we would all be together. My mother was certainly putting on a brave front and carried on as usual with her weekly bridge parties, but Dad was deteriorating fast. I wasn't too surprised when a few weeks later Mum called me to say that Dad wasn't feeling well and wanted to go to the hospital, would I drive them?

Now that they had moved, they were quite a distance away from where I was living, so I suggested calling an ambulance and I would meet them at the hospital. I arrived at the hospital first and had to wait over an hour before Dad was brought in. I could see that he was in a lot of pain, but it would be another few hours before they moved him into a room with three other cancer patients and sedated him. Mum and I stayed with him until he slept, then I drove her back home to the condominium.

I didn't think it was a good idea to leave Mum alone, so much against her wishes I stayed and little by little moved myself in with her, keeping my apartment just in case I needed it. She was 92 years old and had been declared legally blind, not that she couldn't see at all, but had only peripheral vision due to scars behind her irises, so that she couldn't see anything that was immediately in front of her. I had noticed things like pouring milk into the sugar bowl instead of a tea cup, or turning on the wrong burner on the stove. On one occasion she argued with me that she didn't have any Bengay. When I told her I had seen it in her bathroom, she said it was her toothpaste, and she wondered why it burned her mouth. Ho Hum!!! So I think I was justified in wanting to be on hand at all times.

For the next two weeks after Dad was admitted, Mum and I visited him in the morning, had lunch in the cafeteria, then visited him again in the afternoon, and I continued to stay overnight in the condominium. He was obviously in a lot of pain at this time and receiving heavy doses of morphine, which brought on hallucinations. Sometimes we'd take him for a walk down the corridor and he'd say, 'Left, Right, Left Right, do it like Veronica', as if we were marching back in air force days when in fact we were hardly moving at all, but he did seem to be doing quite well. Then there was talk about him coming home at the end of the second week, and Mum was trying to make arrangements for someone to come to the condo to bathe him and turn him over in bed, something she nor I could do.

A couple of days later when we went to visit Dad, he was not in his bed. The nurse told us he had been yelling out Mum's name all night and keeping others awake, so he was moved to a room by himself. It was called the 'last' room, and we knew that meant we were losing him. Later, I was in the room with him by myself, combing his hair while he drifted in and out of consciousness, and I was telling him how much I loved him. I just hope he heard me, because he died that evening. It was March 11th, 1987. He was 82 years old.

While Dad was still fairly lucid he had asked me to be sure to take care of Mum which, of course, he really didn't need to ask. I promised I would. After all, as I mentioned before, I could hardly expect her to be left alone. Although I hadn't given notice at my apartment, I had spent every night since Dad was hospitalized in the condo with Mum because I thought it was the right thing to do. She however, being a feisty little Irish lady, was quite sure she could take care of herself and had other ideas. I put my foot down and let her know that I had promised Dad I would take care of her and I would keep my promise, and that was that!!

We managed to maintain a fairly good relationship with only a few minor spats. After all, we had been good friends in the past and enjoyed some fun times, no reason why we shouldn't now. I took her to her card games and took care of refreshments when it was her turn to entertain the group, as well as drives to interesting places and browsing the big stores, which she loved to do, and I continued with my dance group. Occasionally I'd invite a friend or two home for dinner, which usually turned into a fun evening. It was so good to see her laugh and enjoy herself but I was sure she was missing Dad, after all they had been together 64 years.

Browsing the stores was turning into a slow crawl that was not only boring, but included long stretches of sitting down to rest. Mum had to admit that walking was becoming more difficult, and she was ready to give up. I suggested that if she had a wheelchair, I could push her around to look at everything, and neither of us would get so tired. Much to my surprise she agreed. Mission accomplished, we bought a wheelchair and shopping became more fun after that. The next few months passed without too many upsets and she accepted the fact that we were now living together, under the same roof. I finally gave up my little bed-sitting room.

Christmas was just a few months away, and Mum was determined not to spend it with family, knowing there would be an empty chair at the table. Without my knowledge she had purchased two tickets to cruise the Caribbean for ten days on M/S

Noordam, including Christmas. That was a lovely surprise and I was really looking forward to it. I always enjoyed being on ships and had sailed to Vancouver from Hawaii and back every year I lived there.

When the day came for us to leave, we headed to Victoria airport where we boarded a little puddle jumper for Seattle and our long flight to Chicago, then Fort Lauderdale, Florida, from where the ship would be sailing. Once on board the puddle jumper we met another elderly lady who was heading for the same destination. I don't know how it happened, but when we reached Seattle, I found myself taking care of both of them until we arrived at Fort Lauderdale.

19

ALL ABOARD

Leaving Seattle was not too bad but when we reached Chicago, having ordered two wheelchairs, there was none in sight. I raced up the long ramp from the aircraft to check. The place seemed deserted, and all the crew from the aircraft had departed. I managed to get both ladies up the ramp at a snail's pace and found seats for them, then took off to find help. The time to board our connecting flight was fast approaching and I had no idea how to get to the departure gate, let alone find wheelchairs. Eventually I saw someone heading in the opposite direction pushing a wheelchair, and accosted him, letting him know he was needed, and also a second wheelchair, urgently.

Luck was with us as a young woman appeared around the corner with another wheelchair, and off we went on the double to get the ladies. Then it was a race to the next terminal, and I was wearing high heels! Thank goodness for the moving walkways which took us some of the way, but I swear I must have rushed a good three miles to the departure gate on the other side of the concourse. Needless to say we were the last to board, they had held the plane for us. Immediately we were seated amid cheers (jeers) and clapping from the other passengers, we were off on the next leg of our journey, and arrived in Fort Lauderdale just before midnight.

Most of the passengers from the plane were evidently taking the same cruise as nearly all 300 of us headed like a herd of sheep for the same exit. Busses were waiting to take us to the hotel for our overnight stay, and picked us up again after breakfast next day to board the ship. Well, at least we had made it thus far and after a good night's sleep, a decent breakfast and a nice bus ride through Coral Gables to Fort Lauderdale, we saw our ship for the first time.

It seemed huge, much bigger than the passenger ships I had sailed on from Hawaii, and it was obviously going to be much more comfortable and fun. After going through the preliminary check points, the purser showed us to our cabin. While not large, it was adequate with two beds, table and chairs, a long vanity with drawers, lots of closet space and a bathroom with shower. Plus a big basket of fresh fruit, and a bottle of champagne, compliments of our travel agent!! What more could we want?

It took a while for our luggage to be delivered to our cabin, so we relaxed and read the ship's newspapers and itineraries. We were certainly going to be visiting some exotic places and enjoying some fun activities, there was a lot to look forward to. When our luggage arrived, we unpacked and hung up our party dresses in anticipation of the four Formal Nights, then put our things away in the drawers, freshened up, and left our cabin to explore.

Mum had a wheelchair at her disposal, and we wound our way along the companionways to find an elevator to take us up or down to the next deck. There were beautiful lounges with music for dancing or just listening, card rooms, library, movie theatre, games room, swimming pools with outside snack bars, inside restaurants and of course the casino for gambling, and so much more to see.

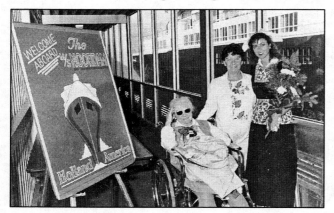

Mum and Veronica arriving aboard Noordam

We sailed on the dot at 6 pm, which was also our dinner time. Through the huge picture windows of the dining room we could see the twinkling lights of Fort Lauderdale receding as we sailed away. I could already feel the excitement and anticipation of a wonderful time ahead and was really looking forward to the next ten days at sea.

There were actually two sittings for dinner, at 6 pm or 8 pm. We chose the 6 pm so that we could go immediately after dinner to the show room and get a good seat for the early Las Vegas style show. The dining room was huge and magnificent, the waiters were impeccable in their white waistcoats and black trousers, everything was served as if we were royalty.

When we arrived at our table for six in the dining room, besides Mum and I, who should be seated with us but the other lady from Victoria, as well as a mother and her teenage daughter. That left an empty seat, so I jokingly said to the maitre d', 'Can you find us a nice gentleman to fill the space?' He brought us a nice gentleman alright, who happened to be the resident Catholic Priest.

He was an extremely amusing Irishman with a very quick wit, and he and my Mother, also being a little bit Irish, hit it off right away. I noticed they were actually flirting with each other. By the way, did I mention that my mother was 93 at this time? The mother and daughter pair did not sit with us at the next meal and had in fact, changed tables. Perhaps they didn't want to be stuck with us 'old folk'.

The first couple of days were spent at sea enjoying the ocean breezes and meeting new people from all corners of the world, everyone was very friendly. Every day, after finding a comfortable chair for Mum to sit on deck, I would find one for myself by the pool and settle down to some serious sunbathing, then I would pick her up for lunch, afternoon tea, or dinner depending upon the time.

Dutch Night on board Noordam, Veronica and Father Ryan

Of course we had to change for dinner, sometimes the dress was formal, sometimes informal, and other times casual. It was entertainment just to see all the different gowns and outfits in the dining room.

One could either eat breakfast in the main dining room or at the outside pool bar as well as the Lido, a huge buffet style restaurant with a terrific assortment of breakfast and luncheon delicacies. There was also an ice cream bar opening at 4 pm where you could make up your own sundaes with a variety of toppings and flavours, and even a pizza parlour. It's no wonder dresses didn't fit by the end of the cruise!!

Speaking of entertainment, a first class show was put on each night after dinner by the cruise staff consisting of four men and four women who called themselves the Pieces Of Eight, mostly dancing and singing, and equally as good as any show you would see in Las Vegas. There were also jugglers, ventriloquists, a fiddler who was fantastic, and singers who

Dutch Night, are we having fun yet?

impersonated people like Frank Sinatra and Dean Martin. There were two shows nightly to accommodate the first and then the second dinner sittings, and the show room was packed for both performances so, if you wanted to sit near the front, it was a race to get there early.

On Christmas Eve, all the crew, consisting of Dutch, English, and Filipino, plus some Americans, put on individual shows in their own ethnic culture, and then they all performed a carol service together, which was very moving. Actually, it was a bit scary too as each person was holding a lighted candle and the flame was very close to the person standing in front of them, plus the ship was swaying quite a bit. I had visions of someone's hair catching fire, but fortunately all went well and there were no mishaps, and the show was excellent. There were monstrous live Christmas trees throughout the ship and beautiful decorations, strolling carolling groups in costume performed at different times throughout the day and everyone, including crew members, were in the festive spirit.

During the day there were trivial pursuit contests, bingo with high winnings, horse racing, cards, movies, you name it, it was available, and if you just wanted to lounge by the pool or take a dip in it, there were three pools to choose from. The casino, where we spent at least two hours after the show winning and losing, mostly losing of course, was open until midnight as long as we were at sea, but closed when we were in port. Mum found her favourite slot machine, pulled up a stool, and there she sat. I think the other passengers steered clear of that particular machine. Mum's name was on it, and you could be sure of finding her at that spot after the first show every night, she was really enjoying herself.

Our first port of call was Playa del Carmen, on the Yucatan Peninsula in Mexico. First we had to go ashore by tender as there were no facilities for a large ship to dock. Once ashore, the bus tour took us to view ancient Mayan ruins dating back to 600 AD. They are built very similar to the pyramids in Egypt, same shape and angled to the sun, with 365 steps to the top of the temple. The ruins overlook the Caribbean Sea, which was an absolutely magnificent cobalt blue - a gorgeous spot.

On to Texum Xel Har, a natural aquarium lagoon, breathtaking in its beautiful setting. The water was so clear and deep, with millions of fish in every colour, shape and size. Several people snorkelled, while I sat on the rocks and drank in the beauty, and took quite a few pictures before the bus took us back to the dock in time for the next tender back to the ship for lunch.

During lunchtime the ship sailed on to the island of Cozumel, Mexico where they were able to dock, and I went ashore for the afternoon. A taxi took me into Cozumel, a typical Mexican town with the usual clothing stores and trivia, but nothing like the border towns of Mexicali and Tijuana on the west coast. When my taxi driver was slowing down to tell me where to meet him for the drive back, we suddenly dropped into a large hole in the road. I was so embarrassed that I jumped out of the taxi. Fortunately the hole was not too deep for me to climb out of. I handed him the fare and started walking away very quickly. When I looked back, about a dozen young men had appeared from nowhere and were lifting the taxi out of the hole. I should have taken a picture of that, it was quite a sight. He was waiting for me an hour or so later for the return trip and neither of us mentioned the 'incident'.

We docked next at the Grand Cayman Islands where, again, I went ashore by tender for the Island tour. The highlight of this trip was the turtle farm where they raise turtles from eggs to 8 feet or more across. I was so fascinated by the ugly things that I almost got left behind, and the bus was ready to leave without me.

We also stopped in Hell - yes, we really did. It's a very small area of about 100 yards around, that looks like there had been a recent fire and left the blackened cinders sticking out of the ground. It's quite eerie. Of course there is a post office from which you can send postcards, postmarked 'From Hell' or 'Best Wishes From Hell, Wish You Were Here!!' The little town of Grand Cayman is quite British with some very nice but tiny stores. Their specialty is beautiful black coral jewelry, very different from the black coral found around the Hawaiian Islands. I didn't buy anything here, I was saving up for a special stop later. There wasn't much else to see on this very small island, except an enormous Hyatt Regency Hotel still under construction, and the Governor's House, which is very ornate.

The next day was spent at sea en route to our next port of call. The weather was gorgeous and a perfect day for sunbathing by the pool or participating in the many ongoing activities. I was trying to relax and read but a noisy pool game was in progress, so I gave up reading and joined in the fun.

It was 8 am, Christmas Eve as we docked in Santo Domingo, in the Dominican Republic. I had a feeling of foreboding even before I joined the others for our land tour, and it didn't take long to realize why. There were armed soldiers everywhere. We found out that the Haitian President was visiting and there could be some trouble, so they were prepared.

While we were sitting on the tour bus, I saw an armed soldier frisking a young man of about 17. The look on the young man's face was one of sheer terror, when I had seen him laughing with a couple of other youths just a moment before. I wanted to get off the bus and tell the soldier to leave the young man alone, but of course I didn't, or I'd probably have been shot.

Garbage was heaped in piles by the roadside, some of it burning and sending up an acrid odour, and there were people lolling about outside run down, filthy buildings with hideous coloured paint peeling from the walls. These people were obviously very poor and no doubt kept that way by a corrupt government and the constant fights with their neighbours in Haiti.

A rickety old bus took us to the home of Christopher Columbus's son. Built in 1509, it was quite impressive, and I'm sure must have been magnificent at one time. Our tour guide spoke very little English so we didn't learn much about the art work and tapestries which we viewed from a roped off area, and there was very little else of interest to show us, as all the furniture had been removed. The rooms, although not large, were quite bare. The tile work and mosaic in the courtyard had obviously been beautiful in its original state, and could be again if restored, but it seemed doubtful that would ever happen.

The drive back to the ship was along the waterfront, where an attempt had been made to decorate in the spirit of Christmas. We were very glad to get back to the ship in one piece. I think it is so sad to see how deprived the people really are, yet living in one of the most beautiful areas in the world. Now I know why there are so many refugees looking for a better way of life.

Of course, if I could have afforded the more expensive shore excursion, I would have seen the other side of the island, which I learned from other passengers, was quite modern and beautiful. I found this to be the case on most of the islands where the Americans had purchased and built properties, but I could see all that nearer home. Now I was seeing how the other half lived, and I certainly appreciated what I had, even having to accept welfare cheques wasn't <u>this</u> bad.

Two weeks prior to our arrival in Santo Domingo there had been a severe hurricane, and quite a lot of damage had been done to the harbour, with debris still drifting loose. It had apparently damaged our starboard propeller, which cut our speed from 20 down to 7 knots. The Captain announced that we would have to bypass the island of Martinique in order to maintain our docking schedule. I had not been to Martinique so didn't know what we would be missing, but some of the passengers were quite upset, and they suggested we could possibly spend more time in St. Thomas, although that was doubtful, again because of scheduling.

Christmas Day was spent cruising at 7 knots on a perfectly calm sea, and what a beautiful day it was. There was something going on all day, pool parties, horse racing, deck games, and lots of prizes to be won. Dinner of course was formal. What a spread, it was topped off by a fanfare, then all the lights went out in the dining room, the doors to the kitchens opened and the stewards paraded in to a rousing recorded version of 'The March of the Gladiators', each carrying a huge Christmas pudding held on high, with a sparkler stuck in it, lighting the way. What a picture it was, cameras were flashing everywhere - the pudding was very good too! That night instead of the usual mint that was normally left on our pillow, we found a little box of chocolates from the Captain with a Christmas card, just one of the many special touches on this delightful cruise.

Boxing Day was our day to visit St. Thomas. This is where I really fell in love, both with the island and the people. I took the island tour, which was part coach and part ferry boat, from Charlotte Amalie, the capital of St. Thomas, to the neighbouring island of St. John. Here I saw some of the most beautiful scenery imaginable. At one point, after we left the ferry in St. John, a new coach took us high up above the coves and we were looking down at seven of the most spectacular little beaches, with pure white sand, and the brilliant blue of the Caribbean Sea.

When we arrived at Megan's Bay we received the usual rum punch (as many as you could handle) and found an area to relax on the beach. Some people went snorkelling and were delighted by the many different fish and coral they saw. As usual, I had forgotten my bathing suit, so rolled my shorts up as far as possible and took off my T-shirt to enjoy the sun and the fabulous view. This had to be Heaven!

Our stay at Megan's Bay was all too short. We headed back to Charlotte Amalie where our first coach met us from the ferry then dropped us off in town, and we were able to browse the many lovely shops. There was a perfumerie that sold fragrances from around the world, world famous Cardew Jewellers, where the gold chains number in the millions, from 10K to 24K. There was Larimar, the famous milky turquoise stone found as recently as 1974 in the mountains of Hispanola, indigenous only to the Caribbean and not yet available anywhere else, and much, much more, all at duty free prices of course. There were Hummels in Little Switzerland, gorgeous linens in The Linen Shop, sequin tops in D'Alley, all at a fraction of the price they were in Victoria, it was a hard decision not to spend, spend, spend, but fortunately my funds were very limited and there were many more places to visit, so I curbed my impulses.

Everywhere was so fascinating. Each street was joined by an alleyway, sometimes tiled in mosaic, with small stores along the sides. I could have spent hours here, but right now it was time to get back to the ship to pick up Mum and change for dinner. Instead of dinner in the dining room that night, there was a terrific party on deck, with lots of food, music, games and entertainment, as we slowly drifted away from this absolutely beautiful island. This is definitely on my list of islands to return to some day.

When we'd arrived in St. Thomas, the divers checked the damage we had sustained in Santo Domingo and it was not as bad as at first thought. Once they had removed the old tires and rope that were tangled around the propellers, everything was fine and we were able to resume normal speed. And so it was on to our next port of call, Puerto Rico.

San Juan, Puerto Rico to be exact. There is an old and a new San Juan. The old one of course dates back to the Spanish invasions, and the Spanish influence is everywhere, as it is on most of the Caribbean islands. The architecture was striking with much use of pink marble and heavy mosaic, outlined in 24K gold. The flowers here were lovely too, in masses of every colour. Streets were very interesting, mostly cobblestone or brick, and very narrow, with steep hills in all directions, and it was very clean everywhere. Obviously San Juan did not have the problems that Santo Domingo experienced. The stores carried the usual array of colourful clothing and souvenirs, and beautiful hand tooled silver jewelry.

In the new San Juan I was surprised to see so many high rise buildings. All the well known hotels, Hilton, Sheraton and Biltmore. This is where the hotel burned and so many people died when they were trapped in the casino on New Years Eve, 1987, just the year before we were there. It was still boarded up with a fence around it and no attempt had yet been made to rebuild.

Morro Fortress was another very interesting structure, overlooking the Caribbean Sea where it meets the Atlantic Ocean. The Fortress was built in 1591 to protect the island from invasion by Sir Francis Drake. I wandered around by myself viewing the stables and living quarters, which looked extremely uncomfortable as the men had to sleep on cement slabs (no straw filled biscuits for them), and they must have been very short too as the slabs were only about 4 feet long. It seemed like I could hear the horses hooves, and the jangle of armour the soldiers wore in those days - what an imagination! It really was breathtaking though, and hard to understand how anyone could think of fighting, while in scenery such as this.

In another area along the cliffs from the castle, squatters huts had been built and stacked on top of each other, looking like big wooden crates, all painted different colours. I couldn't help thinking how poor they must be, but living with a million dollar view.

One of the narrow cobble-stone streets was called the 'Street of Ladies', probably for obvious reasons of the times. Each side of the street was lined with a row of two storey houses all joined together. They appeared to have just one room up and down and a front door, and maybe that's how they were originally built, but now we were told, they had been turned into hotels by leaving the original facade, but opening up the insides to make rooms much bigger and more comfortable for tourists.

The outsides of the houses were painted white and decorated with lots of window boxes full of colourful flowers, really very pretty. I would like to have seen inside but time didn't permit, our bus tour continued on. We saw several churches decorated in a very ornate fashion using bright colours and always lots of 24 K gold, and there were beautiful homes on the hillsides, all with a fantastic view in every direction. Then it was back to the ship in time for dinner and another evening of seeing the show, a little gambling, and an early night. It had been a fabulous cruise so far but the end was only a couple of days away.

Next, a lazy day at sea, perfect for catching up on the tanning before our final formal dinner. We had saved the best dress for last, as it seemed had everyone else, it was a real fashion show in the dining room with all the different gowns and outfits. It was the turn of the Filipino crew to entertain us tonight, the stage show they put on was absolutely spectacular. I was amazed to hear our table steward impersonating Elvis Presley, and to see the wine steward tap dancing to jazz. They were all so talented, it was wonderful.

Since the next night was going to be our last on board, everyone would be rushing around to pack and say their goodbyes to newly found friends, so tonight we were saying goodbye to the crew, from the senior officers to our cabin steward who gives each passenger such wonderful personalized treatment you can't help feeling you are saying goodbye to a special friend. Tomorrow we would be in Nassau, another day to enjoy before we re-enter the real world.

Nassau is a very small island, the capital of the Bahamas, quaint in a very British way. I thought it was very interesting how the part of the Caribbean that was made up of the British Virgin Islands had held on to the British traditions, they even spoke very precise English. Except for the colour of their skin and the colourful clothes we could have been in any little village in England.

The streets in Nassau were anything but straight, and wound around in all directions. It would be easy to get lost, but I had found a companion so we explored together. One of the native residents was handing out leaflets as we left the ship, and insisted that we go and see his 'auntie' at the famous Straw Market. This was a huge outdoor market that sold hats, bags, mats and anything else that could possibly be made with straw, hence the name. We each bought a sun hat, though it was a bit late to do us any good on this trip, as well as a couple of cute straw dolls. At some point we decided we'd like a cup of tea or coffee and, lo and behold, there was a Dunkin' Donut just ahead so, of course, we had to stop in for the special of the day - a jellied donut, with a good cup of coffee!

We hailed a taxi to see what else we could find before returning to the ship. Our driver (driving on the 'other' side of the road) took us out of the town into the countryside, with the beautiful ocean on one side and flat open land on the other. Eventually we stopped at a large sandstone building, which we were told was the castle of the famous pirate, Blackbeard. It did look rather like a castle that Disney might build, but it was about 300 years old, so must be authentic.

Then there was a huge casino where we stopped for a drink of rum, of course, but didn't do any gambling. Across the road from the casino a new Hilton Hotel was being built. It was going to be quite a skyscraper, at that time the only one in Nassau. After a little more driving by the beautiful sandy beaches it was time to return to the ship and our driver took us right up to the gangplank. I had enjoyed this day very much and put Nassau on my list to be seen again some time.

Now we had to finish our packing. The luggage had to be outside our cabin door by 2 am. Tonight being the final night of our cruise, there will be an impromptu show of passenger talent, for which people had been practising all week, followed by the usual hour or two of gambling and the last chance to win the jackpot! Another must is a visit to the ship's stores which are selling off their surplus goods at a ridiculously low price - a great time for bargains.

I know Mum had really enjoyed the cruise. Even though she hadn't been able to go ashore, she had seen everything through my eyes, and decided maybe we should stay on board and keep going, but to her dismay (and mine), found the ship was fully booked for the turn-around. No problem though, she booked for a cruise leaving Fort Lauderdale a month later, covering some of the same islands we had just seen, but adding a few new ones.

Meanwhile, we could stay with my cousin April in Florida for a couple of weeks, and with another relative on the east coast of Florida for a week, and then perhaps visit Disney World. She had it all worked out, now all we had to do was find out if that was OK with our prospective hosts, so we phoned each of them from the ship.

Although April was going to be busy with the theatre during those two weeks, we were more than welcome to stay. We found our way to the airport in Fort Lauderdale and flew in a very tiny plane at a very low altitude across Florida to the town of Sarasota on the west coast. As we flew away I could see our ship still in the harbour waiting for the next shipload of lucky people to board and enjoy themselves as we had. It had been a wonderful ten days.

20

FLORIDA

I had never been to this part of the United States before, and was really surprised at the flat landscape. I soon found that the saying was, 'The only time you're above sea level is when you go over an overpass' but it was quite beautiful and very green. We passed over Alligator Alley, the main freeway running through the centre of the state of Florida, where it was not uncommon to encounter both dead and live alligators when driving. The swamps are full of crocodiles, as well as alligators and snakes. Thank goodness we were in the air, I hoped we'd stay there until we reached our destination!!

April had a nice little home in Sarasota, about 80 miles south of Tampa. It was near some excellent shopping and not far from a beautiful white sandy beach. Although she showed us around as much as she had time for, our two weeks passed much too quickly.

One of the most spectacular places we visited was the magnificent Ca D'Zan which is the former winter home of John and Mabel Ringling, of Ringling Brothers Circus fame. There is an enormous chandelier hanging from the two storey vaulted ceiling in the entry way to the home, which had once hung in the Waldorf Astoria Hotel in New York City. There were also many 17th century Baroque paintings, the most important collection of that type of art in the world, adorning the walls.

Ca D'Zan is very large and quite unique, with much use of pink marble brought piece by piece from Italy, and life size statues, mostly nudes atop the wall surrounding the huge patio of mosaic tiles overlooking Sarasota Bay. The home and its beautiful gardens are open to the public, as well as a museum of various pieces of circus equipment. The original horses used in the very first galiope, and costumes worn by the famous trapeze artist Walenda, who fell to his death from a high wire crossing Niagara Falls, as well as a photo gallery of performers through the years and much more, are well worth seeing. I even saw a photo of my cousin high atop a sway-pole, and one of her riding an elephant which was standing on its hind legs.

There are many other interesting sites in and around Sarasota, such as the Pelican Man's Bird Sanctuary, and the Mote Marine Aquarium, the centre for shark research.

My favourite shopping area was St. Armand's Circle which, as the name implies is a roundabout, surrounded by 145 shops of every description, very high fashion and pricey, but a great place for browsing. There was the Van Wezel Performing Arts Centre, which for some strange reason, was painted purple. It was host to all sorts of productions from jazz to ballet. Also there is the Asolo State Theatre, the area's leading theatrical company. There were so many more things we didn't have time to see, but I was quite sure I'd find myself back here at some future time.

Mum and I left Sarasota by bus, en route to Fort Pierce on the East coast of Florida, tired from all our wonderful sightseeing, we spent most of the four hour ride dozing on and off. It was quite late when we arrived at the bus depot in Fort Pierce but my Dad's cousin was there to meet us and take us to her very nice ocean front home. Unfortunately, both Mum and I had caught bad colds and were feeling pretty lousy.

Since she was 93, I was a bit concerned that we may be overdoing things and not getting enough rest, so it wasn't long before our hostess ordered Mum to bed, where she stayed for most of the week. I too, stayed in bed for a couple of days, and with some heavy doses of a home cure (which tasted awful, but worked) and TLC, we both felt a lot better by the end of the week, and well rested to continue our travels.

The husband of my Dad's cousin, brother-in-law to Great Uncle Henry in Sidney, Vancouver Island, was also a boat builder and took me to see his latest project, which was a huge cruiser being built for a well known politician. The price tag on it was in the millions of dollars, and it was obviously going to be absolutely beautiful when finished. I was learning very quickly that there is a great deal of wealth in Florida and most of the homes near the ocean are enormous mansions, even those in the residential areas were not small. There were many unique types of architecture, mostly with a Spanish flair, lots of terra cotta brick, archways and tile.

After our week of visiting in Fort Pierce we headed for Orlando and Disney World, every kid's dream no matter what age. We stayed in a hotel on the outskirts of Orlando and found that the free shuttle bus to Disney World stopped right outside our door, so we made good use of it. I rented a wheelchair for Mum, and we managed to cover a lot of fascinating territory, especially the EPCOT Centre where the scene was constantly changing on a revolving stage. I was so engrossed in watching the performers, I didn't notice that the wheelchair, which had been parked in the aisle beside me, had suddenly disappeared and Mum was headed, very slowly fortunately, for the orchestra pit. When the chair finally stopped after hitting the rail, Mum just sat there, still mesmerized by the show and never said a word. One of the ushers brought her back and only then did she realize what had happened. It caused a few giggles in the re-telling later on.

We had three-day passes to Disney World, but the second and third days turned quite chilly and it rained, so Mum decided to stay at the hotel and I took the shuttle bus in to see what I could see. A lot of Disney World was being expanded and still under construction, but what I saw was wonderful. I wish Mum had been with me to enjoy the parades, the fireworks, the rides (although she wouldn't have gone on any I'm sure). It's not so much fun doing these things on your own.

The time had come for us to leave Orlando and head for Fort Lauderdale again, and the final week before the next cruise. Fort Lauderdale is known as the Little Venice of the USA, with small quays (or keys) connected by small bridges to the Florida mainland, quite beautiful. One evening we took a paddle steamer ride, with dinner and a vaudeville show, through the inland waterways, passing some magnificent homes, some very large and others not so large, but nothing under a million dollars, each with its own jetty and boat mooring. Unfortunately, the weather was still wet and very windy, and the screens on the paddle steamer obscured our view, so we weren't able to see everything at its best, as we would have liked.

Most of the homes and boats were still sporting Christmas decorations which were extremely elaborate, with millions of coloured lights and animated figures. The homeowners came out onto their patios or their boat decks as we passed by, and we raised our glasses to each other and exchanged season's greetings back and forth. Despite the most un-Floridian chilly weather, we did enjoy the trip, and the dinner and show were excellent. We would like to have time to do it again in better weather; however, our time in Fort Lauderdale was coming to an end.

I had really enjoyed what I'd seen of Florida. There is so much history which involves invasions by the Spanish, British, Indians, battles fought, both won and lost, the building of the railroad by Flagler to transport guests to Ca d'Zan, and from Miami to St. Augustine, where the magnificent Flagler University is named after him, and much more of it to explore but there's no time now. We are leaving Fort Lauderdale, to go off on our next cruise, and the only alligators and crocodiles I saw were at a safe distance in a wild life park!!

21

MORE CRUISING

The weather was still quite cold and rainy when we boarded the S/S Rotterdam and I was beginning to wonder if the sun was ever going to shine, but I knew we were going to be heading south, getting closer to the equator and warmer temperatures. We settled into our new home away from home for the next ten days, feeling like veteran travellers, already knowing the routine.

The first item of business was always boat drill, which meant donning our life jackets and making our way up to our designated gathering place on deck. Unfortunately, this time we took a wrong turn and instead of going up the staircase, went through a door marked Crew Only with a very steep set of stairs which Mum had to manage with great difficulty, and my helping shoulder under her bottom. Reminded me of the rope

Arriving on board Rotterdam

ladder we had to climb up on the Trondanger when we were in the Panama. But we made it eventually, just in time to turn around and head back to the cabin - this time down the main staircase.

Our first port of call was Willemstaad, Curaçao, and by the time we arrived there the weather was perfect. This is one of the most interesting places. The island is divided into two, with Willemstaad on one side and the old Town of Curaçao on the other. The buildings are very clean and colourful, dating back to the 15th century, with a very strong Dutch influence on the Willemstaad side and the older, more historic buildings on the other.

The two towns are joined by a single-span bridge which is opened sideways by a tug to let shipping pass through. Too bad if you don't heed the siren to get off the bridge before it opens, you could be stuck on it for 45 minutes with no-where to go. There is a little ferry to take you from one side to the other, but you have to be quick as it gets crowded and you could still be left behind.

As usual, after finding a good spot and a comfortable deck chair for Mum, I went ashore, browsing through all the stores, which seemed to sell nothing but T-shirts and shoes, and very little of anything else. I also heard my first real steel drum band. It was belting out its rendition of 'When the Saints Come Marching In' - a fellow passenger from the ship got into the spirit and danced her way across the courtyard where they were playing, thoroughly enjoying the moment.

Willemstaad, Curaçao

I was some distance from the ship when I realized it was lunchtime and I would probably be too late for lunch on board, so had to find a place to eat. I was a bit hesitant to go into a restaurant not knowing what the locals might put in their food, and then, just around a corner I found a McDonald's of all things, so had the old stand-by, a hamburger. Of course I didn't know what they put in THAT either, but I didn't get sick, so it must have been OK. Once re-fuelled, I continued my walk about on this really lovely island that I am sure must resemble somewhere in Holland.

I couldn't help noticing how colourfully everyone was dressed, particularly a trio of a man, wife and little boy. The man was dressed in a pink suit right down to his pink shoes, his wife was in a beautiful buttercup yellow silk dress, and the boy was wearing a perfect white outfit. They didn't look at all out of place among the passing crowd. In fact everyone was very well dressed and looked so beautiful. Their skin is a light mahogany with soft features that are probably the result of races intermarrying. They are most attractive, and everyone was smiling and happy. The difference between this island and some we saw on our previous cruise was quite obvious.

Later that evening, as the ship drew away from the dock, there was a party in full swing on deck when the skies suddenly opened up and the rain came down in torrents, everyone dashing for cover. Then it stopped just as quickly, and the party continued under a beautiful starlit sky. As we sailed past the last point of Curaçao there was a spectacular fireworks display, ending with the band playing 'America the Beautiful' and 'O Canada'. It was so moving it brought tears to the eyes. But they soon dried up as we continued playing deck games, watching the ice-carvers and dancing to Caribbean music played by the ship's band, with the twinkling lights of the island receding as we drew further and further away.

This trip was very similar to our last inasmuch as we were at the first seating for dinner, followed by the show lounge and another fantastic show, then an hour or two of gambling then to bed, with Mum of course marking her territory in the casino. She was definitely master of the game now and was squealing with delight every time she won even a few coins, but of course they got put back into the machine again and her bucket was always empty by the time we left the casino for the night.

The ship itself was somewhat older than the M/S Noordam, so the decor was not as modern, but it had several very interesting antiques in glass show cases along the walkways, and many paintings by famous artists. The dining room was elaborate with enormous crystal chandeliers, and the service was impeccable.

Even though Christmas and the New Year were behind us, we still had formal nights, and once again enjoyed the fashion shows. I noticed the passengers were a bit older and the gowns a little less daring than on our last trip. No Catholic priest at our table to regale us with funny stories this time either, but we did have very nice table companions, and our stewards once again treated us like royalty.

Mum still managed to find a good deck chair, where she spent time knitting and snoozing, or finding someone to chat with. I did my own thing, either exploring the activities on the ship or taking a shore excursion. We were getting along fine with this arrangement, that is, as long as I was there on time to pick her up for meals!!

After leaving Curaçao we were off to Venezuela. I had to be up quite early the next morning, as I had signed up for a shore excursion to Angel Falls, near Caracas. Once the tender had taken us to the dock we boarded a bus for a 45 minute ride through the city of La Guaira to the airport, which was surprisingly modern and clean. Our flight in a Boeing 727 took

Colibri Lagoon, Venezuela

a little over an hour, flying over mountains and jungle-like terrain before heading into the valley and a very close (too close) look at Angel Falls, reputed to be the highest water falls in the world at 3,000 feet. I managed to get a couple of pictures through the window as we hovered overhead. They certainly were spectacular.

Our flight took us on to Colibri where we landed on a grass field with no defined runways, then had to walk through the bush to an Indian camp by a very large, lovely lagoon. There were canoes to take us around and under the five spectacular water-falls, which became much more impressive as we drew closer. Although not nearly as big, each one resembled Niagara Falls. We were also served a buffet lunch, which consisted of several meat dishes and vegetables we had never heard of. Even though we had no idea what the meat was (that may be just as well) it did taste delicious and of course, was followed by the inevitable rum punch.

There was plenty of time for swimming and sunbathing on the beautiful beach before making our way back through the bush, boarding the plane for a bumpy take-off and our flight and ride back to La Guaira and the ship. This excursion had been quite an experience, I thoroughly enjoyed it, although the flight in the old 727 was a bit scary. It rattled and shook like nails in a tin can. I couldn't help listening to the sound of the engines and wondering when and who did the last inspection. Once a flight mechanic, always a flight mechanic!

The dock where we had disembarked from the ship was modern and clean with many very attractive shops selling the usual local souvenirs and gorgeous jewellery, as well as beautiful fans for only $7.00 each. I bought several of these to give to friends back home. As I was looking around for somewhere to buy a cup of coffee, one of the vendors offered to make one for me. It turned out to be a demi-tasse of a thick, black and very sweet substance that smelled like coffee, but was impossible to drink. Not wanting to hurt the man's feelings, I hid around a corner after letting him see me take a sip, and then disposed of it in a planter (probably killing the plant), then I hurried back to the ship for a real cup of coffee!

We sailed away from Venezuela on the dot of 6 pm heading for Grenada, which I am sure you will remember reading about when the United States invaded and drove out the Cubans in 1983. The only evidence I saw of the invasion was the gutted residence of the former Governor, who apparently was linked to the Cubans, although I learned from other passengers that there was much more damage at the airport on the other side of the island, which no-one was bothering to repair. The atmosphere in Grenada is still very British, with pillar boxes (mail boxes), and Bobbies (policemen), dressed in the familiar navy blue uniform of the London police.

All the schoolgirls wear uniforms of a tartan skirt with white shirt and tartan tie, and look very smart. I encountered a group of such young ladies and asked if I could take a picture of them, they told me they charge one dollar a person. Because there were eight of them, I declined since I was only carrying travellers' cheques. I did however, manage to capture one of the young ladies on film without her knowledge as she dashed across the street.

Grenada is also known as the Island of Spices, and its spicy fragrance permeated the air. Vendors were everywhere, trying to sell the handmade straw boxes filled with spices, as well as straw hats, dolls, and beaded jewellery. Everyone we met was very friendly, and people were wearing T-shirts saying, 'Thank You America'. This was a far cry from the old 'Yankee Go Home' slogan we used to see. We were only in Grenada for about three hours and sailed soon after lunch, heading for the island of Martinique which, as you may recall, we missed the first time around.

Martinique was nothing like I had expected. My cousin had spent some time there when she was performing with the circus and had really liked the French atmosphere. My first encounter was a large square, lined with stalls selling the usual touristy paraphernalia with local flavour. I bought two little black dolls in very colourful native costumes which cost $4.00 each, then strolled through a park with many lovely trees and flowers, surrounding a large statue of Napoleon Bonaparte's Josephine, as Martinique was her birth place, I understand she is also buried here.

A rather ornate church of no particular denomination, just called The People's Church, caught my eye so I wandered inside. It was beautiful, with lots of stained glass and mosaics. Huge statues of the Virgin Mary and Jesus as a baby. Just like the chapel in the convent when I was six years old, there was soft organ music playing, and I had to suppress the urge to dance down the aisle, but I was afraid the ghost of one of those nuns might be watching, so I left before I found myself in trouble.

The town of Martinique itself was crowded and just seemed like another busy city except for the people's attire and the colour of their skin. There were no big beautiful stores to browse, but lots of small ones displaying everything from fruits and vegetables to clothing and jewellery on the sidewalks, and everything was very expensive. Traffic was bumper to bumper and, with no traffic lights to control the flow, crossing the street was a definite hazard to one's health. The noise of honking horns was deafening. The people of Martinique speak French, and since I'm not fluent in that language, trying to explain that I wanted to buy a certain item was hopeless, so I gave up.

After having a good look around it was getting close to sailing time so I had to make my way back to the ship, but somehow had managed to make a wrong turn, and for a while was hopelessly lost. It was no good asking for directions! I kept telling myself to find a hill going down, which would take me to the waterfront and hope-fully to the ship, and to my relief there it was. I must say I was very glad to be back on board again, and headed for the snack bar and a good cup of coffee, even before I went to find Mum. I was starving.

St. Thomas had really spoiled me. It was by far my favourite island, and I knew that was where we would be docking next. I was among the first in line to go ashore. This time I took my table companion with me, and it felt like I was showing her MY island. In and out of all those gorgeous shops I described before, but this time I really splurged, buying gold chains, perfumes and linens, a gold watch for Mum, and gifts for friends back home, we thoroughly enjoyed ourselves.

We stopped for lunch in a pub down one of the mosaic tiled alleys. The decor was of pirate ships and pirates, and the staff dressed the part, very authentic, right down to the strong smell of rum. Of course we had to have a rum punch along with a big juicy hamburger, before we headed back to the ship. I wondered if I would ever get the chance to come back to this beautiful island.

I just couldn't get enough of St. Thomas, and the few hours went by much too fast. I was very sorry to leave. We'd had a wonderful day, and it made a big difference sharing it with another person.

Next was another day to relax at sea and enjoy some sunbathing, which I had been neglecting again, although I was getting quite brown. It was a gorgeous sunny day, but the ship was rolling quite a bit in a heavy sea. At one point I had decided to do some laundry in the laundromat, situated on an upper deck. Everything was fine for a while, but then went downhill fast, as it did when I fell down the stairs and sprained my ankle. I was supposed to be in the talent show that evening, but after a visit to the doctor and having the ankle bound up, he gave me strict orders to rest, so I ended up in bed at a very early hour. The nice part was ordering room service and having din-ner served in the cabin, just Mum and me.

I had really been looking forward to participating in the talent show, and had rehearsed my Cockney accent to perform a rendition of Liza Doolittle from 'My Fair Lady'. I'd already won a prize for my 'Casper the Friendly Ghost' costume in the fancy dress show (everyone got a prize!!), and I was looking forward to the pos-sibility of another one - too bad they didn't give out booby prizes, I'd have been first choice for that! Actually the day wasn't a total loss as I had won $60.00 on the one-armed bandits in the casino just before I tripped down the stairs, and I was saving it to gamble with on our last night.

The ankle was a little better, but I did need to borrow a pair of crutches from the ship's infirmary, and donning a red sock on the injured foot I headed ashore the following day, once again with Mary, my table companion, to have another look at Nassau, our last port of call. Not being able to walk far, we decided to take a taxi and explore a little further afield. We hailed a taxi and the driver assisted us into the back seat, where we sat for some time, with the driver standing outside smoking a cigarette. I asked him what the hold up was, and he said he wanted to have a FULL cab before taking off, so we sat for several more minutes until I decided we were wasting valuable time, as we would not be in Nassau for very long.

I had overheard another driver mention his price, which was a bit less than what we were going to be charged. Our driver thought he was talking to us, which started a very noisy and heated argument between the two of them. At that point we had waited long enough and got out of the cab. I looked our driver square in the belt buckle (he was at least 6 feet 6 inches tall and I am only 5 feet) and told him if he was going to argue we were going to get another cab, and with that said, we walked across the street to where we could see a couple sitting in a mini bus, and decided to join them.

Then along came the driver of the mini bus, and who should it be but the man our first driver had been arguing with. Oh well, we had a very nice tour through some lovely scenery along beautiful beachfront, past hotels, residences, Blackbeard's Castle (which I had seen before), and of course, a statue of Henry Morgan after whom the rum (or rhum) is named.

We stopped at a place called 'The Queen's Steps', reputed to be the highest point on Nassau. This is a flight of about 20 steps to a plateau from where you could see most of the island - that was it, no buildings, but it was a good point from which to take pictures. We visited a fabulous casino but didn't gamble - just had, what else, a Henry Morgan rum punch of course.

Nassau is such a mixture of old and new, as are most of the islands in the Caribbean. Nearly all of them were discovered some time in the 15th century by Christopher Columbus when they were still inhabited by the Indians. Over the ensuing centuries they have endured invasions by Spain, fires, plagues, and civil wars, but through it all they have managed to maintain the old world charm and dignity. I was quite sorry when this trip came to an end, and we arrived back in Fort Lauderdale on another windy, damp day.

Disembarking a cruise ship is quite a lengthy process. To start with, as on the previous cruise, our bags had to be outside our cabin doors by 2 am, with a certain allotted colour tag, for pick up by the crew before anyone is awake. After breakfast everyone has to report to the lounge, and find others with the same colour coding. There we sit in groups with passports in hand, waiting until our name is called by the Customs Officers (who are usually late arriving), to pass us so we can finally go ashore.

This can take two or three hours, but once cleared by Customs we proceed ashore. According to the coloured tags, the luggage is all placed together in separate sections on the dock, and then comes the task of finding the right colour, then the luggage with your name on it. Once found, the next step is to board a bus to the airport, and as you can imagine the lineups are quite long and everyone is now anxious to get home. The party's over!

By the time you reach the airport and your particular departure gate, either you just missed your flight and have a few hours to wait, or you have to rush to make it with only seconds to spare. Either way it's an anticlimax, the realization that you're back in the real world is apparent. The memories never fade though, and I had made up my mind that there would definitely he more cruises in my future.

22

ONCE MORE UNTO THE BREACH

And so it was back to Victoria where the sun was shining to greet us. Our flight home was quite long and uneventful this time, unlike our cruises which were full of events and wonderful memories. One of my first commitments was to get my films developed. I knew I had taken about 200 pictures from both cruises, as well as our stay in Sarasota and the visit to Disney World. Then I had the task of putting them in order and into an album. I must say I was very pleased with the results. Couldn't wait to show them to everyone and tell them of the great time we had. I think I should apply for a job as spokesperson for cruise lines, I can certainly recommend them.

It took a few days to get into the routine of breakfast-lunch-dinner, shopping, cleaning, laundry, and all those other chores that had been done for me during the past two months or so, but I had no choice. I did still have the dances to look forward to on weekends, taking Mum for drives or browsing the mall via wheelchair was something we were enjoying, but I didn't anticipate her next move.

During afternoon tea one day, she asked me if I would like to take a cruise to Alaska. Well, she and Dad had taken that cruise just a year before he died, and as she was unable to go ashore, I really didn't see the point. I had seen the beautiful movie Dad had taken, which was all I needed to know about glaciers and ice floes. Actually, my response was that I thought she just wanted to take the trip because she would be pampered and waited on, and I did that for her at home, for FREE!!

So we didn't go to Alaska, I was sure that was that, but if you knew my Mum, she always had a Plan B, and this Plan B came about two weeks later. Again during afternoon tea, she said, 'If I decide to go to England would you go with me?' I actually thought she was joking, so joking back I said, 'Well now, you don't think I'd let you go by yourself do you?' at which point she produced two tickets to London leaving in a couple of weeks, and off we went again.

This time I took her wheelchair, and although we had to change planes, we were prepared with our own transportation. The flight was over the North Pole, in which case there is no sunset, daylight all the way. With all the blinds on the plane closed, we did manage to get some sleep and it was a very long, but smooth and uneventful trip. My cousin Monica was at Heathrow to meet us and drove us to her very nice home in Pinner, just north of London. This is the cousin that lived behind us in Rayners Lane at the beginning of the war. Mum had not seen her for several years, although I had seen her just two years earlier when I went on that disastrous trip to get married and didn't - thank goodness.

Monica and her husband Jim, made us most welcome, it was a very happy re-union. We all went out for dinner the first night to one of their favourite restaurants. The next day Monica drove us around London, past Buckingham Palace, Green Park, Piccadilly Circus along Baker Street (where Sherlock Holmes lived), and where Mon-ica's daughter Christine and husband David were now living. We spent a delightful evening visiting with them and dined on fish and chips, which I'm sure you know is absolutely delicious done the English way, although it's no longer wrapped in the 'News of the World' newspaper, smothered with lots of salt and vinegar, as in the 'good old days'.

I was quite surprised during our drive around London to see there were still many empty spaces where buildings had been bombed during the war. Other areas that were devastated were made into nice little parks in memory of those who had lost their homes and lives there. But for the most part, London hadn't changed much from the big bustling city I grew up in. It brought back a lot of memories, both pleasant and not so pleasant. It was also very interesting to see the many different ethnic groups, mostly East Indians in traditional dress.

The following day we visited with Monica's other daughter Jill, who lived in the village of Byfleet near the Blue Lagoon, where my brother was drowned, and we stopped at the little churchyard to visit his grave. We saw the house that we had lived in when the airmen and Canadian soldiers visited us. That seemed so many years ago, almost in another life.

I didn't notice whether or not the Hawker Aircraft factory was still active, prob-ably not. I found it very hard to believe it had been 45 years since I had last been in the village. It hadn't changed at all, except for Brooklands, which has become a very large and impressive museum of automobiles and aeroplanes dating back to when it opened as an automobile racetrack in July 1907 with it's first scheduled race. I wish we had been able to spend some time there; however, I sensed that Mum was feeling a bit depressed, probably because the visit was bringing back sad memories.

She decided we should leave my cousin's house and take a bus trip to Leeds, to try to find the doctors she had worked with when she and Dad had returned to England in 1947. I could hardly believe this possible as she hadn't been in touch with any of them for almost thirty-one years. The likelihood of any of them still being around was quite remote. They weren't exactly young men when she and Dad left in 1958, and it was now 1988, thirty years later.

The bus ride to Leeds, travelling on the main South/North highway, was quite long and not very interesting. The weather was lousy, windy, cold and rainy and a deep depression was setting in on both of us. Once we arrived in Leeds, we took a taxi to the hotel which was some distance out on the Huddersfield Road, not exactly a five star hotel but reasonable except for the lack of heat, and I was freezing. We were both very tired from the bus ride, so after a late dinner of spaghetti and meat balls, and a hot bath, an early night was a good idea.

The next day a watery sun was actually trying to shine. Mum decided we should get a taxi to the Infirmary and see if Dr.Young was still there. Leeds Infirmary is a massive building, almost a block square with a very long flight of stone steps up to the front entrance. Getting Mum up the steps was a one step at a time job, I had to carry the wheelchair and it had started raining again. We finally made it, and let ourselves into the main hall. No reception desk or greeter, in fact not a soul in sight as we started wandering around the corridors.

Eventually we came across a lady in a starched white uniform and asked her if she knew where we could find Dr. Young. She had us repeat the name several times, then to spell it, at which point she said, in a broad Yorkshire accent, 'Oh, y' mean Doctor Yooong, 'es not 'ere'! All that fuss for nothing!! This trip was not going well at all, and I was beginning to wish we were back in Victoria, or preferably the Caribbean.

So it was back to the hotel in time for another pasta dinner. I found out that the proprietor was Italian and pasta was all he served. It was probably all he knew how to cook! After dinner, and a couple of glasses of wine, I found a book to read, took another hot bath (to warm up) and went to bed to read until I fell asleep. Mum was very quiet, and I knew she was disappointed, but there wasn't anything I could do to change the situation, much as I would have liked.

After breakfast the following morning she had me looking through the telephone book to find any one of the seven doctors she had worked for, and eventually came across a familiar name. There was no telephone in our room, so I used the public telephone in the lobby of the hotel, dialled the number then handed her the phone.

To Mum's surprise the doctor recognized her voice right away, amazing after a 31 year absence. They chatted for a few minutes before he had to see another patient, but promised to stop in at the hotel and visit on his way home that evening. When the allotted time came, we had tea ordered in the lounge. Mum was like a schoolgirl waiting for her first date. It was really sweet the way they greeted each other after so many years. I was obviously in the way, so left them to enjoy their visit, and went back to the room to read.

I do believe that became the highlight of our trip, but there was more to come. We had only been in England a week and Mum's mission was already accomplished, so we had to find something to do for the next two weeks of our vacation, although personally, I was ready to go back to Canada right away.

I suggested the Lake District would be nice at this time of year, so off we went to catch a train to Windermere in Cumbria. Not having made reservations we were lucky enough to find bed and breakfast accommodation in a pretty little country cottage, and settled in to enjoy the beautiful Lake District for a week. Of course the streets were all cobblestone and very hilly, as are most villages in England, and either Mum had put on weight, or I was getting weak from pushing the wheelchair, so had the bright idea that it might be fun to rent a car.

After all, how hard could it be to drive on those country roads? Not like driving in the city! I walked the three miles to the hotel where the car rental office was located, and had to wait a while for a car to be returned. When it did, a young couple got out and saw the stricken look on my face, but they assured me it was 'a piece of cake, you'll be fine'. Putting the key in the ignition with shaking hand, I realized I was sitting on the 'wrong' side, this wasn't natural to me. Clenching my teeth, I put my foot gingerly on the gas pedal, and off I went.

Downhill to the traffic light was OK, but then I had to turn right and go up a steep hill with cars parked on either side and busses going up and down the street, not to mention the masses of pedestrians who insisted on walking in the middle of the road. I was nervous to say the least. Much to my surprise, I made it back to the house without incident, so decided that I would take Mum for a nice drive around the lakes after dinner. Shouldn't be too much traffic around at that time of the evening, or so I thought.

Everything was fine until I got out onto the main highway, when a convertible full of young men flew past and yelled, 'Step on it Grandma'. That did it, I made a U-turn as soon as possible and drove straight back to the house. Not even bothering to park the car, I jumped out, raced in and found the man of the house. Then I asked him to return the car to the rental place immediately, and get my money back. Well, he did and I did. That was the end of my driving in England!

The Lake District is made up of several really beautiful lakes, the largest being Lake Windermere, which is very long and narrow. On a lovely sunny afternoon, I pushed Mum in her wheelchair the three miles, all the way into Bowness, where we boarded a steam boat for an afternoon relaxing on the lake and enjoying the scenery.

The village of Ambleside is at the other end of the lake. Here all passengers went

ashore to enjoy a delicious afternoon tea of scones with
strawberry jam and Devonshire
cream on the grounds of a really
old country mansion. After tea
and a tour of the mansion, which
was magnificent and probably
dates back to the 17th century,
we returned to the boat and
made our way back to Bowness.
Finally we were relaxed, and

The stern wheeler on Lake Windermere

our moods improved. It had been a beautiful day.

We also took a bus trip to Wells Cathedral and Bath, where the Roman Mineral
Baths are located, and visited Dove Cottage, the 17th century cottage in Cocker-
mouth which was home to William Wordsworth the famous English poet laureate.
Like so many places in Great Britain, history abounded and we spent a lot of time
admiring not only the architecture and beautiful stained glass windows, but reading
inscriptions on tombstones in Wells Cathedral where many warriors of 'olden days'
are buried, along with recognizable names of people one reads about in history books.
Despite a heavy rain shower in the afternoon, which thoroughly soaked us, this had
been another enjoyable day and I was sorry to have to board the bus for our return
trip to Bowness.

Not to miss out on any sightseeing, and since it was obvious I wasn't going to be
doing any driving, we hired a taxi on our last full day in the Lake District, and spent
a wonderful few hours being driven around the different lakes, stopping frequently to
take pictures. There were very narrow wooden bridges to cross, with room for only
one vehicle at a time, little cottages with thatched roofs, pubs with funny names at almost every turn, and everywhere the most gorgeous, colourful gardens with flowers
of every description imaginable. The air was fragrant with perfume from the apple
blossoms and syringa. We stopped for tea at a cute little pub before continuing our
tour of the countryside, and by the time we had completed a very large circle back to
our bed and breakfast home, we could truly say this was by far the best day yet, but
our week was up and we were leaving this beautiful part of England the next day.

The train from Windermere to Bournemouth, our next destination, was quite
an experience. Gone were the noisy old steam trains with plush seating in narrow
coaches, and the rhythmic clackity clack of the wheels on the rails. This was an
electric train, and was very open, with unpadded seats that were very uncomfortable,

the only advantage being that the windows ran all along either side so you could see the view of the English countryside in every direction.

There was a Snack Coach which served sandwiches and tea or coffee, not very appetizing, but no dining car where you could sit and have a decent meal like in the old steam trains with Pullman coaches. We had to take our lunch back to our seats and balance it on our laps. Plus it was very cold, so by the time we reached Bournemouth we felt like we had been bounced around in a blender with a bunch of ice-cubes. However, we had arrived safe and sound all ready for whatever came next.

Bournemouth, situated on the south coast of England, is one of the nicest and most popular of all the seaside resorts. During WWII nearly all the hotels were taken over by the military as staging posts, prior to the troops being sent overseas if they were Army, or to Operational Training Units if they were Air Force, it was also a target for the German fighters to bomb in daylight air raids. Since then everything has been rebuilt, upgraded and returned to its former glory.

We stayed in a really lovely hotel, right across from the nice sandy beach and the English Channel. Our room and beds were very comfortable, but as in most very old hotels like this one, we had to share the bathroom with the other guests on our floor, and we had to wait our turn before we were able to enjoy the much needed soak in a hot tub.

The city of Bournemouth was quite a distance from the hotel, I didn't realize how far until I started walking with Mum in the wheelchair. By the time we reached the centre of town I was ready to drop, and of course, had to stop for a cup of tea before exploring the shops. I must say I was very impressed. There were stores of every description in magnificent old buildings three or four storeys high, and the architecture was stunning. In the centre of town was a huge roundabout, in the middle of which was a very large white pagoda, surrounded by colourful flowers and a perfectly manicured lawn.

We made several visits to town shopping for woollies in our favourite store, Marks and Spencer, as well as discovering others, and lunching in quaint restaurants and pubs. At one point during our last trip to town, a screw had come loose on the wheelchair from bumping over the cobblestones and I came perilously close to tipping Mum out as I manoeuvred another high curb. It was fortunate that we were due to leave for our plane back to Victoria the next day because it would be impossible to get the chair repaired in the short time we had left. Needless to say, we had to take a taxi back to the hotel, for which I was truly thankful. I needed the rest, and was feeling a bit queasy.

During our stay in Bournemouth, there were two special people we had to visit.

One of them was John, the son of the farmer where I used to stay during school holidays in Somerset. It had been at least 41 years since we had last seen each other and, although he had been through some pretty hard times, had managed to survive. We had of course, corresponded with each other, at first frequently then it dribbled down to a Christmas card with a brief note in latter years as happens so often, but we had known each other since I was 11 and he was 13, so we could find plenty to reminisce about.

Actually, when I joined the WAAF in 1943, he had tried to join the RAF but, being a farmer's son he was exempt from service, or so his father thought. However, when the recruiting officers came to the farm to talk with his father, John told them his Dad wasn't there but had said it was OK (which was not true), so they signed him up. Of course, his Dad was furious. The idea in John's mind was that maybe we would be stationed together, but that never happened, we were actually at opposite ends of the country the whole time. When I left for Canada the second time, in 1955 we still had not caught up with each other, even to say goodbye, and a lot of water had gone under the bridge since then.

Our other special person to visit was a gentleman who had been a very close friend of my Mother's sister when they were both young women, and even though her sister had been dead for many years, Mum had still kept in touch with him. Unfortunately, this was a sad visit as he had been bedridden for several years. It was obvious he would not be around much longer. They shed a few tears together, and we didn't prolong our visit. Mum was very relieved to have been able to see him. Those visits became very special to us because, a few weeks after we arrived home, we learned that both these gentlemen had died.

We had really enjoyed our week in Bournemouth, and it was over much too soon. We were due to leave early the following morning for our return to Canada, but some time during the night I started getting sick, I mean REALLY sick. I kept asking Mum to call the doctor. I knew the hotel would have someone on call, but she kept insisting I was just having a bilious attack and it would pass. It didn't. By 9 am I was too weak to move and unable to crawl back into bed after my latest visit to the washroom, so she finally relented and called the doctor. When he arrived, I was delirious, but I distinctly remember him saying he was going to call an ambulance as he jabbed a needle in my rear end, and my Mother telling him not to be ridiculous. But that's all I remember, until I woke up in the hospital.

Apparently, I had suffered a gall bladder attack and the gall bladder was infected. I spent the next ten days in a little country hospital in a very nice ward with fourteen beds, occupied by a friendly group of women who were happy to see me finally wake up. Evidently I had been 'out' for a couple of days. I was only allowed a sip of water 4 times a day for the first two days after I came to, but no food until the fourth day of my stay, and the pain was excruciating, but the doctor did not want to operate. He just wanted to get me well enough to return to Canada as soon as possible.

My first concern when I woke up was that we had missed our plane, and I asked the husband of the lady in the next bed to me when he visited, to please call my Mum and tell her what she must do to re-book our flight. Unfortunately, Mum was in no mood to listen, and was actually very cross with me for leaving her alone in the hotel. I later learned that the manager and staff of the hotel were taking very good care of her, but as a result of being left alone she did not intend to visit me, although she did manage one visit to bring me a toothbrush and comb, and some clothes for when the time came for me to be released. The secretary in the hospital office came to talk to me as soon as I was feeling better, and took over making our arrangements. She re-booked our flight and made sure Mum and I would be taken care of when we arrived at Heathrow. She really was a life saver.

When the day came for me to leave the hospital, heavily sedated and not feeling too much pain, Mum arrived in a taxi, and I was sitting in my wheelchair just inside the door waiting for her. I got up to open the door to let her in and she immediately sat in my wheelchair, announcing in a very loud voice, that she was, 'Not about to pay any bill' (which I had just handed her), 'I'm English and have paid into the National Health Service for years'. Fortunately the corridors were empty, but she could be heard some distance away in the office.

The secretary arrived and calmed her down, and sat me in another wheelchair while taking care of Mum, who found herself signing away the rest of our travellers cheques to pay the bill before they could release me. She was definitely not a happy camper. The taxi had waited for us and we returned to the hotel in dead silence. I spent the rest of the day, and half the night trying to remain as still as possible, I wasn't supposed to lift anything, even my handbag. The hotel staff took care of everything for us, and made sure we were ready to leave at 5 am.

The hotel manager had ordered a limousine to take us to Heathrow Airport, rather than a bumpy ride on a bus, and we were met there by two luggage vehicles with drivers who deposited us at the restaurant and got us our breakfast, then came back to take us to the plane. We were certainly getting first class treatment and assistance right up to the time we boarded the plane for home.

Mum was still smouldering and wouldn't say a word to me during the flight back to Vancouver, but since I slept most of the way, I didn't really mind. However, when we arrived in Vancouver it was a different story. Someone at the hotel in Bournemouth had managed to fix the wheelchair (temporarily), and as soon as we were off the plane she was ready to sit in it. That left me taking care of the suitcases, and of course, there were no redcaps in sight. So I placed the two smaller suitcases on Mum's lap and she had a larger one with wheels on either side holding onto the handles as we made our way out of the terminal. We must have made a comical sight. Progress was slow because the bags didn't want to cooperate and kept getting in the way of the wheelchair. I didn't dare exert myself too much, I was still having some pains.Once outside the terminal we had to find the bus to the ferry.

Again I had to lift the suitcases and wheelchair onto the bus with no help from the driver, then off the bus and onto the ferry, then off again when we reached Vancouver Island, by which time I was feeling pretty weak. I found a taxi, and our driver took care of everything from the ferry right to our front door. It was quite an anticlimax to a very strange vacation and I was never more glad to be home. The frigid atmosphere soon passed when we again adopted our 'normal' routine, although I did overhear Mum telling our story to someone on the phone, adding that I wasn't really sick, it was just a bilious attack. I soon set that record straight!!

23

THE PARTING OF THE WAYS

One of the first things I had to do upon our return was see my own doctor, and within a couple of weeks I found myself back in hospital having the offending gall bladder removed. Dr. Lott found 33 gall stones which I should have kept to prove to Mum that it was not a bilious attack that had made me so sick, but I'd decided I had them long enough, thank you. Once again I spent ten days in the hospital rather than the usual seven. I think I had one visit from Mum when a neighbour brought her to see me, but I fell asleep during the visit, and missed her scolding me for leaving her alone again.

I heard about it from the girl in the next bed, who thought it was quite funny to see this little old lady shaking her finger at 'sleeping beauty' and getting no response. My doctor was well aware that I would not be able to take care of myself properly once I returned home, so kept me in the hospital a few extra days, just adding to poor Mum's dilemma. Finally, I was released from the hospital wearing a large muumuu and carrying a little cushion over my wound. I called a taxi and went home alone.

Of course the first day out of the hospital is pretty awful, you're not quite sure if you should be doing this or that, or if you should still be in bed.

I had no choice though, but to get back into the routine immediately, and resume taking care of Mum just like nothing had happened to me. I was really afraid I would pop the stitches I was still wearing, not to mention the constant pain, but what's a gal to do?

The day after I was released from the hospital, a friend of Mum's had been invited for coffee, which I had to prepare and serve, of course. I should mention that coffee was always served to visitors from the big silver coffee pot which was rather heavy even when it was empty, and in addition I had to toast and butter scones, all with difficulty, while trying to hold my little cushion over my stitches with one hand, and serve with the other.

During this coffee clache Mum said to the visitor, 'Would you like to see the rest of the place?', and they both got up from the dining table. Mum showed her visitor through the rooms, out onto the patio where all the Martha Washington geraniums were in full bloom, creating quite a picture. She was answering questions and offering information about strata fees and other expenses as they went from room to room.

On their return, they sat down at the dining table again, and I poured them each another cup of coffee. The visitor then got out her cheque book and wrote a cheque which she passed to my Mother, and they shook hands, in a 'gentleman's agreement'. I thought Mum had just sold something but I had no idea what, until after the lady left and Mum announced that she had just sold the condominium! Oh Boy - now what?

It seems Mum had made the decision to go into a retirement home and I could go back to live in the United States. Which is exactly what happened, but not for another few months as she had to wait for accommodation to become available in the retirement home she had chosen. Eventually the day came for Mum to move into a very nice suite with similar layout to the condo, but with only one bedroom. She was still able to use most of her furniture, even though the rooms were smaller. An antique dealer had been contacted and had taken away the rest of the furniture and a few things I would like to have kept, but there were plenty of knick knacks left to make her new home cozy and attractive.

The following week after Mum had moved into the retirement home I spent alone in the empty condo, sleeping on the floor after all the furniture was gone, with a sweater for my pillow. The only things working were the telephone and electricity, which I had not yet had disconnected. I was waiting for responses from Arizona, which is where I would be returning after my absence of almost five years.

By coincidence I had seen an ad in the Victoria newspaper for a townhouse to rent in Scottsdale, Arizona. When I phoned the local number I was invited by the owners to view some photos of the townhouse and decided it would be perfect for my friend Carol and me to share. I was also anticipating going back to work at the hotel where I had previously worked as a secretary. Everything seemed to be falling into place. I was looking forward to returning to Arizona and resuming my old lifestyle of dancing, and exploring the desert, which I loved.

I attended my last dance at the Crystal Gardens and said goodbye to the friends I had made during the previous five years, although I knew I'd be back to visit Mum, and would keep in touch with them. Several told me they would visit my Mother too, which I certainly appreciated. When Dad died I had inherited his car (the 'old folks car' I mentioned before), and I decided to trade it in on a more appropriate one, which turned out to be a huge station wagon, a Mercury Marquis. I packed it full of the belongings I'd managed to accumulate, and with my good friend Cy, who accompanied me to help with the driving, left Victoria on a very cold rainy day.

As we boarded the M/V Coho, the ferry which crosses the Straits from Victoria to Port Angeles, in Washington State, and the same one I had arrived on five years earlier, the customs officer, huddled up against the chill, asked us where we were headed. We said, 'South to Arizona to find some sunshine', and with a 'Lucky B-s', he waved us on. I suppose he was thinking we were snow-birds just leaving for a month or two and I didn't think to mention that I was a returning resident of the United States. Hence I arrived in Arizona without the required paperwork to register a Canadian vehicle. This proved to be a problem later on.

The Highway 1 route south, through Washington State, Oregon and California, takes you down the coast road bordering the Pacific Ocean through some beautiful scenery, especially in California, such as Carmel, Monterey and Santa Barbara. I had travelled this road many times and was quite familiar with all its twists and turns, and where the best places were to stop overnight or for a meal. The most hair-raising part though, is going through San Francisco where the hills are so steep you are almost standing up to drive, and dare not take your foot off the brake.

At one point going through San Francisco, we had turned off the highway to find a washroom at a service station, only to encounter a very narrow winding hill, so steep that we had to run off into a driveway for fear of losing control, and not being able to stop. When we did reach the bottom of the hill and the gas station, we were rather surprised to find we had not burned out the brake drums - they smelled like it though! We found we could have come down a much less hilly street if we had taken the next turn off, and were very glad we didn't have to go back up the hill to return to the freeway. OK! We'd certainly know better next time!!

By the time we reached Scottsdale, Arizona, three days after leaving Victoria, it was getting dark and we had no idea how to find the address of the town-house I had rented, sight unseen through the newspaper ad. We were driving around in circles getting totally frustrated, even though we had phoned for directions from Carol, who moved in earlier that day. She was very glad to see us when we did finally arrive, tired and hungry. So we sent out for pizza, accompanying it with a glass of wine and a toast to our safe, but late arrival.

The pictures I had seen of the town-house did not do it justice. It was lovely and was beautifully decorated. The two bedrooms upstairs were large and bright with comfortable King size beds. The large living room and kitchen downstairs were equipped with everything we needed, I loved it. Carol had already chosen the front bedroom, so I had the other one which was actually bigger and had more closet space - something I always need, being a 'clothes-horse'. We discovered the sofa in the living room was a sleeper, so Cy occupied that, and being nearest the kitchen, was up first to make the coffee in the mornings. The next two weeks were spent settling in and showing Cy around this lovely area, and revisiting some of my old haunts.

Although he liked Scottsdale very much, the temperature got the better of him and he flew back to Victoria sooner than intended. I had already secured a job at the hotel where I had worked before, but since my job as a secretary had already been filled, I now found myself working in the gift shop. This suited me fine, I loved meeting people and always enjoyed retail work. However, it was only for three days a week, either morning, afternoon or evening shift, and no more than 24 hours a week which didn't bring in a very big pay cheque. I was hoping that it would eventually work into a full time job.

I couldn't be happier, being back in familiar surroundings. There were quite a few people still working at the hotel who were there at the time I left five years earlier and it just seemed like I was carrying on where I'd left off. It was a relief to know that Mum was being well taken care of so I could get on with my life again. A good friend of mine had also transferred here from the Rancho Mirage hotel and we started socializing together. There was plenty to do and see, and we kept busy.

The beautiful Sonora Desert

There is a sign on the Scottsdale Road claiming this to be 'The Most Beautiful Desert in the World'. It really is, with lots of interesting plant life and flowers that blossom after the first spring rains, and every kind of cactus imaginable. Of course it does get extremely hot and the local saying is, 'the only thing I don't like about Arizona is July and August', when the temperatures are stifling.

Well now, I'm always prepared to expect the unexpected, and the unexpected in this case was that Mum had decided she wanted to come and live with me in Scottsdale. After a few conversations both with Mum and with the manager of the retirement home, it was decided that I would fly up to Victoria and bring her back to Arizona with me.

All her possessions were dispersed among the other residents of the retirement home, except for some special things she wanted to keep. I had the brilliant idea that it would be nice to travel by bus and see some of the country en route, remembering what a wonderful trip I had across Canada by bus in 1956. Unfortunately this trip turned into one disaster after another, starting off with the Customs Officer at the border accusing me of trying to smuggle my Mother into the States, he was serious! And there were other events all too horrible to mention. I must say though, Mum was a real trooper and never complained once, and this time she certainly had cause to.

I had intended to give Mum my bedroom and I would sleep on the sofa-sleeper, but decided it would be too difficult for Mum to climb the stairs. We also felt the sofa would not be comfortable enough, so I rented a very nice suite for her in an adjacent building. As soon as I returned from my morning or afternoon shift at the hotel, I would pick Mum up and we'd spend the rest of the day together until I returned her to her suite for the night. This was not the best arrangement and fortunately, only lasted for the first week. Then something happened where I found it necessary to ask Carol to leave. We had been friends for a number of years, but after a rather nasty confrontation in which things were said which could not be retracted, that friendship came to an abrupt end, and she left me with a fine mess to clean up.

After she had gone, Mum moved into the town-house with me, managing to climb the stairs to her bedroom, where she was much more comfortable. She was glad she didn't have to keep going out in the heat which was beginning to have an adverse effect on her, as it had on Cy. Knowing that my six months' rental was coming to an end, and as the town-house had already been rented to another party, I was concerned about what I was going to do on my own when Mum returned to Canada.

Since she was not a landed immigrant as I was, she was only allowed to stay in the United States for six months less a day, although I'm sure I could have made special arrangements, considering her age. Anyway it was she who decided we should buy a mobile home. It didn't take us long to find a very nice double wide, in a beautiful park on the outskirts of Scottsdale and Tempe. As this too was completely furnished, all it needed was our own personal touch and the accessories that Mum had brought from Canada.

As soon as our lease was up on the townhouse, we moved into the mobile home and began to make friends in the park. Mum loved it, and I'm sure would have stayed indefinitely, but then she got sick. She thought she was having a heart attack, and I had to call an ambulance for her. She spent the rest of that night in the emergency room being ignored, and I was very worried as she looked like she was about to draw her last breath. The emergency room was very busy accepting victims of a horrendous crash on the freeway, and the injured were being flown in by helicopter. There were at least a dozen casualties, some with very serious injuries. All beds in E.R. were occupied, and the staff was totally absorbed in helping them, which was quite understandable.

It wasn't until well into the next morning that they finally took Mum into a room by herself and started taking tests. Fortunately it had not been a heart attack, though I have no idea what made her sick. She seemed very much better the next day, and I breathed a sigh of relief. Although her stay in the hospital was for only two nights, we received a bill for $7,000.00 U.S. I was stunned, especially as I knew her medical bills were fully covered in Canada, a hospital stay would not have cost her anything. Unfortunately, a person of her age was not eligible for travel insurance, so we were committed to paying the price.

We had a little chat about that, and decided it would be best for Mum to return to Canada and have her own doctor take care of her. After recuperating for a few days at home, getting the OK from my doctor who had been treating Mum, that she was well enough to travel, we headed back to Victoria.

This time I drove the Mercury Marquis station wagon, and took a leisurely drive back up the coast road. I had phoned the owner of the retirement home, who happened to be a friend, and he was more than happy to have Mum back again. I knew she was very popular with the residents there, and had missed her card playing friends so this was a good thing we were doing. They had been able to scrounge up her furniture, except for the brand new TV which Cy had bought her, and her suite was ready and waiting.

Her many friends were glad to see her back again and I'm sure she was really glad to be there. I stayed for a week, caught up with my friends at the dance, left my station wagon with Cy to be sold in Victoria because as I mentioned before, I didn't have the necessary papers to register it in the U.S, so couldn't sell it there either, and I flew back to Scottsdale and my new home, alone again.

24

SCOTTSDALE AND PALM DESERT

When I returned to Scottsdale, I bought myself another car which turned out to be a real lemon. It let me down so many times, making me late for work or unable to get to work, that I eventually decided to quit my job and return the car to the dealership. However, they were not about to take it back or refund my money.

Before accepting the vehicle at the next dealership I visited, it was put up on the rack to be checked out, and it was discovered that the vehicle had received quite a lot of damage, and had obviously been in a serious accident. They told me it really wasn't roadworthy and they would have to send it to the 'car dump'. Fortunately, they gave me a good deal on another car which I made sure WAS roadworthy.

I drove home in my 'new' car, a Chevy Caprice, then wrote a letter to the Better Business Bureau about my bad experience. A few weeks later I learned that the dealer that sold me the 'lemon' had been shut down. I couldn't help wondering what happened to the rest of the 'lemons' on his lot, I'm quite sure there were more and that some poor unsuspecting, naive individual would fall victim to another bad deal.

I had been driving 13 miles to work as secretary in a real estate office, having left the hotel gift shop a few weeks earlier when it became apparent I would not be able to exist on my own with such a small part-time salary, and there was no likelihood of it becoming full time. As I was the only one in the realty office and had very little to do, it became rather boring, so I wasn't sorry to leave. Although the pay was far more than I had ever received before, I have to be busy, so driving all that way to read a book or do crossword puzzles wasn't my idea of a day's work. I couldn't imagine why they even needed an office since the phones never rang, so I started job hunting once more.

I soon found a job as a sales assistant nearer home in a very nice high fashion boutique in the Fifth Avenue area of Scottsdale where there were lots of unique art galleries and unusual stores, which were great tourist attractions. This job was much more interesting, especially during the season when it became extremely busy. I really enjoyed it, and was once again meeting people from all corners of the world.

Life in the mobile home park was good too. There was a huge clubhouse with monthly functions, pot-lucks, dances, costume parties, and trips to places such as Laughlin (rather like Las Vegas). I enjoyed them all. There was also an Olympic size swimming pool, and although I can't swim I really enjoyed spending time in the pool after dark (skinny dipping of course!), when the air was still warm but not hot, and the stars so near you could almost pull them out of the sky. They were good days and I was very happy there. I had made a lot of friends, and enjoyed socializing with them, especially at the off beat events held in the clubhouse.

I also had a very special friend. We would take an evening walk around the park together before our dip in the pool, and long drives visiting the Desert Museum, or the Air Museum, which was my favourite. There was a huge RAF Vulcan Bomber on display there as well as several WWII planes, but unfortunately no Wimpys.

There was also the Bionosphere, an enormous 'balloon' type structure which was climatically controlled and sealed, the idea being to see if people could be self sufficient in another atmosphere. There were about 12 men and 12 women, not all related, who undertook this experiment. They kept several animals, such as chickens, goats, and pigs, as well as a vegetable garden which produced large crops of all types of vegetables for their consumption. Sleeping

Views of the Bionosphere, Oracle, Arizona

quarters were rather sparsely furnished with a mattress on a raised platform, and very little privacy. I'm sure there must have been bath houses and toilets, but I don't remember seeing any.

I imagine that being closed off from everything as we know it in the 'outside' world for an extended period of time, with no phones, newspapers, TVs and unable to go for long walks or shopping was more than some of them could handle, and after a few weeks were asking to be let out. Once the seal was opened to let just one person out, the whole project had to be scrapped, and millions of dollars

Veronica beside the 'Bumble Bee' at the USAF Museum, Tucson, Arizona

were wasted. The entire structure, once it was vacated, had become quite overgrown and the smell of animals still lingered in the air. It was an interesting concept, and worth seeing, but not something I would volunteer to do.

I had been living in the mobile home park for about three years when a lady came along who wanted to buy my home. At the time I really wasn't thinking of selling and couldn't understand why she wanted mine in particular, since she was already living in her own mobile home in the same park. She kept insisting that mine was bigger, nicer, had two store-rooms instead of one, was better furnished, and on and on. Then she offered me a price quite a bit more than I had paid for it, and making a nice little profit, I decided to go for it, even though I was very happy and hadn't been giving any thought to moving again.

My romance had ended a couple of months earlier when my special friend had moved to Las Vegas and married an old flame. Once again I had no one to consider but myself, so I returned to Palm Desert, which I had always loved even though things were not always as they should have been there. I was able to go back to work at the hotel in Rancho Mirage where I spent so many happy years earlier, but not as a secretary, once again that position had been filled and there were no vacancies in the Sales Department.

Funnily enough the man who had been my boss when I was a secretary in the hotel in Scottsdale had also returned to Rancho Mirage and was now Manager of the Gift Shop. He was happy to give me a job at my old stomping ground. Seemed like this place was a magnet that kept drawing me, and others, back.

I purchased a mobile home in the same park where I had lived before in the triple wide with the stained glass windows I'd made. My ex had been long gone in the meantime, and no likelihood of running into him, but some of my former friends were still there and it didn't take long to get back into the swing of activities in the clubhouse.

I was able to take a trip to Victoria to see Mum. She seemed very happy, and settled in the retirement home among her old friends and card playing partners, but as usual, my days of 'normal routine' didn't last long and soon after I returned from that visit, I received a call from her doctor telling me that she had been hospitalized and was quite sick.

Of course I was on the next available flight out again. When I reached the hospital, she was in the hallway in a wheelchair waiting for me, feeling much better now that I'd arrived. I was told she had developed a bad bout of 'flu and they were afraid it would turn into pneumonia, especially dangerous at her age. The nurse informed me that Mum would not be able to return to the retirement home as a new restriction had been applied that didn't allow wheelchairs there, so it would be necessary for me to find a nursing home for her.

There are several very nice nursing homes in Victoria and Sidney. I looked at all of them, especially the one in Sidney, which I thought would be ideal since there were family members still living close by who would visit. Mum had other ideas though, wanting to go to the nursing home where my grandmother had been, and that was that. It was fairly centrally located and I think she chose that one so that her former bridge playing friends could take a bus to visit her. Sidney, about 17 miles from Victoria, was not so convenient.

And so she went to Sandringham. I had the task of packing up all her belongings from the retirement home. I also had to give a lot of things away as she was allowed only a few items and changes of clothes in the nursing home. She had made most of her outfits, which were cute little pant suits and knitted sweaters. I had to make the choice of what to keep and what to give away, that was very hard to do. Fortunately, a young lady who had taken care of Mum in the retirement home was the same size and was more than happy to receive several nice outfits, and I knew Mum would be pleased for her to have them too, which made me feel a lot better.

Once more Mum settled in, and was being well taken care of. She even found a 'boy-friend' and together they enjoyed racing their wheel-chairs down the corridors, much to the consternation of the nursing staff. I returned to Palm Desert, but phoned every Sunday evening at 6 pm, and she would be sitting by the telephone waiting for my call. Sometimes it was very hard for me to hear what she was saying as her voice was fading. After all, she was now 97 years old.

One Sunday when I called it was obvious she had a very bad cold. With her heavy breathing in my ear, I could not make myself heard by her any more than I could understand what she was trying to say to me, and it was very frustrating for both of us. I told her I loved her and to get over her cold, and I would call again next week, but sad to say, that was the last call I made. Her doctor phoned me two days later to say Mum had died of pneumonia, which I suppose was really no surprise. The date was February 23rd, 1992. She had celebrated her 97th birthday the previous September. Again, I was on the next available flight to Victoria, and was met at the nursing home by the lady I had employed as companion to take Mum for walks and out to lunch. She was quite upset with the fact that my Mother had been in the middle of telling one of her stories about her interesting and exciting life with Dad, when she seemed to fall asleep, so of course, never finished the story. She wanted to know if I knew the end of it, but it wasn't one I had heard before. Mum had a lot of stories to tell, she and Dad could and should, have written books of their own.

As much as I loved my Mum, there were times when she and I almost came to blows. Both of us having Irish tempers, there were some fairly hot and heavy arguments which she, of course, always won. As Dad used to say, 'Whatever Amy wants, Amy gets', and she usually did. On the flight back to Palm Springs we ran into a heavy thunder storm and the plane was struck by lightning. There was a loud THUMP right behind my seat, all the lights went out except for the strip lighting along the aisle. The pilot checked the fuselage with the aid of a searchlight along each side and fortunately found that we had sustained no damage, and very soon the lights came back on. When I related the event to our friends, they joked, 'That was your Mum having the last word' - I'm inclined to believe it!

For a few seconds after the lights went out there had been a deadly hush, but then everyone started talking at once and a long line began to form for the toilets, which I thought was rather amusing! I was sitting in the very last seat by the toilets and could hear the conversations. It seemed that absolutely everyone in line had a story to tell about the time their plane was also struck by lightning.

I called my cousin April in Florida after I got home and told her of Mum's death. After chatting for a while she suggested that I sell my home in Palm Desert and move to Florida since I no longer needed to be on the west coast and available to fly north when needed. I certainly had enjoyed my stay in Sarasota, and as I now had no other ties anywhere, it seemed like a good idea.

It didn't take long to sell my mobile home. I had spent a considerable amount of money redecorating the inside and adding new appliances as well as landscaping the huge corner lot it occupied. It all looked very nice, plus the fact that I was selling it fully furnished. After all the i's were dotted and t's crossed, I packed up once again and drove to Florida, and another adventure was about to begin.

25

BACK TO FLORIDA – AGAIN

I contacted Marilyn, a friend whom I had known for several years when we worked together at the hotel in Rancho Mirage. She had moved to Florida from Palm Desert a year or two earlier, and we had kept in touch. She flew out to Palm Springs and drove across the country with me, this time in my brand new Chevy Cavalier for which I had traded in the Caprice. Once again, we left in the wee small hours of the morning to get a good start before the heat of the day developed.

The route across the southern States is quite boring, one straight road, the I-10 from coast to coast, only occasionally passing through towns or points of interest. However, it became extremely interesting after we crossed from Arizona into New Mexico. Hurricane Andrew was already heading towards the Florida coast and the spin-out of the wind and rain was reaching far inland.

The rain was so heavy at times that I had to drive with the window open, and my head outside so that I could see the centre line in the road. It was no use trying to follow the tail lights of a car in front, which could hardly been seen anyway, because they may be pulling off the road or ending up in a ditch, so I had to rely on that white or yellow line to guide me. This kept up for about three days, and although we were able to find overnight lodging, motels were getting filled up quickly with people from the coast evacuating inland.

Eventually we made it to Marilyn's house, south of Sarasota on 5 acres of very soggy, muddy land. My white car was caked in mud, and we were totally soaked, but fortunately, all in one piece. I stayed there for a few days, enjoying the country atmosphere, and a well earned rest. I hadn't realized how nerve wracking the driving had been. It took a few days for my body to stop trembling and finally relax. We were both exhausted.

Staying with Marilyn was not really convenient for her, so when another friend offered me her mobile home all to myself, as she was going to be away in New Jersey for a few months, I accepted. April, in the meantime, was anticipating me staying with her, but we worked things out. I moved into my friend Kiki's mobile home just a week before Hurricane Andrew struck southern Florida, demolishing an entire mobile home park in Homestead near Miami.

Although I had no idea what to expect, and no-one to tell me if I should evacuate and where to go if I did, I sat up all night watching the devastation on TV, and didn't feel so much as a puff of wind, for which I was truly grateful. Mobile homes don't fare too well in hurricane force winds, so I was very fortunate that Venice (just south of Sarasota) was in a sheltered area. The local supermarket lost part of it's roof though, and a row of houses not too far away from where I was staying, received some damage. I learned that from the month of November through to February, hurricanes are constant and every year Florida, the Panhandle, and the Gulf Coast of Texas are hit hard and millions of dollars in damage is incurred, as well as loss of life.

A very good early warning system is in place. Once the order to evacuate is given, all roads become clogged with the mass exodus of vehicles heading inland, although the rains and winds will already have started. This continues for hours either getting stronger as the storm picks up speed, or weakening once it hits land. Then it becomes a tropical storm, but it is unpredictable and it's not wise to disregard the warnings.

There is usually time for people to stock up on water and essentials, as well as plywood with which to board up their windows. Stores like Home Depot and other suppliers are mobbed with customers desperate to protect their property and get out of town as quickly as possible. Then there are other diehards who have experienced hurricanes before, and think they can ride it out despite the fact that police are risking their lives driving around neighbourhoods to warn everyone to leave. TV newscasters are also putting their lives in harm's way to bring a blow by blow (pardon the pun) account of damage as it happens. Its definitely not a pretty sight.

When my friend Kiki returned from New Jersey, I stayed on for a little while to keep her company in her mobile home, then rented a very nice condominium in Sarasota near my cousin's house. I also got a job in the fashionable Sarasota Square Mall, settling down to a more normal routine. April had quite a social life and I was invited along on several of her outings, mostly to wherever there was ballroom dancing. I mentioned before that she and her family had been involved with the Ringling Brothers Circus, whose winter camp is in Venice, and she would get tickets for us to attend the dress rehearsals of some of their performances. Don't you love the circus? It brings out the 'kid' in all of us.

When the lease on the condominium I was renting expired at the end of the year, and Mum's affairs were settled, I inherited a small sum of money, and bought myself a condominium in a complex which surrounded a very pretty lake. My new home needed a lot of TLC, so I set to work totally redecorating it. Painting and papering, browsing second hand stores for special pieces of furniture and making it into the home I had always wanted for myself. There were two large bedrooms, one en-suite, and one full bathroom, a big living room with sliding glass doors into a screened in patio (to keep the alligators and other beasties out) just a few steps from the lake.

I started by using a very large hammer to knock down a partition between the kitchen and living room. The partition was made up of 2 x 4s with lopsided shelves at odd places and it looked terrible. I couldn't believe that all the nails I extracted had to be at least 6 inches long. It took a lot of pounding to remove them before I could discard the pieces of wood. Whoever built the partition was definitely no carpenter!!

The kitchen was hideous, with the most outrageous wallpaper imaginable. I soon changed that into a very pretty kitchen with an eating area, and folding doors hid the washer and drier. I also had a large walk-in closet in the master bedroom, what a luxury. Finally, I had it all finished and was very proud of my accomplishment. Now I really had a place to call home, and it was all mine. I also bought myself a new car and drove all over Florida visiting many of the wonderful historic areas, such as St. Augustine, St. Petersburg and Orlando, as well as Miami, but never made it as far as the Florida Keys.

The following Christmas I went to work part time selling decorations in the Christmas Shop of a very beautiful department store. I had so much fun there that I wished it could be Christmas all year, and I also made two very good friends. Over lunch one day, I was telling them about the trips I had taken with my mother, when one of them said, rather wistfully, that she had never been anywhere, and would love to take a cruise. My reply was 'O.K Bernie, save your money and we'll go', and by golly, it wasn't long before she said she was ready. The following April, she and I sailed through the Caribbean together. It was the same cruise that I had taken with Mum, but this time I was seeing it all again through Bernie's eyes. We had a ball. I know that even though she may never take another cruise, she won't forget that one. We have reminisced about it many times since.

I also met Monica, a wonderful lady from England who had already travelled all over the world, but more for business than pleasure. We enjoyed each other's company tremendously, and spent many hours together talking about England before the war, as well as during and after, and all the interesting places she had visited. We found we had so many things in common there would never be an end to a conversation. We became the best of friends. Eventually the three of us went our separate ways, but have always kept in touch as good friends do.

I held several different jobs during the seven years I spent in Florida. They were mostly part-time temporary retail positions in the beautiful department stores, just for the tourist season, mainly because I kept trying to retire, and then I'd find myself bored with nothing to do. But there came a time when retirement was a must. I had to make the big decision of 'where was I going to retire?'

I didn't really want to stay in Florida, even though it is a very interesting place with lots of history and places to visit. I loved my home, but there is little in the way of entertainment for single people to socialize, especially in my age group. I don't like bars or singles clubs, and after all those years in a convent, I didn't feel that I wanted to affiliate myself closely with a church. We did have a very nice clubhouse in the complex with lots of activities, but I was beginning to feel that I was in a rut. My feet were getting itchy again.

Just about that time I received a letter from Cy, my good friend who had driven to Arizona with me. We had kept in touch over the years. He had visited my mother often when she was in the nursing home, which both she and I appreciated. He was writing to tell me that his brother, with whom he shared a house, had passed away, and if ever I thought of visiting Victoria again, could stay at his house rather than bother with hotels. He also said he was looking for a good looking housekeeper (though tongue in cheek, I believe!).

Later that same day, I was taking a drive and stopped for a cup of coffee, sharing a table with a stranger, and we started talking. She asked me if I was Canadian, as she had noted my different accent. I told her I was, and had lived in Victoria, BC. Her response was, 'How could you possibly leave such a beautiful place.......?' to which I had no good answer. Then that evening I was attending a party at a friend's house when I was introduced to a young man from Victoria. Well, that was three signs within 24 hours all pointing to Victoria. After giving it some serious thought, I came to a conclusion.

I wrote back to Cy accepting his offer of a place to stay (but didn't mention the housekeeper part), sold my beautiful condominium fully furnished, shipped my car to Victoria and once again was heading back to my roots. I must say, of all the moves I've made, this is the best and, as you can tell, I've made a lot of moves!!

26

A FRIEND INDEED

Cy was at Victoria airport to meet me when I arrived, but I could tell he was not well. I carried my luggage to the car and hoisted it into the trunk, as I watched him having a lot of trouble getting into the driver's seat. I was so excited to be back in Victoria after a nine year absence, that I was chattering away like a magpie, when I realized he was not responding and seemed to be in another world, driving well below the speed limit. If it had been an automatic drive instead of a stick shift, I would have taken over the driving, but I had never driven a stick shift, so had to trust that we would arrive home safely. We did, this time!

It's quite a long drive from Victoria Airport into the city, about 17 miles. I was relieved when we finally reached Cy's house. After putting my suitcases in the tiny bedroom I was to occupy, I made myself at home as offered, and put the kettle on for a much needed cup of tea. As we sat drinking it, Cy had me read him his Will, which I did, although all the legalese didn't make a lot of sense to me. I returned the Will to the drawer where he kept it, only to have to get it out and read it again. This went on several times, before I had to make an excuse to leave the room, hoping he would have forgotten about it by the time I returned, but he hadn't!

The following day I accompanied him to his doctor's appointment, and learned that Cy had emphysema and short term memory loss. He would soon need an oxygen tank. This accounted for the Will scene being repeated over and over again. It became obvious that he needed more professional assistance than I could give him, and I arranged for a care giver to visit him twice a day, making sure he ate and took his medication. The doctor started making house calls rather than Cy being taken to him, and Cy was getting plenty of care and attention.

When the care giver took over on a permanent basis and a young neighbour started spending more time with him, I moved into an apartment close by, visiting often. Cy was a good friend that I was very fond of, and wanted to be there to bring a smile to his face. He remembered his childhood, and his time in the Royal Air Force during the war, so we reminisced together. I even had him singing old wartime songs. He actually remembered all the words, but he was deteriorating fast.

A few months after I'd moved out, he had a bad fall during the night and went into a coma. His care giver found him unconscious the next morning, called an ambulance and he was rushed to hospital, but did not recover. He died a few days later. I was so glad I had been able to spend even a short while with him, and I was going to miss him.

The apartment I'd moved into was in a very nice high rise building in James Bay, which is one of the oldest districts of Victoria, and has many interesting heritage homes. It's also within walking distance of beautiful Beacon Hill Park where I had spent many happy hours with my daughter when she was a very little girl, soon after we'd arrived from Toronto. The building was the same one Vivienne and I had lived in briefly the summer she graduated from high school, and the view from the 14th floor was the same one that had made us homesick for Hawaii, but this time I knew there was no going back.

It was just a short walk into downtown Victoria past the famous Empress Hotel, the Royal British Columbia Museum, and Madame Tussaud's Wax Museum, and of course, the magnificent Parliament Buildings designed by Francis Rattenbury, and opened in 1898, dominating three sides of the square forming the Inner Harbour, touted as one of the most beautiful harbours in the world. And it really is!

'Symphony Splash' is one of the many events during the summer season. It is performed by the Victoria Symphony Orchestra on a floating barge moored in the harbour, and ends with a rousing performance of the 1812 Overture accompanied by a fabulous fireworks display. Other major summer events in the area are a Food Fair, Jazz Festival, Summer Olympics, Vintage Automobile Parade, Christmas Light Parade and of course, the Canada Day Parade on July 1st.

I participate in several parades a year with my group of ex-WAAF and other veterans for the anniversary of VE Day on May 8th, D-Day on June 6th, Battle of Britain Parade in mid-September, Remembrance Day on November 11th, and others. We march along Government and Douglas Streets to the Cenotaph at the Parliament Buildings where wreaths are laid at the foot of the Cenotaph while we listen to a brief service. Some of these parades draw a crowd of up to 40,000 cheering and clapping spectators.

In my second year in Victoria, I was asked to carry a standard in the Battle of Britain Parade. After the very moving service in the Cathedral, we formed up and marched off to the sound of the bag-pipes playing a rather slow march. A strong wind was blowing the flag in all directions and it soon became quite heavy. I was having trouble keeping step with my short legs trying to take long strides. Half way to the Cenotaph I started feeling a heaviness in my chest and I knew I was in trouble, but wanted to make it all the way. I did, but as soon as we halted, I collapsed after practically throwing my standard to the man beside me.

He assisted me to the grassy curb, an ambulance was called and the whole parade was disrupted, waiting for it to arrive and cart me off to hospital, where I was diagnosed as having a stress related heart attack. The first three days I spent in the Intensive Care Unit, and another three in the Continuing Care Unit, before returning home with strict instructions to take it easy. It was not a pleasant experience, and I certainly won't be carrying any more flags bigger than a paper one on a stick.

There is always a funny side to a story, and I have chuckled about this one many times since. It's impossible to buy a woman's shirt that will accommodate a heavy tie, such as the RAF tie I had to wear, so I was going to wear a man's shirt which had just been bought. When I was dressed and ready to leave the house on that fateful day, I inspected myself in a full length mirror and was horrified to see that the long tail of the shirt was causing an ugly bulge around my hips. Not having time to get undressed and re-dressed, I got the kitchen scissors and cut the tail off while still wearing the shirt, and tucked it back into my slacks. Of course, the first thing the paramedics did was pull my shirt out. I could hear my Mother's voice saying, 'How many times have I told you ...!!'

It didn't take long for me to start enjoying my new life and retirement in Victoria, but I had to find something to do, I couldn't look at the beautiful view ALL day. My mother had introduced me to the Senior Centre when I was here before, but I didn't feel I was ready for it at that time (I was much too young at age 55!), but now, 20 years later, it seemed like an excellent idea to become a member and meet people.

I became a volunteer cashier in the Fern Café, the very nice little restaurant at the Monterey Senior Centre in Oak Bay, and enjoyed the three hours a week, meeting and getting to know people. I also attended all the dinners and functions celebrating such events as Valentine's Day, St. George's Day, St. Patrick's Day and anything else they could think of to have fun. There were coach trips that took us to several lovely places for a few hours outing including lunch, and I was getting reacquainted with this beautiful island, as well as making friends.

Oak Bay is a lovely village on the outskirts of Victoria, so typically English it is known as 'behind the tweed curtain'. The stores that line Oak Bay Avenue are mostly antique stores and arty-type shops, with several very classy and high priced clothing stores. Nearly all the buildings are heritage, built in the 1800s, and bear the name of the original owners across the portico. There are many stately homes of course with gorgeous gardens. Even the newer homes are built to conform to the old style architecture.

The first Christmas I was back in Victoria, the Senior Centre was taking a bus trip to Harrison Hot Springs, a resort beside a lake in the interior of British Columbia. This sounded like a great way to avoid spending Christmas alone, so I signed up for the three day trip, and joined a bus load of happy wanderers as we went on the bus, first on the ferry to Vancouver, and then through the fabulous scenery of British Columbia to our destination, the Harrison Hot Springs Hotel. The hotel was beautifully decorated and ablaze with sparkling coloured lights as we arrived and checked into our very comfortable rooms.

I had arranged to meet up with one of the ladies for a drink in the lobby of the hotel prior to our Christmas Dinner in the Copper Room. As we left the lounge and were on our way to dinner, I noticed a gentleman walking toward us, whom I had seen sitting by himself on the bus. I said, 'Hello', and told him if he wanted dinner he was heading in the wrong direction, so he turned around and joined us. During dinner we chatted and danced later to the trio playing in the ballroom, and arranged to meet after breakfast next morning for a dip in the hotel pools.

There were five pools all together, starting with a HOT inside pool, and an adjacent pool which was slightly cooler. The three outside pools were progressively colder, until the last one was downright freezing. We took a dip in all of them in turn and it really was most invigorating. I forgot to mention that my new friend has only one arm, having lost his right arm in a farm machinery accident at a very early age. As we spent more time together on this and other trips, I really had to admire the way he managed to open one of those tiny milk containers with one hand, or scooped out the butter and jam in the little plastic holders and spread it on his toast. He never asked for help. Some people can't even do that properly with two hands.

Christmas Day at the hotel was a round of activities, carolling in the lobby, hot rum punch by the fire in the lounge, more carolling and pictures taken around the huge Christmas tree, and of course a walk by the lake. Snow had fallen overnight but it wasn't cold and I thoroughly enjoyed it, despite the fact that I hadn't seen snow in all the years I'd lived in the States. The last time was at the opening of the Coquahalla Highway twelve years earlier.

That evening was the big Christmas Dinner in the ballroom, with all the trimmings. The room was packed with our group and other revellers who'd arrived by the bus load. After dinner we were entertained by two very funny comedians, one a Scot, the other Irish. They had everyone in stitches, and following them was music for dancing. The night ended on a high note with everyone in excellent spirits, or should that be, the excellent spirits were in everyone!! Boxing Day was our last day in Harrison Hot Springs, and I had to have a final dip in the pools. As usual, when I've had a good time, I was sorry to be leaving, it really had been fun and I had a few new friends I would see back at the senior centre, including my gentleman friend, whose company I had enjoyed. This was just the first of many trips I took with the group from the senior centre over the next couple of years.

The following Christmas a trip to Leavenworth, an Alpine village, high up on the mountains in Washington State, was beautiful. The snow started falling as we wound our way up the mountain road at a very slow pace, and we found ourselves knee deep in the stuff as we alighted at our hotel. After dinner we explored the village of Leavenworth which has mostly Christmassy shops and Bavarian restaurants, all gaily decorated with millions of coloured lights. We slithered and slid our way around to browse them all. There was entertainment everywhere with groups of carollers at every corner, and people dressed in Bavarian costume. Mr. Kris Kringle himself greeted us when we returned to the hotel.

On Christmas Day we were taken to see a performance of *A Christmas Carol* at a log cabin theatre, followed by the bell ringers from the local church ringing carols, while hot punch was being served to all. The show was excellent and the setting of the theatre deep in the forest surrounded by snow was like a picture postcard. This was one of my most enjoyable trips, and I promised myself I would come back to see Leavenworth in the Spring when all the mountain flowers were in bloom. I'm sure it would be quite beautiful in a different way.

After living in my 14th floor apartment for a couple of years, I felt it was time I had a property of my own again, instead of putting money into someone else's pocket. I enlisted the help of a realtor who found me a really nice condominium just on the outskirts of Oak Bay, close to town as well as handy for the Senior Centre where I continued to volunteer. Once more I was packing up and moving, determined to stay put this time.

I didn't tell you that I have a small Maine Coon cat that was rescued after the big earthquake in Northridge, California in 1994. We had felt the quake in Palm Desert, where I was living at the time, and a neighbour had found the wee thing wandering in the middle of the road. I don't think the kitten could have been more than four weeks old. My neighbour was allergic to cats. She knew I had been wanting a kitten, since I'd lost my beautiful Persian Princess in Arizona just a few months earlier, and she brought it to me. Of course, being a lover of animals, I was overjoyed and christened her Little Missy which soon got shortened to just 'Missy'. She has accompanied me on all my moves since then, and adjusted well to each of her new homes.

It didn't take long for us both to settle in and I really enjoyed living in my first condominium in Canada. I didn't have the greatest view, overlooking a main road and hearing the sirens of ambulances and fire trucks on a daily (and nightly) basis, but the noise no longer sent me diving under a table. The location was perfect and I was happy. I had two very nice bedrooms, as well as two full bathrooms, a living room with windows on two sides, so it was very bright and cheerful. There was also a small galley kitchen with an eating area, and a large tiled entry way off which was a laundry area with a washer and dryer and a large clothes closet, which I certainly needed. I also had two patios on which I put several pots of flowers, and once again I had a home of my own.

Of course I am never satisfied with the decor and it doesn't take long before I find myself papering and painting. This condo was no exception, though I decided to have it painted professionally this time, just the way I wanted. It also had a wood burning fireplace, which I was rather reluctant to use as such, so I installed a very attractive electric fireplace, which certainly added to the comfort and looks of the place. I was delighted with the end result.

I had also discovered that my old dance club was still very active, and to my surprise, was holding their bi-weekly dances at 'my' senior centre. I had seen a brochure listing names of the executives, on the wall of one of the restaurants in Oak Bay, and recognized a name, so I called her and made arrangements to meet at the next dance. I also enlisted my gentleman friend, Herb and for the next couple of years we had a routine of dinner at my place every other Sunday, followed by an evening of dancing. The Sunday between, we would take a drive to some of the many delightful spots on the island, places I didn't even know existed. He has lived on the island all his life and knew exactly where to go, while I could never have found such beautiful locations by myself.

Life was good and I was very content. For the first time in ages I did not have any desire to make any changes. Then I had a phone call one day telling me Herb was in the hospital after suffering a heart attack. He was OK, but they kept him in the hospital for a couple of weeks. I visited almost every day until he was due to be released, then drove him to his home and made sure he was comfortable.

His daughter had also been visiting him in the hospital, and decided it was time her Dad sold his home and found a nice retirement home to move into. As I believe I mentioned before, there are several very nice retirement homes in and around Victoria, and Herb and I drove around to view a few, mostly new ones in addition to those I viewed when I was looking for a retirement home for my Mother.

He finally decided on one which was close to shopping and also to the senior centre which, if he had to give up driving, he could still reach by bus. He had also decided that I too, was going to move into the retirement home, and was quite upset with me when I made it clear I was happy in my condo, and had no intention of moving into a retirement home for at least another 15 years. I don't think he had realized that he was that much older than me. His home sold quickly and he moved without my help. From then on our friendship deteriorated. I was sure he would make new friends within his own age range once he was settled, and wished him well, but I was sorry to lose his friendship.

We would still run into each other at the senior centre when I was cashiering in the café. He did his best to avoid me, until one day when I saw him lunching alone, I joined him at his table and we had a nice conversation. We didn't renew our friendship or continue where we'd left off, but at least he wasn't avoiding me deliberately after that, and we'd each moved on with our lives.

27

THE LAST WORDS

It seemed everyone I knew had a computer and although I wasn't interested in learning 'programs' and 'sites' I thought it would be a good idea to have one also, mainly so that I could type on the word processor and correspond with my friends south of the border, by writing one letter and making copies with personalized paragraphs instead of having to write individual letters by hand which virtually said the same thing to all of them. So I shopped around and finally purchased one along with the necessary monitor and printer.

When the computer was delivered, I was on my own to set it up. I figured if I could be a flight mechanic in the WAAF and make an aircraft engine work, I surely could put this thing together and make IT work. It took a while, but with the instructions spread out on the floor, I finally had it all plugged into the right places and was ready to start. I think I must have called my server for help at least fifty times that first week, to where we were on a first name basis, but little by little I was teaching myself how to press the right keys, and was amazed at all the information available. This really is an awesome invention if used properly.

Soon I had an extensive list of pen pals to correspond with via e-mail, some of them as far away as Texas and Nova Scotia, as well as the friends I'd left behind. It was interesting learning about their daily lives, there certainly was variety. One evening while I was in the middle of such correspondence, a screen popped up advertising a 'Singles Site'. All I had to do was type a brief profile about myself and 'send' it. Nothing ventured, nothing gained, I typed the profile as requested, mentioning that I had served in the WAAF, loved cruising, dancing, and a few other words of interest, hit 'send', and off it went.

Almost immediately I received a response signed 'Cruise Nut'. This person had also been in the air force, loved cruising and dancing, etc., or so he said! This all seemed too good to be true, so I sent a rather snotty little note back to the 'Singles Site' suggesting that, 'If this is a sprat to catch a mackerel, you will not get me to sign on or send money; however, if this is for real, here is my phone number, please call me', and I went back to whatever I'd been doing before.

After about half an hour I signed off my computer and immediately the phone rang. Lo and behold, it was the 'Cruise Nut'. We discovered we lived just a few blocks apart, and had many common interests and should definitely meet to discuss this further. We arranged to meet the following Thursday outside the Dutch Bakery, a nice little restaurant on Fort Street in Victoria. It seemed an awful long time to wait, this being only Monday, but wait I must.

Thursday finally arrived. I decided to be early, and wait in the store adjacent to the bakery. If I didn't like what I saw, I was going to stay inside until he gave up and left. WELL, I definitely liked what I saw and came out of the store quicker than I went in, and approached the gentleman who had just arrived. He was very well dressed in blue blazer and grey slacks, sparkling white shirt and an air force tie, not too tall, a head of wavy white hair and the most beautiful smile. I was already hooked, but first we had to talk. I suggested we cross the road to the Eaton Centre, rather than sit with strangers sharing a table in the Dutch Bakery, and this we did.

When we reached the cafeteria, he helped himself to coffee and proceeded with it on a tray to the end of the shelf, only to have it drop off the end and cover him with hot coffee. Since the waitress was closest she started to wipe him down with a cloth, and I heard him say, 'Don't worry, it didn't burn anything important'. I had to hide my face to cover my giggles, I knew right away we were going to hit it off. This man had a good sense of humour, VERY important.

About two and a half hours later, having talked ourselves silly, not mentioning the spilled coffee once, we decided to take a walk in the sunshine to the Inner Harbour, still talking and discovering common ground. We had umpteen things in common, not only that we both enjoyed cruising, but had been in the same place at the same time over 60 years previously when he was a Navigator stationed in the Royal Canadian Air Force just seven miles from where I was at Honeybourne. We had also frequented the same pub, the Dirty Duck, though of course, being an officer he was in the White Swan side and we didn't meet then, nor once when his plane was diverted to Honeybourne. I may very well have been on crash duty for that pre-dawn landing, and attended to service the aircraft. In fact, there were so many coincidences it was uncanny.

I had moved from Florida back to Victoria just two years earlier, he had moved from Ontario more recently and here we were, just a few blocks apart in our condos. Surely this was meant to be!

Our first meeting lasted about five hours. As I didn't want to overdo a good thing, I suggested we part company, for now. So he went his way and I went mine, but not before he gave me a kiss, right at a busy intersection while waiting for the light to change. Bells Clanged; Horns Blared; People Cheered - well, not really, but I know I was floating on air as I walked away.

Soon after I arrived back in my condo, there was a delivery of a huge bouquet of flowers and a card wishing me, 'Happy Birthday, with love Ron.'

I had mentioned that my birthday was the next day, and I was delighted that he remembered, considering all the topics we had discussed. Of course, I immediately phoned to say thank you, and from then on you could say we were inseparable, we spent some time together every day. We were getting along perfectly, and as Ron says, we are like two peas in a pod, and feel like we have known each other forever.

One evening just three weeks later, after I had cooked a nice dinner, and we were relaxing watching TV, he actually proposed to me the old fashioned way on bended knee, and of course, I accepted. We were now engaged. I knew the minute I had seen him through the store window that he was my Mr. Right.

We set our wedding date for October 24th, 2002, which was also the date of my parent's wedding in 1924. After all the invitations had been sent out, reception reservations and other plans made, we discovered that because I was a divorcee we needed permission from the Bishop to be married in an Anglican Church.

Several people tried to talk us out of a church wedding, but I was determined I was going to get it right this time. I even bought a long ivory wedding dress with a lace bodice, covered with sequins and pearls, long lace sleeves, and three peplums cascaded down the back of the skirt. It was beautiful and I couldn't wait to walk down the aisle in it and feel like a bride is supposed to feel.

It took until the week before the wedding for the letter from the Bishop to arrive giving us his blessing. We heaved a big sigh of relief, and Reverend Glenn Sim married us as planned. It was indeed a beautiful ceremony with Ron's relatives and my friends, including my best friend Monica from Florida, filling the little local church.

I arrived in a stretch limousine, along with my matron of honour who was also my hairdresser, my bridesmaid who was Ron's teenaged grand daughter Becky who, with her mother had travelled all the way from New Brunswick for the occasion, and my friend David from Sticky Tape days, who was to give me away ('reluctantly', he said). The limousine was decorated with burgundy and white ribbons which matched Becky's long satin dress. My friends Norma and Monica had helped me into my beautiful wedding dress, and the only jewellery I wore was a double row of pearls in my hair, and the little pearl stud earrings that Vivienne's father had given her the Christmas before we lost her. She had never had a chance to wear them and I felt that she was there with me as I 'danced' down the aisle. This time I wished the nuns could have seen me. I do believe they would have approved.

David escorts Veronica down the Aisle.
© Frances Litman Photo

The service was perfect, although the weather outside was dull and chilly, but just as we were exchanging our vows a brilliant ray of sunshine filtered through the stained glass window onto us both. It certainly seemed like a very good omen, or maybe it was Mum having the last word again, giving us her blessing. I'd like to think so.

Our photographer led the procession of cars from the church to an area of her choice to take the pictures which, despite the fact that it was very chilly and a bit foggy, came out very well. As soon as the photo session was over we led the way in the limousine to a lovely waterfront restaurant, which was decorated for the occasion with an arbor of flowers and looked lovely. The food was delicious, and the champagne flowed, accompanied by music for dancing. We all had a wonderful time, as one of my new brothers-in-law said, it was The Event of the Season.

We were so busy enjoying ourselves that we didn't realize the time, and before we knew it, nearly all the guests had departed. We found ourselves among the last to leave, which was rather untraditional. It was quite late by the time we arrived at our hotel in Victoria, where we had reserved the honeymoon suite for our first night as Mr. and Mrs. It was complete with a basket of goodies and a bottle of champagne, compliments of the manager. I hadn't even tasted the champagne at our reception or eaten any of the wedding cake, my glass and plate disappeared while I was dancing, so of course we had to open this bottle and toast each other. It had been the wedding day of my dreams and I couldn't be happier.

After the ceremony. Photo, Morag Pfeiffer
(also on back cover)

Our out of town guests stayed on for the rest of that week, and since we were not going away for our honeymoon until later on, we spent it showing them some of our beautiful island. Included was a trip to Chemainus, with all its wonderful murals on the buildings, and other points of interest that we had discovered. They departed with some very happy memories.

We had each sold our condominiums in Victoria and bought a nice little home in Saanichton, a very countrified area on the Saanich Peninsula of Vancouver Island. The

little seaside town of Sidney, where my parents had lived, is just 15 minutes north; the city of Victoria, 30 minutes in the opposite direction. My cat, Missy, walked into our new home and immediately spoke her approval. In fact, the first time Ron visited me at my condo, Missy greeted him warmly and gave him her rub of approval. Funny how she realized, as I did, that this was my Mr. Right. I do believe she fell in love with him at first sight too.

For the first time in my life, I was absolutely sure I was doing the right thing. I had met my soul mate, and all the last pieces of the puzzle of my life fell into place. Now I know that all those moves I made were not running away from something, but running to my destiny. I really believe we were meant to meet.

Ron & Veronica before the reception.
© *Frances Litman Photo*

We spent our belated honeymoon the following January taking a cruise beginning in Sydney, Australia and ending at Auckland, New Zealand, visiting many interesting ports along the way. They were twelve blissful days.

The two years since then have been filled with activities, including the dance club every other Sunday, the Senior Centre for dinners and outings, as well as our Air Force Wing, comprising a group of ex-air force personnel, to which both Ron and I belong. They hold a TGIF, and any other reason they can think of to have a party. I join my ex-WAAF group for luncheons once a month, and of course, there are all the parades we participate in, including the very important one - the 60th Anniversary of VE-Day, May 8th 2005, which also happens to be the Year of the Veteran.

A very interesting and poignant few minutes occurred during the service after that parade. As we veterans sat under the marquee, a gentleman spoke to us. He had been a young boy in Holland when the Canadian troops marched in to liberate that country from the German occupation. He gave a very moving speech of his experiences at that time.

The children were fearful of the German soldiers, but all of a sudden, here were the Canadian soldiers handing out chewing gum to all the children. As a child he had never heard of chewing gum in Holland. He popped his into his mouth, chewed and then promptly swallowed it. He soon learned that you had to keep chewing, and chewing, and never swallow it, so a soldier gave him another stick of gum, and this one he chewed 'for ever'. Today he was handing out a stick of gum to each veteran at the event to say, 'Thank you' to all the Canadian soldiers who participated in the liberation of his country.

Cruising has continued to play a major part in our lives. We cruised through the Panama Canal in 2004, which I had first traversed in 1945 with my parents. Among the many interesting ports of call on this trip were my favourite island of St. Thomas, also Acapulco where we saw the cliff divers, Puerto Vallarta where the movie, *Night of the Iguana* was filmed starring Richard Burton, Cabo San Lucas which is so clean and beautiful, and much more.

We also took a trip to Hawaii for two weeks in the fall of 2004. I was able to bring my daughter's ashes back to be scattered on the waters in Sidney, where she and I had spent so many happy times in our sailboat.

Ron also has a daughter who lives on the Saanich Peninsula with her husband, as well as a sister and her husband, who was Ron's 'best man', not far away in Victoria. We meet frequently for dinner or coffee, and catch up on the family news.

Something else Ron and I have in common is the fact that we both celebrate our birthdays in May and, as I mentioned before, we met the day before mine. This year was a particular milestone for me, so we decided to have a big party and combine all three celebrations, Ron's 84th birthday on the 19th; 3 years since we met on the 30th, and my 80th birthday on the 31st.

We rented the big hall at the senior centre and invited 40 guests, including the new friends we have met since each of us arrived from other parts of the continent not that long ago, and a good time was had by all. In fact it was so much fun we have decided to do it again next year for Ron's 85th and maybe for all the 'milestones' thereafter. We celebrate our 'anniversary' on the 24th of each month as if it were for another year. After all, I doubt that we will be around to celebrate our actual quarter-century anniversary.

I have acquired other brothers and sisters-in-law, and two granddaughters, Holly, who came from Vancouver for our wedding, and Becky, from New Brunswick. With each of us having computers, we can keep in touch via the internet. Now, I not only have a wonderful husband, but the family I have always wanted and never had.

This year we took a trip to England and enjoyed a reunion there with my cousin Monica, and April joined us from her home in Florida. One of the highlights of this trip was a visit to our old stomping ground of 60 years ago, the White Swan/Dirty Duck pub in Stratford-upon-Avon. It brought back a lot of memories to both of us, but hadn't changed much over the years except for the addition of modern indoor plumbing which replaced the spooky one-holer that I remember.

For our third wedding anniversary (2005), a return trip to Hawaii is planned. This time we will be staying in Kailua-Kona on the coast of the Big Island of Hawaii, near the Volcano National Park where Mauna Loa, the active volcano is located, as well as the Kiluaea Crater. I have seen fantastic pictures of the volcano erupting, as it does quite frequently, and hope it will perform for us.

In 2006 we have two Air Force reunions to attend. The first one is in York, England at Ron's old base of Linton-on-Ouse, probably the last reunion of 6 (RCAF) Bomber Group. Among other events, it will include a visit to East Kirkby where my Dad was stationed as a Flying Control officer with 617, the Dam Buster squadron. The second will be that of Ron's 408 Squadron, one of the squadrons in 6 Group, in Edmonton, Alberta on our way home.

Life is wonderful, and as long as we can stay as healthy as we are now, I know we will have several happy years to enjoy travelling, marching and dancing together .... we have been truly blessed!

DON'T YOU JUST LOVE HAPPY ENDINGS!!

EPILOGUE

Though my memoirs are finished, and I have just celebrated my 80th birthday, my life is far from finished. There is so much more I want to do and much more that I want to see.

Reflecting back over these past years I can't help wondering what would have happened, and where would I be if there had been no World War II. That event affected everyone and the course of our lives was changed forever. Most of us were able to pick up the pieces and move on, but for others, that wasn't possible. Hearts, minds and limbs were shattered beyond repair, as is the aftermath of any war. There have been so many wars within my lifetime. Even as I write, lives are still being lost in Iraq.

I consider myself extremely fortunate that my parents and I survived the air-raids in Great Britain. We had some scary times of course, but that was to be expected. Losing my cousin in Tunisia and my brother in the Blue Lagoon were the closest we came to personal tragedies in those dark days, but we also lost many friends and neighbours.

The loss of my little brother weighed heavily on my conscience and I felt guilty for not being able to protect him, regardless of the fact that I'd been told there was nothing anyone could have done at the time. It's odd though how life works and I'm sure now that our destinies are planned. When he was a little more than two years old I had taken him to the local swimming pool and we were sitting on the side of the pool dangling our legs in the water, when someone nudged him from behind and he fell head first into the pool, disappearing to the bottom. I too jumped in to save him but couldn't see him, the pool being crowded that day. Fortunately, someone had seen it happen and jumped in saving both of us. Although it took a little while to catch our breath, we both recovered.

A couple of years later, when Adrian was at Taplow Grammar School, he fell into a well and would have drowned except for a quick thinking teacher who rescued him. But from that ordeal Adrian caught scarlet fever and was hospitalized for several weeks, and had to learn to walk and talk again, fortunately making a full recovery with no long lasting effects.

At the beginning of the war, many children were being evacuated out of England via ship to Canada and Australia. Adrian and I were supposed to be leaving for Canada to stay with my grandmother in Vancouver, but by some strange coincidence our papers were lost and we were left behind. The ship, The City of Benares, full of children, was torpedoed and sunk by a German U-boat (submarine) and all were lost. Again, he had dodged what evidently was his inevitable fate.

Being able to live in my Dad's homeland of Canada was a wonderful healing process and my experiences in those first two years were so far removed from anything else I had ever done, that I have to pinch myself and ask, 'Was that really me?'. When I told my friends at Sticky Tapes about life on the dude ranch, I don't really think they believed me, but it was all true.

The years I spent in the WAAF both during wartime and post-war, were all part of an education in many ways, but mainly, being able to get along with others in all walks of life. We were all so different, yet wearing the same uniform and marching to the same drummer for the same cause.

There was no such thing as 'class distinction', unless of course, you wore three stripes or a few 'rings'. Many friendships were formed and love affairs started, only to come to an end when a new posting happened and there was a parting of the ways. Trying to maintain contact was virtually impossible, there was so much going on.

Despite all the potatoes and carrots I peeled and the other penalties paid for breaking rules, I wouldn't have missed the experience for anything. Now that I've finally settled down after all my moves and travels across the United States, I am able to relive those days with my friends in the WAAF Association here in Canada. Our monthly luncheons are a noisy affair, it seems as if we have all suddenly become those 17 and 18 year olds again as we recount a funny event. We all have stories to tell. This one is mine. I hope you enjoyed it.

From Veronica, with Love

PS: Because I didn't want to disclose the final chapter of my book, I have saved this acknowledgement until last. Of course, that is to thank my husband Ron for all his help and encouragement to finish my book, and without whom there would have been no happy ending.

The British Memorial to the women members of the Allied Air Services

British Memorial to Women of WWII

ISBN 141206860-6